The Garland Library
of Medieval Literature

General Editors
James J. Wilhelm, Rutgers University
Lowry Nelson, Jr., Yale University

Literary Advisors
Ingeborg Glier, Yale University
Guy Mermier, University of Michigan
Fred C. Robinson, Yale University
Aldo Scaglione, University of North Carolina

Art Advisor
Elizabeth Parker McLachlan, Rutgers University

Music Advisor
Hendrik van der Werf, Eastman School of Music

Corpus Christi College, Cambridge MS 425, p. 97, showing the beginning of Chapter 1 of *Vita Sancti Hugonis*, with an illuminated initial letter representing St. Hugh with mitre and crozier, his right hand raised in blessing. (Reproduced by permission of the Master and Fellows of Corpus Christi College, Cambridge.)

Gerald of Wales
(Giraldus Cambrensis)

THE LIFE OF ST. HUGH OF AVALON
Bishop of Lincoln 1186–1200

edited and translated by
RICHARD M. LOOMIS

Volume 31
Series A
GARLAND LIBRARY OF MEDIEVAL LITERATURE

Garland Publishing, Inc.
New York and London
1985

Library of Congress Cataloging in Publication Data
Giraldus Cambrensis, 1146?–1223?
The life of St. Hugh of Avalon, Bishop of Lincoln 1186-
1200.

(Garland library of medieval literature ; v. 31.
Series A)
Translation of: Vita Sancti Hugonis.
Bibliography: p.
Includes index.
1. Hugh, of Avalon, Saint, 1140?–1200. 2. Christian
saints—England—Biography. I. Loomis, Richard Morgan,
1926–   . II. Title. III. Series: Garland library
of medieval literature ; v. 31.
BX4700.H8G5713 1985   282'.092'4 [B]   84-21130
ISBN 0-8240-8916-2 (alk. paper)

Printed on acid-free, 250-year-life paper
Manufactured in the United States of America

211200

For My Family

The Garland Library
of Medieval Literature

Preface of the General Editors

The Garland Library of Medieval Literature was established to make available to the general reader modern translations of texts in editions that conform to the highest academic standards. All of the translations are original, and were created especially for this series. The translations attempt to render the foreign works in a natural idiom that remains faithful to the originals.

The Library is divided into two sections: Series A, texts and translations; and Series B, translations alone. Those volumes containing texts have been prepared after consultation of the major previous editions and manuscripts. The aim in the editing has been to offer a reliable text with a minimum of editorial intervention. Significant variants accompany the original, and important problems are discussed in the Textual Notes. Volumes without texts contain translations based on the most scholarly texts available, which have been updated in terms of recent scholarship.

Most volumes contain Introductions with the following features: (1) a biography of the author or a discussion of the problem of authorship, with any pertinent historical or legendary information; (2) an objective discussion of the literary style of the original, emphasizing any individual features; (3) a consideration of sources for the work and its influence; and (4) a statement of the editorial policy for each edition and translation. There is also a Select Bibliography, which emphasizes recent criticism on the works. Critical writings are often accompanied by brief descriptions of their importance. Selective glossaries, indices, and footnotes are included where appropriate.

The Library covers a broad range of linguistic areas, including all of the major European languages. All of the important literary forms and genres are considered, sometimes in anthologies or selections.

The General Editors hope that these volumes will bring the general reader a closer awareness of a richly diversified area that has

for too long been closed to everyone except those with precise
academic training, an area that is well worth study and reflection.

James J. Wilhelm
Rutgers University

Lowry Nelson, Jr.
Yale University

Contents

Corpus Christi College, Cambridge MS 425, p. 73, showing the beginning of Chapter 29 of *Vita Sancti Remigii*, "On Baldwin the Cistercian and Hugh the Carthusian." (Reproduced by permission of the Master and Fellows of Corpus Christi College, Cambridge.)

INTRODUCTION

Life of the Author

The medieval Latin author known as Giraldus Cambrensis, or
Gerald of Wales, names himself Giraldus de Barri. He uses the
title of archdeacon (of Brecon or its diocese St. David's)
even after resigning that office in 1203. In his preface to
the lives of St. Remigius and St. Hugh, addressed to Stephen
Langton and written about 1214, Gerald names himself "G. de
Barri dictus, archidiaconus Sancti David" (*Op.* 7: 3; see also
SD 2, 156, 190, 262).* He was born about 1146 at his father's
castle of Manorbier on the coast of southwestern Wales, between
Tenby and Pembroke. The year of his birth is inferred from his
own imprecise estimates of his age. In *De Principis Instructione*, he notes that he was nearing the end of his twentieth
year when in August 1165 he witnessed the midnight rejoicing
of the people of Paris upon the birth of an heir to the French
throne (*Op.* 8: 292). This heir, of whom Gerald frequently
writes, became King Philip II of France, known as Philip
Augustus, who reigned from 1180 to 1223 and waged persistent
wars against the Angevin kings of England. Gerald was studying
the liberal arts in Paris and would later study and lecture
on canon law there. His father, William de Barri, belonged
to a Norman family that had settled at Barry Island, southwest
of Cardiff. His mother was the daughter of the Norman castel-
lan of Pembroke, Gerald of Windsor, and Nest, the daughter of
the Welsh prince Rhys ap Tewdwr. Knights belonging to this
notable family gained eminence in the Norman invasion of Ireland, an achievement chronicled by Gerald in his *Expugnatio
Hibernica*. But in boyhood, while his older brothers built
play castles, Gerald built churches and monasteries in the
sand (*Autobiography* 35). His mother's brother, David FitzGerald,
was bishop of St. David's for twenty-seven years, from 1148 to
1176. At his uncle's death in 1176, when Gerald says (again
loosely reckoning his own age) that he had not yet completed
his thirtieth year, Gerald was chosen one of four nominees to

*All references keyed to the Select Bibliography.

succeed Bishop David (*Autobiography* 59). Not then, nor after
his second election in 1199, did Gerald manage to be actually
consecrated bishop of St. David's. Although Gerald was appointed to serve the royal court of England, especially in
diplomatic missions to the Welsh, Henry II opposed him upon
his first election to the bishopric of St. David's. The archbishop of Canterbury, Hubert Walter, opposed his consecration
the second time, whereupon Gerald appealed the case to Rome
and openly championed the recognition of St. David's as a
metropolitan church independent of Canterbury. That claim was
seriously investigated at Rome, where Gerald himself searched
the papal registers, but Innocent III finally called for a
new election and Gerald withdrew his candidacy. What counted
against him from the beginning, he observed with frank vanity,
was his popularity, his independence, his learning, his courage,
and his high birth (*Autobiography* 60). England evidently did
not want an assertive Welshman at the head of the leading diocese of Wales; Anglo-Norman monks were chosen for the post
instead.

Bishop David FitzGerald had appointed Gerald archdeacon of
Brecon about 1174. Such nepotism was common, and Gerald even
calls it a tradition at St. David's (*SD* 256). Nearly thirty
years later, having failed to become bishop of St. David's,
he resigned the archdeaconry and persuaded Hubert Walter to
approve the appointment of his own nephew, also named Gerald,
to succeed him as archdeacon.

Hubert Walter agreed but won a concession from Gerald that
he would pledge not to raise again the issue of metropolitan
status for St. David's. Gerald made the pledge. Among the
witnesses to the still-extant agreement was his nephew, Gerald
FitzPhilip, the new archdeacon (see Appendix 2 of Richter).
But though the nephew had the title, it was his uncle's understanding that he would continue until his death to administer
and receive the revenues of the archdeaconry (*SD* xxvi-xxviii).
Gerald looked forward to a tranquil retirement, away from the
storms of secular and ecclesiastical strife that had whirled
around him for most of his nearly sixty years.

As the sand-churches of his boyhood suggest, he had long
dreamt of peace. In his account of the journey through Wales
he made in 1188 with Archbishop Baldwin of Canterbury to preach
the Third Crusade, Gerald often pauses to describe affectionately
some feature of the land of his birth. Especially moving are
his descriptions of quiet places he has known. There was his
birthplace at Manorbier near the western sea, with all the resources of a great castle--fish-pond, orchard, hazel grove,
stream and water-mill in a secluded valley, the region rich in
wheat and fish from the sea, its climate tempered by warm currents from Ireland (*Wales* 150-51). Near Gloucester, where he

had gone to school at St. Peter's Abbey, there was the Austin
Canons' priory of Llanthony Prima ("the first convent of St.
David on the River Honddu," founded in 1103 by two hermits, a
second or daughter-house being later established at Gloucester).
It stood in a deep narrow valley enclosed by high mountains,
the site swept by rain, winds, and clouds, yet bracing and
healthful, its vistas of mountain tops and grazing deer con-
ducive to a life of contemplation (*Wales* 96-98). And there
was Gerald's own little house at Llanddew near Brecon, his
residence as archdeacon, where he wrote *The Journey Through
Wales*. It was small but suited to his studies. Here he enjoyed
the *aurea mediocritas* of Cicero and Horace--moderate circumstances free of care, midway between excess and scarcity. It
was a house that served his needs in this world but kept him
mindful of the next (*Wales* 107).

A decade before his resignation as archdeacon, Gerald of
Wales had retired from service with the royal court. He reports that he studied at Oxford and then settled in Lincoln
(*Autobiography* 139), where he remained until the St. David's
suit took him to Rome in 1199. He chose Lincoln because the
bishop of Lincoln, Hugh of Avalon, had assembled a group of
scholars there who were distinguished for both learning and
virtue. Gerald had hoped to resume his studies in Paris, but
the outbreak of fresh hostilities between Richard I and Philip
Augustus prevented that (*Autobiography* 127). Among St. Hugh's
scholars was a theologian with whom Gerald had studied during
his former years in Paris, Master William de Montibus.

The fullest evidence for Gerald's years of residence in
Lincoln, both before and after the St. David's suit (1199-
1203), is provided in Gerald's *Speculum Duorum*. The work is
not included in the Rolls Series edition of Gerald's writings,
since it was thought that no manuscript had survived. But the
Speculum Duorum is extant, in a manuscript at the Vatican
Library that is part of the collection previously belonging
to Queen Christina of Sweden (cataloged *Cod. Reg. Lat. 470*).
It has now been edited with full commentary and English translation, published by the University of Wales Press in 1974,
under the general editorship of Michael Richter. As Yves
Lefèvre demonstrates ("Un brouillon"), the manuscript was prepared with the author's supervision and incorporates many
significant amplifications of the text. The revisions are
part of a process by which Gerald transformed a private letter
of remonstrance to his nephew into a public defense of himself,
and among the latest revisions are some of Gerald's most
passionate and candid revelations.

Gerald reports that when he resigned as archdeacon and
recommended that his nephew succeed him, his friend Walter Map
judged it an unwise move. Map had much in common with Gerald.

He was a man of letters, a canon of Lincoln Cathedral who became archdeacon of Oxford in 1197 and who sought unsuccessfully
to become bishop of Hereford. His wit has come down to us in
the volume entitled *De Nugis Curialium*, containing satiric
vignettes of the age. Like Gerald, Walter Map exempts only
the Carthusians from his bitter attacks on the religious orders. The friendship of Gerald of Wales and Walter Map is
questioned by A.K. Bate (1972), who argues that the claim of
friendship was a pretence to enhance Gerald's reputation. It
is true that Gerald of Wales often advertises himself with
bravura and bad taste, but Gerald's assertion that Walter Map
said that his resignation was unwise seems plausible and suggests more than a casual acquaintance. According to Gerald,
Walter Map publicly said it was imprudent for Gerald to resign
his office in favor of his nephew and cited the example of
Henry II and his rebellious sons to demonstrate how sons can
despoil a father (*SD* 10).

The analogy was relevant, for Gerald and his nephew were
as close as father and son, and Gerald acknowledges his im-
prudence. But affection had moved him. He had secured his
nephew's promotion at the tearful request of the boy's father,
Philip de Barri, who had named his son for Gerald and entrusted
him to his care so that he might have a career in the world of
letters (*SD* 146, 194). That implied also a career in the
church. Gerald had received the boy into his own household
when he was first at Lincoln in the 1190s. Later, while he
was in Rome, he arranged for the boy to be taught by tutors
at Lincoln. But after the title of archdeacon of Brecon was
conferred on the young man in 1203, Gerald FitzPhilip manifested
a stubborn disinclination to study. His uncle patiently designed another regimen of study for him under a teacher at
Lincoln. But when he returned in 1206 from a two-year visit
with relatives in Ireland, he found that his nephew had not
followed this prescribed regimen (*SD* 44). He then appointed
yet another tutor, named William de Capella, the son of a
priest from Breconshire. For two years, Gerald of Wales got
on well with this tutor, who had such pleasing manners that
he won the old man's heart (*SD* 86). After a pilgrimage to
Rome, in the course of which he became a brother in the English
hospice founded by Innocent III and, like Thomas Becket, resigned all his benefices to the Pope (*SD* xxxii, n. 72), Gerald
returned to Lincoln to find himself betrayed.

The new bishop of St. David's, Geoffrey of Henlaw, formerly
prior of Llanthony Secunda, had appropriated funds belonging
to the income of the archdeaconry of Brecon. When Gerald pro-
tested, Bishop Geoffrey suggested that he send Archdeacon Gerald
FitzPhilip to Wales to investigate. The trip would cost more
than the funds in dispute, Gerald complained, but the nephew

and his tutor were eager to go and Gerald provided them with
horses for the journey. They met Bishop Geoffrey at Hereford,
and in the chapter there, before clerics who included old
friends of the elder Gerald's, the nephew made a formal appeal
to the Pope against his uncle. The complaint, of which no
legal statement survives, appears to have been that the uncle
was withholding funds of the archdeaconry from his nephew
(*SD* xxxii). In other words, the nephew wanted to enter into
possession of the goods of his office. Both Bishop Geoffrey
and William de Capella supported him in this. Since his uncle
was settled in scholarly seclusion at Lincoln and enjoyed
income from other benefices, a reasonable case might be made
that now, five years after being installed, the nephew was
entitled to exercise full authority in administering the archdeaconry and its revenues. Subsequent records of the archdeaconry indicate that this happened (perhaps after the lifting
of the interdict in 1214) and that Gerald FitzPhilip discharged
the duties of the archdeaconry as his principal occupation
until 1246 or 1247, when he was about sixty-five years old
(*SD* xxxvii, xxxviii).

But his uncle saw the concerted maneuvers of nephew,
bishop, and tutor as a betrayal of him and a violation of the
agreement of 1203 upon which the dignity and security of his
retirement rested. He had been a benefactor to them all. He
had fostered and secured ecclesiastical preferment for his
nephew; he had cast the deciding vote in the election of
Bishop Geoffrey, who was occupying the see Gerald had once
sought for himself; and he had hired his nephew's tutor, whom
he had also endowed with benefices. He saw their actions as
ingratitude prompted by greed, pride, and ambition. The love
he had felt and shown for Gerald FitzPhilip, the trust and
solicitude, the intimate sharing of home and table, books and
conversation, the generosity in giving the nephew clothes and
horses as well as food and lodging and education, the very act
of providing for his nephew's future by having him installed
in the important office of archdeacon--all these deeds of love
were to be the fuel for Gerald's hatred, once he perceived that
his nephew had turned against him.

The *Speculum Duorum* is a "mirror of two men," namely, the
nephew and his tutor (*SD* xxxiv), like Hamlet's mirror for his
mother, "a glass/Where you may see the inmost part of you."
For all its bitterness, the modern editors find a stubborn
honesty in the work (*SD* xxxix, xl). They estimate that the
original letter was composed about 1208-10. The reworking
and expansion of this letter, as preserved in the Vatican
manuscript, they date as written about 1216-18 (*SD* xxi, lxi).

How else was Gerald occupied during those years? He was
writing the *Life of St. Hugh* about 1210-14. He revised, ex-

panded, and rededicated his four earlier books on Ireland and
Wales. He wrote three autobiographical works concerning his
fight for St. David's. He wrote a manual on good government,
De Principis Instructione, that tells with some detail the
tragic case of King Henry II and also comments on the un-
successful invasion of England by the son of Philip Augustus
in 1216-17 (which reached as far as Lincoln Castle and was
repulsed there). He began a book on the religious orders,
Speculum Ecclesiae. And the editors of *Speculum Duorum* present evidence suggesting that after composing the *Speculum
Duorum* Gerald may have prepared a second edition of his manual
on priesthood, *Gemma Ecclesiastica* (*SD* 102, note to lines
433-61). The *Gemma Ecclesiastica* was first issued before
Gerald's trip in 1199 to Rome, where he presented a copy to
Innocent III. The only extant manuscript of the *Gemma* is
Lambeth 236, which contains a passage that seems to have been
originally composed in these pages of the Vatican manuscript of
Speculum Duorum. The passage is the concluding paragraph of
Chapter 6, Part 2 (*Op.* 2: 190-91). In his preface to his
edition of the lives of St. Remigius and St. Hugh (*Op.* 7:
xiii-xiv), James F. Dimock notes that at the end of *De Iure
et Statu Menevensis Ecclesiae* (the third and last of Gerald's
books on the St. David's controversy), Gerald speaks of his
lives of Remigius and Hugh as having been completed when he
was about seventy years old. That, says Dimock, would be
about right for the volume containing the lives of Remigius
and Hugh; but Gerald adds that he also issued the *Gemma
Ecclesiastica* when he was about seventy. Only if there had
been a second edition could that age be correct for *Gemma
Ecclesiastica*, and Dimock knew of no copy of a second edition.
But the text of *Gemma Ecclesiastica* in Lambeth MS 236 may well
be one, as the *Speculum Duorum* editors suggest. In that case,
the second edition of *Gemma Ecclesiastica* could be contempor-
aneous with *The Life of St. Hugh*, and Gerald's estimate of his
age--about seventy--when completing these works would be approximately right.

Even in his old age, Gerald was productive. Though the
dispute with his nephew may have disturbed him, it did not
silence him. *Speculum Duorum* shows, on the contrary, that
the case of his nephew's malfeasance provided him with matter
for writing and that the writing, as it always did, consoled
him. His establishment at Lincoln was that of a literary man
of substantial means (*SD* 116). Once during a famine in the
1190s, while he was studying in his chamber, he heard destitute
people clamoring at the doors and windows of his residence.
Moved to pity, he ordered that all his fur-trimmed cloaks and
hoods be sold and the proceeds given to the poor (*Autobiography* 128). He maintained careful household accounts and was

attended by servants (*SD* 78). He entertained guests in his
solar or private upper room (*SD* 30, 126-28), fed his household
well, including the ungrateful William de Capella (*SD* 96),
presided like a lord in whose presence all but his wayward
nephew rose (*SD* 126), kept a fine Lombard sword that William
de Capella stole (*SD* 96), though Gerald had once saved his
life from robbers (*SD* 92). He apparently had a well-staffed
scriptorium, judging from the numerous scribes whose hands
have contributed to the *Speculum Duorum* manuscript that was
assembled under his supervision (*SD* xix).

But his nephew did not share his uncle's taste for the
learned life. He would not learn Latin or French, the pre-
eminent tongues of the educated (*SD* 32, 132). He preferred to
play on his harp rather than attend to the instructive words
and urbane tales exchanged by the wits into whose company his
uncle brought him (*SD* 132). The nephew would tell ribald
folk at Lincoln--who later spread the story--that he wanted
control of his revenues quickly, rather than leaving them in
that old man's hands. With a boyish lisp that he would not
overcome and that grated on Gerald, the nephew made public
fun of his uncle's theological discourses and even of his
witty remarks (*SD* 32).

Why would the nephew not behave like his good brother
William, who used to memorize his uncle's aphorisms and anecdotes (*SD* 52-54)? Or like that Irish cousin who misbehaved
but humbly accepted correction from his uncle Gerald (*SD* 190-
92)? Gerald FitzPhilip liked the company of actors (*SD* 50),
exercised himself in archery and hunting (*SD* 138), and in the
evenings only studied to elicit barbarous melodies from his
Welsh harp (*SD* 138). His features, even in childhood, were
not admirable: his neck turned too easily; his head was too
elongated and rounded, his eyes too restless and unfixed, his
mouth devilish (*SD* 24). But he could wear a pretence of
liberality and was actually thought by some to be a modest
and decent young man (*SD* 160).

A modern reader might take him for a spirited youth im-
patient of school. His uncle's portrait, sheathed though it
is in moral texts and outrage, reveals a nephew of some charm.
And this takes us to the heart of the problem. Twice in
Speculum Duorum, Gerald quotes from the *Glossa Ordinaria* a
comment by Bede on betrayal by family or friends: worse than
other injuries are the pains of lost love (*SD* 6, 182). Gerald
loved his nephew and in that love had not only given his
nephew all, but he had told him all. All that Gerald had
boldly written, all that he had fearlessly said at his own
table regarding the faults of the great ones of the earth,
pope, Roman curia, kings, princes, all the home-truths of his
books and conversation were open to his nephew as to a trusted

friend (*SD* 144). And that trusted friend, with his tutor's
literate assistance, had copied out excerpts from Gerald's
books and conversation. Wounding him with his own weapons,
they prepared a dossier that showed Gerald of Wales to be a
traitor to the rulers of church and state (*SD* 144). Even the
letter from which *Speculum Duorum* grew was used against Gerald.
Some of the canons at Hereford Cathedral to whom the nephew
showed it judged it libelous and more injurious to the uncle
who wrote it than to the nephew whom it attacks (*SD* 160-62).
De Invectionibus, his book on the St. David's controversy that
precedes *Speculum Duorum* in the Vatican manuscript, was criti-
cized by some, Gerald complains, just because of its title.
Are there to be no invectives allowed on earth? (*SD* 162).

The tutor, William de Capella--whose last name Gerald
reads as "she-goat" or "whore" (e.g., *SD* 78)--dared to call
the *Speculum* a *spiculum* (dart). "What does he know of word-
play?" retorts Gerald (*SD* 196). Does he know what species of
verbal figure it is to substitute one letter for another?
The figure is classified as one of several varieties of pun
(*adnominatio*) in the *Rhetorica ad Herennium*. It was one of
Gerald's favorite devices, and he uses it to denote the
present unrest in his life: the dispute with his nephew has
turned his study (*studium*) into a stadium (*SD* 208).

He longed for peace, but now he is slandered and laughed
at and maligned. Not indifferent to fame, he finds himself
thought by many to be a mad and fatuous old man, whom they
once knew to be strong and full of life (*SD* 220). Ingratitude
has turned spiritual joy and brotherly love into implacable
hatred (*SD* 258), reverses trouble his mind, the light of noble
leisure is clouded and darkened, and every day old age wears
away the power of his memory (*SD* 186-88). Saddest but most
honest are Gerald's admissions of his own guilt, his indis-
cretions, his irregularities, his mistakes, his spiritual unrest. He wishes he were not so vengeful. He wishes he could
turn the other cheek. He knows the apostle Paul's injunction
not to return evil for evil, but he cannot reach that perfection. Additions to the manuscript show his turbulent rage
breaking out even as he polishes the little book. Wishing he
could bear injuries patiently but acknowledging that he still
loves his friends and hates his enemies, he adds "especially
when they keep attacking us" (*SD* 260). He complains that his
nephew has rewarded his unworthy tutor by giving the tutor
clothes that Gerald had given the nephew.

A bishop should be perfect. As he is of high rank, a
bishop should excel in wisdom and holiness. This translates
a text from the canonist Gratian that Gerald quotes in a
letter to Bishop Geoffrey of Henlaw, lecturing Geoffrey on
how a bishop should behave (*SD* 232). For Gerald sees himself

as betrayed by his spiritual father, the bishop of St. David's,
because that bishop has sided with Gerald's nephew. He has
not acted as a mediator. Worse, he seems to resent the very
existence of Gerald. Is it because Gerald had played a part
in Geoffrey's becoming bishop? Gerald declares that Geoffrey
has gone so far as to ban Gerald's letters from the diocese
of St. David's and to deny him permission to preach there.
Publicly, the bishop complains that Gerald is complaining
(*SD* 256). But he cannot keep Gerald from the writing that is
his consolation (*SD* 194). Posterity may read what he writes
and judge the case as he does (*SD* 238-40). Gerald will complain, then, driven to the solace of a song of grief, like a
dying swan (*SD* 208).

He was a man not perfect, but with a vision of perfection.
His ideal was the saint at peace with himself and others--
learned, generous, prudent, patient, courageous, and loving--and
such a civilized and happy man of God haunts the labored pages
of *Speculum Duorum*. He is the man the author would have his
nephew be, the man he wishes the bishop of St. David's were,
the man he wishes he himself could be. The texts Gerald
thrusts upon his nephew from the classics, scripture, the
fathers, and modern canonists delineate features of that happy
man. But Gerald did not have to meet him only in books. He
had known such a man. He had seen with amazement how a swan
behaved in his presence. He had seen the wonderful beauty of
the cathedral he rebuilt. He had observed the cheerfulness and
happiness that were almost always in his face. He was a man
such as few men are. For the bishop of Lincoln, St. Hugh of
Avalon, whose distinguished community of scholars had drawn
Gerald to Lincoln, was a civilized and happy man of God.

Gerald's high regard for St. Hugh is manifested dramatically in his last book, *Speculum Ecclesiae* ("Mirror of the Church"),
completed about 1220. This is a survey of the church past and
present, distant and near. The one extant manuscript is de-
fective, but it remains a big book. The often-echoed judgment
of the Rolls Series editor, J.S. Brewer, that it is little
more than a "collection of monastic scandals" (*Op*.4: viii)
does not do justice to the book's range. It has four parts.
In the preface, Gerald announces that the first part will deal
briefly with the various kinds of religious life and orders;
the second and third will deal with monks and prelates, particularly Cluniacs and Cistercians in England and Wales; and
the fourth, which he calls far the most important part, will
discuss the Church of Rome, the mother and mistress of all
other churches. In this fourth part, he notes that certain
topics have been developed in the now badly damaged first
part--for example, the donation of Constantine and how the
Christian church was prefigured in the Mosaic tabernacle and

the temple of Solomon (*Op.* 4: 284). It would appear that the
first part summarized the origins of ecclesiastical institu-
tions, such as the papacy and monasticism, while sketching
the patristic origins of such issues as the respective merits
of the active and the contemplative life, or how evangelical
poverty could be reconciled with the rightful use of temporal
goods and how the Bride of Christ could wield power in human
society. Gerald cites decrees of the Lateran Council convened
by Innocent III in 1215. The issues he examines were issues
of the day. They were issues that engaged the soul of Francis
of Assisi at the very time Gerald was writing. In his preface,
Gerald deplores yet again the rising currents of Aristotelian
logic then reaching Paris from Toledo; he wonders whether
heresy may lurk there and pleads for the older rhetorical
tradition in which he had been trained half a century before.

In Parts 2 and 3, he tells something of the history of the
monastic orders and illustrates with vivid reportage the
abuses into which some of them had fallen after the glory of
their pristine days had passed. He paints, for example, an
amusing picture of the monks at Canterbury feasting wordlessly
but with frenzied gesticulations and whistling. Wouldn't it
be better just to talk quietly at table, like gentlemen? The
Cistercians, whose diet is spare and whose hospitality is
generous, he shows to be prone to cupidity, as they add field
to field and grange to grange on their vast farm estates. He
tells of monks guilty of scandalous lust, monks who pose as
physicians and wander about peddling nostrums, monks who prefer
the freedom of an outlying grange to the discipline of their
home cloister, monks who mix craftily in politics when they
should be at their prayers. But he describes one order that
has suffered no decline from its original purity: the Carthusians, the order to which St. Hugh had belonged. Gerald
finds in their statutes the wise provisions that account for
their constancy.

The Carthusians resemble the Cistercians in their austerity
and simplicity of life, notes Gerald, but the Carthusians are
more eremitical. They eat no meat nor animal fat, even when
sick, and they wear only robes made from the skins of animals.
Each has an individual cell or hermitage, though they share a
common kitchen. In their fields, says Gerald, they can keep
oxen, sheep, and goats, but not cows, mares, studs, or pigs.
They tend guests and the poor in a modest manner and try to
avoid entering into disputes regarding their lands and possessions. Thus, concludes Gerald, they remain more free than other
orders to devote themselves to contemplation and the love of
God.

To prove that the church can find great leaders outside
the monastic orders, Gerald cites in *Speculum Ecclesiae* the

achievements of St. Thomas Becket and Stephen Langton, the learned and valiant archbishop of Canterbury to whom Gerald dedicated the volume containing his *Life of St. Hugh*. But that monks can be great contemplatives and also serve in the active ministry is demonstrated by the career of St. Hugh, the Carthusian who became an exemplary bishop. Gerald praises St. Hugh's stern reproof of the monks of the venerable St. Alban's Abbey, who, jealous of their prerogatives, says Gerald, were reluctant to admit him as their bishop to their cloister and altar (*Op.* 4: 94-96). While Gerald opposes the interference of secular rulers in the choice of bishops, St. Hugh, favored by Henry II, was indeed a worthy candidate. Choosing Hugh was a moment of grace in that monarch's reign, says Gerald. And it is probable that the other bishop promoted by Henry from a contemplative order, Archbishop Baldwin, is now a saint. Gerald recalls the death of Baldwin at Acre, on the Third Crusade. If Baldwin's heavenly crown is but a probability, it is certain--*hesitari vel ambigi non permittitur* ("one cannot hesitate or doubt")--that Hugh is a saint (*Op.* 4: 345). For God has verified his triumph *aperte per signa et prodigia multa* ("openly by many signs and wonders"). The tribute to the Carthusians at the end of Part 3 of *Speculum Ecclesiae* and this confident allusion to Hugh's miracles and sainthood near the end of Part 4 may be read as Gerald's endorsement of the contemporary event of the canonization of Hugh of Avalon. The papal bull of canonization by Honorius III is quoted by Dimock (*Op.* 7: 243-45). It is dated February 17, 1220.

A few years later, it was recorded in the register of the bishop of Lincoln that the church of Chesterton in Oxfordshire was vacant through the death of Master Giraldus de Barri, certified by the dean of Hereford. Had he died in Hereford? We do not know. The institution of his successor as rector of Chesterton occurred in Hugh of Wells's fourteenth year as bishop of Lincoln (December 20, 1222, to December 19, 1223). The exact date is not given. (The reference, which Kathleen Major has confirmed for me, is *Rotuli Hugonis de Welles*, ed. W.P. Phillimore, F.N. Davis, and others, Lincolnshire Record Society Publications [1912-14], Volumes 3, 6, 9; the entry relative to Gerald's death is in the second of these volumes, pp. 9-10.) Years before, Gerald had defended his right to the Chesterton benefice in a letter to Hugh of Avalon written about 1194 (*Symbolum Electorum*, *Op.* 1: 259-68). We have no other evidence regarding his death, and his place of burial is not known. But in his honor, modern statues of him have been erected at St. David's Cathedral and Cardiff City Hall.

Latin distichs of his own composing that he liked to quote as the words of an eloquent *sapiens* (as in his letter to Stephen Langton, *Op.* 1: 403) may stand as his epitaph:

> Semper adest homini, quo pectoris ima gemiscat;
> Ne possit plena prosperitate frui.
> Gaudia nunc luctu, nunc mutat amara secundis,
> Versans humanas sors inopina vices.
> Sola venire solent, et vix, et sero, secunda;
> Sed simul et subito, et semper, amara fluunt.
> Ergo ubi nil varium, nil vanum, nilve nocivum,
> Sint ibi fixa tibi spes, amor, atque fides.

(A man always has something to make him groan deep in
his breast, so that he cannot enjoy complete well-being. Unexpected chance, making human fortunes revolve, now changes
joys into sorrow, now turns bitterness to joy. Happy things
come one at a time, just barely, and late; bitter things rush
together, suddenly and continuously. Upon that place, therefore, where nothing changes, nothing is vain, nothing is hurt-
ful, fix your hope, your love, and your trust.)

Artistic Achievement

Hugh of Avalon has been continuously remembered and honored
by the Carthusians, and biographies of him survive in medieval
manuscripts and early printed editions. But when James Dimock
published his edition of the *Metrical Life of St. Hugh* in
1860, Hugh was so little known in the English-speaking world
that the editor could speak of the saint as: "forgotten almost,
un-noted save in the brief annals of his church, unmentioned
almost, save sometimes in his own cathedral city, or when
some stranger has asked and borne away the name of the man who
built the holy and beautiful house of God that crowns the hill
of Lincoln" (p. xii). Six years before, in 1854 in Paris, the
life of St. Hugh had been published in Migne's *Patrologia
Latina* (153: 937-1114), a reprint of an edition published by
Bernardus Pezius at Ratisbon in 1733. This was an abbrevia-
tion of the principal life of St. Hugh, known as the *Magna
Vita Sancti Hugonis*. The author of the *Magna Vita*, as established by Dimock, was Adam, monk and abbot of the Benedictine
house of Eynsham Abbey (near Oxford), who was St. Hugh's chaplain and confessor during the last three years of Hugh's life.
Adam recorded Hugh's words and deeds with the devotion, exacti-
tude, and candor of a Boswell. With equal care, James Dimock
was to revive interest in St. Hugh in nineteenth-century
England, through his edition of the *Metrical Life of St. Hugh*
(1860) and the Rolls Series editions of the *Magna Vita Sancti*

Hugonis (1864) and the *Vita Sancti Hugonis* by Gerald of Wales (1877).

In 1870, availing himself of Dimock's edition of the *Magna Vita*, James Anthony Froude published an article on Hugh, "A Bishop of the Twelfth Century" (*Fraser's Magazine*, New Series, 1 [February 1870]: 220-36). It is a brilliant retelling of scenes from Hugh's life and has doubtless made Hugh known to many readers who would never have ventured upon Adam's medieval Latin biography, in which Froude found himself "brought face to face with authentic flesh and blood" and gained acquaintance with a man of "the sunniest cheerfulness" who was yet "one of the most beautiful spirits that was ever incarnated in human clay." John Ruskin read Froude's article and shared Froude's admiration for St. Hugh. In his autobiography, *Praeterita*, Volume 3, Chapter 1, Ruskin recounts his own visit to the Grande Chartreuse in 1849 in the company of his father. He was disappointed with both the mountain setting and the monastic buildings, which were not so striking as he had expected. The monk who was their guide pointed out that the Carthusians did not come there to look at the mountains. Ruskin found that attitude incomprehensible. Yet he observes that from the eleventh to the fourteenth century the Carthusians "reared in their mountain fastnesses, and sent out to minister to the world, a succession of men of immense mental grasp, and serenely authoritative innocence; among whom our own Hugo of Lincoln, in his relations with Henry II and Coeur de Lion, is to my mind the most beautiful sacerdotal figure known to me in history" (Ruskin 35: 482).

The earliest extant accounts of the life of St. Hugh are the work of Gerald of Wales. During his first stay in Lincoln (ca. 1196-99), Gerald wrote a history of the Norman bishopric of Lincoln, a work known under the title *Vita Sancti Remigii*, "The Life of St. Remigius" (*Op.* 7: 1-80). Remigius was a monk of Fécamp Abbey in Normandy who supplied troops for the invading army of William the Conqueror. He was consecrated bishop of Dorchester in 1067. The see was transferred to Lincoln in 1072, and Remigius died there in 1092, having begun the building of the great Romanesque cathedral, which was consecrated four days after his death (*Op.* 7: 21). In the *Vita Sancti Remigii*, Gerald endeavors to demonstrate that this founder was worthy of canonization, and then he proceeds to summarize the history of the see down to the bishop of his own day, Hugh of Avalon.

After 1166, the see had been vacant for many years. An illegitimate son of Henry II, Geoffrey Plantagenet, was elected bishop in 1173 but was never consecrated. At last, in 1183, Walter of Coutances was installed as bishop of Lincoln (while Geoffrey Plantagenet was to go on to a stormy career as arch-

bishop of York). The following year Walter of Coutances was
transferred to the see of Rouen. Hugh of Avalon was consecrated
bishop of Lincoln on September 21, 1186, and served till his
death in 1200. In Chapter 26 of the *Vita Sancti Remigii*,
written while Hugh was still alive, Gerald gives eyewitness
testimony to Hugh's remarkable character and leadership.
Here is my translation of the chapter (the Latin text is in
Dimock's edition, *Op.* 7: 39-42):

Hugh of Burgundy

The successor of Walter [of Coutances] was Hugh,
who was born in Burgundy to a noble family of knightly
rank. From childhood, he was devoted to virtue and
religion. Lest he be corrupted by the degeneracy of
the age, he bound himself to the strict rules of the
monastic life of the Grande Chartreuse. Later he was
sent from there to be prior of the Carthusian convent of
Witham in England. King Henry II used to hunt in the
forest where the convent was located and took the occasion to visit the place and its prior. Hugh soon
gained the king's friendship and favor and was promoted
to be bishop of Lincoln. Here he was a firm advocate
of justice. He would not yield in the least to royal
agents or courtiers or government officials who were
accustomed to attack the church or the clergy. With
all his strength he effected and implemented whatever
he saw would promote decency and religion and the good
and honor of his church. He added two canonries with
fixed and perpetual benefices, namely with lands and
churches formerly lost that he recovered; and he canceled two others that his predecessors had endowed with
money from the cathedral treasury. He vigorously held
on to the monastery of Eynsham, which had earlier been
lost and was due to come under the king's control;
with expensive but effective and fruitful efforts, he
restored to the church of Lincoln the granting of the
pastoral staff [i.e., authority to install the abbot of
Eynsham]. He also rebuilt the head [the east end] of
his church with Parian [i.e., white] stones and [black
Purbeck] marble columns of remarkable craftsmanship,
and raised from the foundations a completely new structure, very richly executed. Similarly, he launched the
building of a fine episcopal palace and with the help
of the Lord confidently planned to finish one far more
spacious and noble than those preceding. Using sound
judgment, he also retrieved that mantle of [Bishop
Robert] Bloet and [Bishop] Alexander. It was once im-
providently and unwisely contributed [to the government]

and on that pretext was owed forever. With one payment
he canceled this perpetual and subservient tax, by means
of a charter confirmed with the king's seal that affirms
--if faith reigns on earth--the liberty of the church of
Lincoln and its perpetual immunity. He also raised as
trustworthy pillars for his church outstanding persons
renowned for learning and integrity, chosen for this
purpose with great care from throughout the kingdom.
He did not give first consideration to blood-ties, as
others carnally do, nor to offspring, but, led by the
Spirit and with reason his guide, he weighed learning
and merit instead. He was free of greed and ambition.
Firmly keeping his hands clean of every bribe, every
imposition and exaction upon those subject to his
authority, he so dreaded the snares of simony, in which
today almost all who govern are caught, that he would
spontaneously and habitually refuse most gifts offered
to him, lest any sign of supposed wrongdoing arise. He
was generally wary even of being bound to an exchange
of gifts or under an obligation in spirit or by natural
relationship. But why do I review particulars? He shone
with so many notable signs of goodness and probity,
virtue and integrity, as to be virtually the one pillar
of the English church in his days and a unique mirror
shining with a reflection of the divine light. In almost
everything, he had no need to look for an example, but
to give an example. Among the bishops of Lincoln up
to his own time, he is now rightly regarded as first
and foremost after blessed Remigius, if his end should
agree with his beginning. Having put on the vestment
of a bishop, may he bring to a happy conclusion what he
has begun so admirably. Pressing steadily forward and
not looking back, let him exert himself and beg God's
help, so that in the course of a good life, "the middle
may not differ from the beginning nor the end from the
middle" [Horace, *Ars Poetica*, 152]. As he nears the
end, may he from day to day approach Christ as his end,
with larger strides of virtue and a finer zeal in good
works, his burning love not growing cold.

In Chapter 5 of his later *Vita Sancti Hugonis*, Gerald sup-
plements a paragraph on the rebuilding of the cathedral with
a paragraph on how Hugh built his clergy, an architectural
analogy already used in the above chapter on "Hugh of Burgundy."
It is apt. Hugh built the clergy of his cathedral into "sound
and reliable pillars for his church" (*VSH* 21) by administrative
actions that parallel the steps taken in rebuilding the cathedral. A system for the government of the church existed but

needed restoration; Hugh contributed to the definition and
implementation of this system of government. The design was
that of the cathedral chapter as it had been established in
England in the eleventh century, on the model of churches in
Normandy.

There had been an important Saxon church at Lincoln dedicated to St. Mary. Bede tells that Paulinus built a stone
church at Lincoln in the seventh century. The probable site
was the hilltop where in the first century *A.D.* the Romans
had built a fort. Two major Roman roads meet at Lincoln:
Ermine Street, the route north from London to York and Scotland,
which is joined just south of the city by Fosse Way, crossing
the country from the southwest to Lincoln, its southern ter-
minus being Exeter. Ermine Street, whose path is followed
rather closely by modern roadways of the city, is the main
street of Lincoln to which Gerald often refers. It climbs
the hill and crosses the site of the Roman fort (with the medieval castle on the left or west and the minster to the east),
and then, through a Roman gate whose arch is still intact,
the road proceeds to Yorkshire. Before the Norman Conquest,
St. Mary of Lincoln was recognized as a mother church of the
parish (Hill, 20, 67, 72, 77). But it was not a cathedral
church until the Normans made it one.

We can trace the elements and evolution of the chapter
system at Lincoln in a fourteenth-century collection of
statutes and customs of Lincoln Cathedral known as the *Black
Book*. It was transcribed by Henry Bradshaw and printed in
the *Statutes of Lincoln Cathedral*, Volume 1. The color is
that of the medieval binding; a macaronic phrase in a fifteenth-century statute refers to the volume as "le blak boke
vocatus" (*BBL* 7). The first sentence of the first part of the
Black Book as transcribed by Bradshaw reads: "Dignitas episcopi
est in choro Capitulo et in omnibus locis supra Decanum et
omnes personas ecclesie et canonicos in exhibitione honoris
habere preminenciam" (*BBL* 273). (In the choir, the chapter
house, and all places, it is the privilege of the bishop to
have preeminence in marks of honor, above the dean and all
dignitaries and canons of the church.)

This encapsulates the government of the cathedral. The
bishop presides over a body of clerics whose principal member,
second to the bishop, is the dean. All the principal officers
are named in a later passage (*BBL* 279), which I translate: "In
the church of Lincoln there are four principal dignitaries,
the dean, the precentor, the chancellor, and the treasurer;
there are eight archdeacons, of Lincoln, Northampton, Leicester,
Hungtingdon, Buckingham, Oxford, Bedford, and Stow; and there
is a subdean." The precentor presides over the liturgy, the
chanting, and the choir school (*BBL* 283-84). The treasurer

is responsible for the safekeeping of precious objects belonging to the cathedral, such as relics, vestments, missals,
and chalices (*BBL* 285); when these treasures were seized by
the king in the sixteenth century, the office of treasurer
ceased to exist (*BBL* 103). The dean is elected, subject to
the bishop's ratification (*BBL* 279); otherwise the canons
and officers are appointed by the bishop (*BBL* 274). The canons
are endowed with prebends, which would be churches or manors
(or in some cases cash payments). The responsibilities of a
prebendal church could keep a canon away from the cathedral;
a charter of St. Hugh's requires that in such cases the canon
provide adequate maintenance for the vicar who would take his
place in choir (*BBL* 308). The bishop himself was often compelled to be away from Lincoln. His diocese, extending from
the Humber to the Thames, was very large. As a leading
prelate, he was summoned to royal councils and on occasion
had to follow the court to the Angevin territories on the
continent. The second sentence in the *Black Book* prescribes
how the bishop is to be received at the cathedral when he returns from overseas (*BBL* 273). The day-to-day administration
of the church was in the hands of the dean and chapter. Their
rights and immunities are affirmed in twelfth-century charters
of St. Hugh and Bishop Robert de Chesney (*BBL* 308-10). Hugh
had good reason to choose his men cautiously.

He petitioned Baldwin--the archbishop of Canterbury who
had consecrated him bishop of Lincoln--for men to assist him
at Lincoln. From among his own clergy, Baldwin assigned him
Roger of Rolleston and Robert of Bedford (*MV* 1: 112). Ironical-
ly, when Baldwin's archdeacon expected Hugh to give him a
palfrey as the customary tribute for episcopal consecration,
Hugh had refused such a simoniacal payment, obeying instead
the strict decrees of the Lateran Council of 1179 (*MV* 1: 104).
Adam of Eynsham tells of a master in Paris who desired to become a canon at Lincoln Cathedral; knowing him to be less virtuous than he was learned, Hugh declined to offer him a place
(*MV* 1: 120-21). Hugh opposed an effort by the government of
Richard I to have twelve of his canons serve as royal ambas-
sadors abroad, that they not be drawn from their duties at
Lincoln (*MV* 2: 110-13). To the important post of chancellor,
he appointed the Paris master William de Montibus. The chancellor not only superintended the official correspondence,
records, and library of the cathedral chapter, but also had
authority to license persons to lecture in Lincoln (*BBL* 284-
85). Hugh's success in recruiting men of William's stature
made Lincoln a center for the study of theology and canon law.

An ancient custom existed at Lincoln of daily offering a
mass and a recitation of the complete Psalter for the benefac-
tors of the cathedral. The psalms were divided among the

canons, but the exact distribution of psalms had fallen into
question. At some time between 1195 and 1200, under Dean Roger
of Rolleston, the chapter made a distribution that Hugh rati-
fied in an *antiqua constitucio* included in the *Black Book*
(*BBL* 300-06). The opening words of the psalms as thus assigned
may still be seen inscribed in Latin above the choir stalls
named for the prebendal churches. The bishop's psalms are
the first three of the Psalter, *Beatus vir*, *Quare fremuerunt*,
and *Domine quid multiplicati sunt*. Hugh would accordingly
have recited these psalms daily. The opening verses of
Beatus vir are appropriate to him. In the translation of
The Book of Common Prayer, they read:

> Blessed is the man that hath not walked in the counsel
>   of the ungodly, nor stood in the way of sinners: and
>   hath not sat in the seat of the scornful.
> But his delight is in the law of the Lord: and in his
>   law will he exercise himself day and night.
> And he shall be like a tree planted by the waterside:
>   that will bring forth his fruit in due season.
> His leaf also shall not wither: and look, whatsoever he
>   doeth, it shall prosper.

The chapter on "Hugh of Burgundy" in *Vita Sancti Remigii*
might have ended Gerald's history of the bishops of Lincoln,
but he appends an essay reflecting his own interest in the
role of the bishop, as well as his fascination with Hugh.
It is entitled *De episcopis tergeminis*, "On three pairs of
bishops." Dimock believes the essay contains revisions
written after Hugh's death, since near its end there is an
allusion to Hugh's not winning the reward for martyrdom (*Op.*
7: 80). But perhaps Gerald simply perceived in Hugh a leader
whose diplomacy would forestall an impasse that in his circumstances might occasion martyrdom. At all events, the essay is
a comparison of six bishops of twelfth-century England, the
most famous being the martyred archbishop of Canterbury, St.
Thomas Becket. The others, in addition to Hugh, are Henry of
Blois, bishop of Winchester (1129-71); Bartholomew, bishop of
Exeter (1162-84); Roger, bishop of Worcester (1164-79); and
Baldwin, bishop of Worcester (1180-84) and later archbishop of
Canterbury (1185-90). The bishops are described in pairs:
Thomas of Canterbury and Henry of Winchester; Bartholomew of
Exeter and Roger of Worcester; and last, two bishops who were
members of contemplative orders, Baldwin of Canterbury, who
was a Cistercian, and Hugh of Lincoln, a Carthusian.
   Gerald had personal acquaintance with both Baldwin and
Hugh. He had accompanied Archbishop Baldwin through Wales
in the spring of 1188, when Baldwin was seeking recruits for

the Third Crusade. Chapter 29 of Gerald's *Vita Sancti Remigii*,
comparing Baldwin and Hugh, begins thus (*Op.* 7: 67-68; my
translation):

> But not long after the time of these men [Bartholo-
> mew of Exeter and Roger of Worcester], the king arranged
> for two men to be promoted bishops from the ranks of
> monks, one a Cistercian, the other a Carthusian. One
> became the bishop of Worcester and afterward archbishop
> of Canterbury; and the other, bishop of Lincoln. The
> first had been abbot of Ford, and the other, prior of
> Witham. In his last years--though it seemed more from
> a concern for opinion and show than out of piety--King
> Henry II had resolved to bestow cathedral sees upon
> members of these two monastic orders, to redeem his
> reputation thus, since he had previously made many un-
> worthy men bishops. These two seemed to be equally
> good and religious, but they were quite different in
> the style of their virtues. Each was learned enough,
> but the second [Hugh] was very learned. The first
> [Baldwin] was slow to speak and brief; the other was
> full of wit and playful talk. The first was almost
> always rather sad and apprehensive; the other, good-
> humored, with nearly constant cheerfulness and assurance.
> The first was a Diogenes, the other a Democritus; the
> first was cautious and restrained in anger, as in nearly
> everything; the other was provoked by even a slight
> occasion. The first was mild, lukewarm, and slack; the
> other, keen, ardent, and strict.

Gerald proceeds to discuss Baldwin's tenure as archbishop
of Canterbury. His verdict is that Baldwin dissipated the
gains won by Thomas Becket at the cost of his blood. He
quotes Pope Urban III as addressing Baldwin by the titles
"most fervent monk, warm abbot, tepid bishop, and slack archbishop" (*Op.* 7: 68). After the commentary on Baldwin, Gerald
returns to Hugh, with a celebrated description of Hugh's pet
swan. This description he incorporated into his later *Vita
Sancti Hugonis* (*VSH* 50-52), omitting one passage that I have
restored in brackets in my text of the *Vita Sancti Hugonis*.
Adam of Eynsham quotes Gerald's description of the swan in
its entirety in the *Magna Vita*, adding observations of his
own that confirm Gerald's (*MV* 1: 103-09).
    After describing Hugh's swan in Chapter 29 of *Vita Sancti
Remigii*, Gerald tells a dream of Hugh's (*Op.* 7: 76-77):

> When he became a monk in his youth, he often suffered
> the opposing attacks of flesh and spirit within himself,

not without great pain. At last a man like an angel
appeared to him in a vision and instantly seemed to
cut off his genitals with forceps that he carried in
his hand. In fact, it was a happy cure granted him by
God. For from that hour, though he was afterward made
a bishop and transplanted to the extravagances of English
wealth at a passionate age, he never felt the attacks
of carnal desire, or, what was a greater wonder,
scarcely even the first impulses. On this topic,
Augustine writes: "It is not from nature but from grace
than any rational creature is granted the power not to
sin."

In the *Magna Vita*, Adam says that it has been incorrectly
asserted that Hugh dreamt he was relieved of carnal torment
by being made a eunuch by the Virgin Mary (not the "man like
an angel" of Gerald's version). Rather, says Adam, Hugh
dreamt that Prior Basil, who received Hugh into the Carthusian
Order, appeared to him and removed something like red hot
cinders from his bowels (*MV* 1: 51-52). Subsequently, says
Adam, though he did feel the first impulses, he was not vio-
lently tempted again. This may be meant as a correction of
Gerald.

Gerald rounds off his essay on the six bishops and his
whole history of the church of Lincoln in the *Vita Sancti
Remigii* by an interesting estimate of Hugh and his episcopacy
--interesting in part because it records a change in Hugh's
manner, from an earlier asperity to a tempered forbearance
(*Op.* 7: 77-78):

But the bishop of Lincoln, who as I said was ardent
and strict when he was first made a bishop, took thought
and reflected that the head of the church [Christ] was
submissive on earth; and he realized that he might have
no peer in the kingdom whose companionship could comfort
him or whose virtue could strengthen him, nor any
superior whose authority could fully support him. As
time passed, he decided to observe the custom of the
land. Since it is wrong that each part not fit the
whole to which it belongs, he decided in patience and
modesty to conform himself more fully and serenely to
the company of his fellow bishops. More reasonably,
then, he preferred in most cases to submit willingly
to forcible rule than by openly resisting alone (for
"Woe to those who are alone!" [Ecclesiastes 4: 10]), to
endanger himself and his people, whom he had already
rooted in the good things of the kingdom [of heaven].

Here follow two and a half pages of quotations from scripture and scriptural commentators in praise of patient endurance.
Gerald concludes with an ornate contrast that also figures in
his preface to the *Life of St. Hugh* (*VSH* 2): Hugh may not win
(as Becket had) the red crown of martyrdom, but he should be
rewarded with the white lily of innocence and purity (*Op.* 7:
80): "If the bishop of Lincoln should not in fact obtain the
purple and rose-colored crown [of martyrdom], may he at least,
inspired by grace from above, happily win the snowlike tribute,
made beautiful with the radiance of the lily, in that garden
of delights and that flowering field of thrones above, where
according to merits both rewards and garlands are generously
distributed."

Gerald left Lincoln in 1199 on his first trip to Rome to
defend his right to be consecrated bishop of St. David's. For
four years, this quest was to be his chief occupation. It was
followed by a two-year stay in Ireland and a pilgrimage to
Rome. As I have already noted, when he returned to Lincoln
about 1207, he had not only withdrawn from the fight to pre-
side at St. David's but had resigned his office as archdeacon
of Brecon in favor of his nephew. He would devote his last
years--some fifteen now remained to him--to his books. It may
have been the dean of Lincoln Cathedral, Roger of Rolleston,
who at this time commissioned Gerald to write a life of St.
Hugh. Roger was dean from 1195 to his death in 1223, the same
year Gerald may have died, so that their friendship was one
of many years' duration (see *VSH* 90 for an allusion to this
friendship).

The tomb of Hugh of Avalon at Lincoln Cathedral had become
a shrine visited by pilgrims. The custodians of the tomb recorded miracles attributed to High's intercession, and the dean
and chapter were often called upon to hear and evaluate reports of miracles. Concern for authenticating miracles would
derive both from distrust for superstitious credulity--Hugh
himself, like his hero, St. Martin, had sternly put down the
superstitious cult of a reputed local martyr (*MV* 2: 201)--and
from the desire to assemble testimony that would meet the cri-
teria for canonization promulgated by recent popes (see Farmer
87-88).

The special character and purpose of Gerald's *Life of St.
Hugh* are expressed in his preface (Paragraph 1): the miracles
by which saints are manifested to the world should be cherished,
and the love that animates saints should be made known *dignis
laudum preconiis*, with worthy tributes. Gerald's *Life of St.
Hugh* is to be a work of praise that will make the saint known
and loved. At the end of the preface to Part 1, Gerald states
that he will write of Hugh in very plain and unpolished words,
planis admodum verbis et non politis (*VSH* 4). Similarly, in

the preface to the second part he announces that he will report the miracles of St. Hugh in a straightforward account,
tractatu dilucido (*VSH* 57). The preface to the third part
notes that he will summarize the later miracles in the style
of the schools, *scolastico quoque digerere stilo* (*VSH* 90).
Plain prose is what we find in most of *The Life of St. Hugh*.
But the work has rhetorical enrichments as well. In a stylistic
analysis of the *Gemma Ecclesiastica*, John Hagen observes that
Gerald uses a plain style in the main body of instruction and
illustrations in that manual but occasionally displays a more
ornamented style (*Jewel* xxiv-xxxi). A like mixing of styles
is evident in the *Vita Sancti Hugonis*.

Stylistic enrichments in *VSH* include quotations, com-
parisons, balancing of phrases and sentences, and poetic
repetitions of sounds. The quotations include scriptural
echoes and *sententiae* from the Latin fathers and poets.
Twice Gerald clusters quotations (*VSH* 37, 106). Several times
he quotes St. Hugh. The words ascribed to Hugh--as in *VSH* 18,
25, 44, 46, which I discuss below--often have verbal embellishments that could be of Gerald's composing but may be faithfully
preserved instances of the wit for which Hugh was noted.

Amplification by comparison appears in *VSH* 37. Antono-
masia, or the use of personal name in place of a common noun,
appears twice: Dalila (Delilah) for "sensuality" (*VSH* 5) and
Mars for "fighting" (*VSH* 8). Gerald uses litotes often: "sub
silencio pretereundum non putavi" (*VSH* 50); "Non enim misterio
carere potuit" (*VSH* 52); "non incompetenter" (*VSH* 90); "nec
inmemor nec ingratus" (*VSH* 100). He uses paired synonyms with
great frequency. An interesting example is the following
sentence (from *VSH* 7) in which adverbs, nouns, and adjectives
are paired in parallel phrases, with the synonyms separated
by a verb:

> Quam incontinenti tam *provide* rexit et tam *mature*,
> ut quam *pauperem* susceperat et *exilem*,
> possessionibus amplis *opulentam* in brevi redderet et *opimam*.

Anaphora appears in the gracious words of St. Hugh in
VSH 44: "Bene comedatis, et bene bibatis, et bene ac devote
Deo serviatis." Anaphora is combined with parallelism in the
ornate second paragraph of *VSH*:

> Sicut igitur inter metalla conmunia aurum rutilans et
>   obrizum,
> sicut inter arenas innumeras preciose virtutis gemma
>   reperta,
> sicut inter nubes et nebulas procellosas sol clarius
>   erumpens et diem irradians ...

The last phrase, "sol clarius erumpens et diem irradians," is paralleled by the main clause of the sentence: "sic sanctus hic ... insulam Britannicam ... illustravit." Gerald's best-known quotation of Hugh uses parallelism: "Martinus osculando leprosum curavit eum in corpore. Leprosus autem osculo sanavit me in anima" (*VSH* 46).

Twice Gerald quotes Hugh as using puns. In *VSH* 18, Hugh puns with the verb phrase *tenere terram*, in these senses: to hold land by legal possession, to hold some earth in one's hands, and to be spiritually attached to this earth. In *VSH* 25, Hugh uses the punning device of changing one letter in a word, the device to which Gerald refers in *Speculum Duorum* (*SD* 196): "festive pocius hoc festo et non festine agendum." An instance of punning repetition together with alliteration and rhyme is this passage from *VSH* 67: "inter signa insignia quasi primum et precipuum hoc admirandum et annotandum." Alliteration sometimes links several words in a phrase: "nisi facili et frivola forsan offensa" (*VSH* 33); "tam effrenis et efferus et fere tirannicus" (*VSH* 42). In the *Poetria Nova*, Geoffrey of Vinsauf cautions that excessive alliteration is a vice and recommends modest use of this ornament (see the translation by Margaret F. Nims). Geoffrey and Gerald were contemporaries. Though the *Poetria Nova* contains later revisions, it appears to have been substantially completed early in the reign of King John and features a famous apostrophe on the death of Richard I (Geoffrey of Vinsauf 12, 29-31). Many of Geoffrey's principles of decorum and amplification, which derive from the same rhetorical tradition as that in which Gerald of Wales had been trained, are illustrated in Gerald's works. John Hagen observes that alliteration and assonance distinguish Gerald's original compositions from texts he is only quoting (*Jewel* xxv-xxvii).

Though it has survived in only one manuscript, the *Vita Sancti Hugonis* exercised significant influence. When the papal commissioners wrote their canonization report on Hugh in 1219, they drew details and incidents from Gerald's work. From it are derived the specifications as to Hugh's birthplace and the incident involving kissing a leper at Newark (Farmer 95, 97). The commissioners' language describing Hugh's building the chapter of canons at Lincoln is similar to Gerald's (Farmer 96). Of the thirty-seven miracles recorded by the commission, seven are the same as ones described by Gerald (*VSH* 68, 73-76, 77, 78, 83, 84, 101). Farmer observes that both accounts may be drawn from the same source--the records at Lincoln. He also characterizes Gerald's account of the miracles, in comparison with the "bare minimum of information" in the commissioners' report, as "more vivid and picturesque but less trustworthy" (Farmer 88). The *Metrical Life* written after Hugh's canonization

in 1220 retells in verse many of Gerald's anecdotes (see my
appendix on the *Metrical Life*). I have already mentioned the
use that Adam of Eynsham makes of the description of the swan
from Gerald's conclusion to the *Life of St. Remigius*. Both
Gerald and Adam refer to others who have written or may write
about St. Hugh, and each acknowledges that his own treatment
is limited (*VSH* 87, 88; *MV* 1: 3, 45; 2: 232). Adam concen-
trates on Hugh's spirituality, while Gerald is attracted to
Hugh's character and personal style. It is possible that Adam
and Gerald knew of one another's work, both of them being
engaged in writing lives of Hugh early in the thirteenth century and each completing his work by about 1214. The modern
editors estimate that the *Magna Vita* was completed "soon
after" 1212 (*MV* xii); Dimock judges that Gerald's *Vita Sancti
Hugonis* was completed in late 1213 or early 1214 (*Op.* 7: xiii).

Gerald is the professional writer, whose finest work resembles modern journalism at its best. In the *Life of St.
Hugh*, the formal constraints of composing *dignis laudum preconiis* forbid him the excursions into vituperation, gossip,
and folktale that mark so many of his books. By way of contrast, his *Life of Geoffrey* [Plantagenet], *Archbishop of York*
(*Op.* 4: 355-431) is not only a defense of that most loyal
of the sons of Henry II but also a scurrilous indictment of
Geoffrey's enemy, the unpopular chancellor of Richard I, William
Longchamp. But the absence of raciness and satire in the
Life of St. Hugh manifests Gerald's versatility: he can also
recount with grace a good man's good deeds. Though short,
his *Life of St. Hugh* is complete in outline and offers a lively
portrait of Hugh that is our unique source for several valuable
anecdotes.

Adam of Eynsham, on the other hand, was not comfortable
as a writer, and his literary flourishes are labored. One
wishes it had never occurred to him to apologize so often and
at such length for not being a good writer. He need not have
apologized. His virtues as a biographer are the primary ones
of accuracy and, within his range of interest, fullness of detail (see *MV* 1: viii). For Adam was with Hugh constantly
during the last three years of Hugh's life and as his confessor knew Hugh's inner life as Gerald could not. Adam records faithfully what he saw himself and what Hugh told him
(*MV* 1: 43, 45; 2: 74). Hugh liked to retell incidents of his
own life, Adam reports. While Gerald must also have been among
the privileged auditors of Hugh's reminiscent conversations,
Adam's access to the bishop's stories about himself was obviously closer.

He never learned to play, Hugh would tell his friends.
The old prior of Villarbenoît who was his first teacher kept
him from the games of other boys, saying that he was training

him for Christ, not play (*MV* 1: 7-8). Yet Hugh had a gift
for playful behavior that often served him well. Upon becoming
bishop of Lincoln, he proved a strict minister of justice
and defender of the church's integrity, scrupulous in conferring
benefices (*MV* 2: 97). Because foresters used violence on some
of his people, Hugh excommunicated the king's chief forester.
Later he refused to give a church living to one of the members
of the royal court, though he might thereby have appeased the
king. Henry II was infuriated at this twofold boldness. He
summoned the bishop to him. Just as the bishop arrived, the
king led his lords to a nearby glade (the scene was at his
manor at Woodstock) and had them sit in a circle, refraining
from any greeting to Hugh. Hugh followed and greeted them.
Receiving no response, he took a place for himself next to
the king. With ostentacious indifference, Henry began to
stitch a bandage on his finger. Hugh remarked quietly, "How
you resemble your cousins at Falaise now." Henry collapsed
in laughter. When his attendants stared at him, he said,
"You don't understand the insult this barbarian has given us,
do you? I will explain." And he explained that his great-
grandfather, William the Conqueror, had been born to a tanner's
daughter from Falaise, a town in Normandy known for its leather-
work. The birth was illegitimate as well as humble. "That
mocker saw me stitching and made fun of me for being like my
cousins at Falaise!" With the king's approval, the offending
forester did penance and became a fast friend of Bishop Hugh's
(*MV* 1: 114-19).

Children were as much at ease with Hugh as were animals
or disarmed kings. They would gaze at him, laughing and
clinging to his hand, in an intense communion (*MV* 1: 129-31).
As bishop, Hugh kept a sumptuous table--a point noted in Gerald's
Life (*VSH* 44)--and during the feasts musicians and actors
performed, though Adam stresses Hugh's detachment during those
entertainments (*MV* 1: 125). Hugh treated women with warmth
and deference, observing that to no man had the privilege been
granted of being God's father, but to a woman had been granted
the privilege of being God's parent (*MV* 2: 48). Unlike narrow-
minded enthusiasts for the monastic life, he taught that the
kingdom of heaven was not for hermits only. Three virtues
alone counted, as possible and as necessary for layfolk as for
religious: love in the heart, truth on the lips, and chastity
in the body (*MV* 2: 46).

Yet he loved the contemplative life. Once or twice each
year after becoming bishop, he would return to Witham to live
again for a while the simple life of a Carthusian. His cheeks
would flush with joy as he drew near the monastery (*MV* 2: 49).
So he had thrilled to Carthusian life years before, when his
joining the community at the Grande Chartreuse had had the

character of a flight. He had promised the prior who had been
his teacher since boyhood that he would not become a Carthusian.
But when Hugh felt sure of his calling to the Carthusian life,
he avoided an encounter with the prior of Villarbenoît and went
secretly to the Grande Chartreuse. His old teacher had been
the one who took Hugh for his first visit to the Carthusian
monastery, and he saw at once that Hugh was enraptured by the
austere serenity of Carthusian life. He extracted a vow from
Hugh not to join the Carthusians but to stay with the canons
of Villarbenoît. Hugh broke this vow without scruple, as
being enforced, not free, and contrary to what Hugh perceived
to be God's call to a more perfect life (*MV* 1: 26-27).

Adam tells us--with an unnecessary apology for stooping
to such homely details--that during his retreats at Witham,
Hugh wore a plain sheepskin garment rather than his usual lined
cloak; preferred to take the dry leftover crusts of bread for
his weekly portion--preferred them, for they were tastier;
and enjoyed (*delectabiliter gaudebat*) washing his own vegetable
bowls, and any bowls that needed cleaning, polishing them as
if each were a chalice (*MV* 2: 49-50). It was his rule always
and everywhere to do what had to be done at each moment (*MV* 1:
76, 126). Quiet attention to ordinary tasks and contentment
with ordinary comforts fostered that peaceful discipline.

He had a disdain for such wonders as blood seen on the
eucharistic host. He taught that it was a greater thing to
see Christ there by faith (*MV* 2: 95). The holiness of the
saints was miracle enough for him, and the universal miracle
that he always treasured was creation itself (*MV* 1: 90-91).

Realist that he was, he knew what dangers beset the church
of Christ. The authorities of the state would allow the church
liberty only temporarily and on their terms only, which could
change in a day. He would not simply surrender to the royal
party, as other churchmen urged him to do, nor seek by bribes
to win the king's favor, even to secure the promotion of so
notable a cleric as Walter Map, archdeacon of Oxford (*MV* 2:
131-33). As he dealt forthrightly yet graciously with Henry II
and Richard I, so he sought, with a father's authority and
concern, to counsel the wayward John. After Richard's death,
Hugh preached a sermon in John's presence on the virtues of a
good ruler. The restless prince, soon to be king and needing
good advice, sent word three times to the bishop to end the
sermon, as John was ready to go to dinner (*MV* 2: 143). When
Hugh was on his deathbed at his London residence at the Old
Temple, he was himself counseled by the archbishop of Canterbury, Hubert Walter, who was John's justiciar and had also
been a minister to Richard I, and who had often been at odds
with Hugh. Now he told Hugh to break his Carthusian abstinence
and take some meat. Though Gerald says he did not do so (*VSH*

54), Adam says that Hugh did consent to take some meat on
that occasion, in obedience to his ecclesiastical superior.
But the archbishop also advised Hugh to repent of the anger
he had often shown against Hubert himself. Hugh declined.
All that he might repent of in that connection, he told the
archbishop, was not having been *more* angry at him (*MV* 2: 189).
Hugh realized that he had a temper. He confessed that in
conducting business in chapter, he was often like pepper with
his canons; but he loved them and they knew it, and so they
lived and worked together in peace (*MV* 1: 124).

No incident in Hugh's career so dramatically illustrates
his audacious spirit in resisting violent men as his quelling
of the anti-Jewish riots that broke out in his diocese, as
elsewhere in England, after the death of Henry II (*MV* 2: 16-18).
Henry's government had protected the Jews, as his son Richard
also attempted to do. If the royal motive was self-interested
--since Jewish financiers supplied needed capital to institu-
tions of the kingdom--it was humane and enlightened self-
interest compared with the selfish fury of the mobs that
mercilessly pillaged and killed the Jews when Henry's death
and Richard's departure on the Third Crusade left them less
protected. A mob burst into the cathedral at Lincoln, and
Hugh met them there, fronting their threats and their weapons
with his own unarmed body. While some of his priests scurried
to hide under the altars, Hugh dashed right into the raging
mob, pronouncing excommunication against those who persisted
in this violence. His tongue and his self-possession (and
Adam adds, his guardian angels) preserved him from harm and
subdued the mob. Though terrible massacres of Jews occurred
elsewhere, there were disturbances but there was no massacre
at Lincoln.

It should be noted that Adam of Eynsham does not specify
that Hugh's valor in facing down a riotous mob in the cathedral
at Lincoln was against enemies of the Jews, but that was probably the case. Anti-Jewish riots did break out in Lincoln and
elsewhere in Hugh's diocese in 1190 (see *MV* 2: 17, n. 1). And
Hugh did suppress the cult of a thief who had pillaged Jews
and whose murder by a fellow-thief was falsely blamed on the
Jews (*MV* 2: 201, n. 6; Thurston 276-82). Later, in the mid-
thirteenth century, a boy was found slain near the Jewish
quarter in Lincoln, located on the hill-slope south of the
cathedral. An anti-Semitic legend developed according to
which this child was a martyr of Jewish hatred for Christians,
and he is the subject of an English folksong titled "Little
Sir Hugh." Chaucer's Prioress invokes "yonge Hugh of Lyncoln"
at the end of her tale of a similar martyrdom. But Chaucer
nowhere alludes to St. Hugh of Avalon. It is a sad irony
that medieval anti-Semitism should have had a longer life in

popular tradition than the memory of the bishop whose many
well-authenticated noble deeds include the suppression of an
anti-Semitic cult.

The Jews of Lincoln remembered Hugh's valor in their behalf. When his body was brought to the cathedral for burial,
many nations were represented among the mourners: English, Normans, French, Burgundians, Slavs, Scots, Irish, Welsh (*MV* 2: 207;
Thurston 547). The Jews also came and cried out that Hugh
had been a true servant of the great God (*MV* 2: 228).

His funeral was so extraordinary an event that Gerald
calls it the first of Hugh's miracles (although Adam of Eynsham
attributes miracles to Hugh during his lifetime, one of which
he reported to the canonization commissioners in 1219 [*MV* 2:
126, n. 1]). The justice of Hugh's funeral being so honored
lies not only in his virtue and the love he inspired in many
hearts but in the care he took to show reverence for the dead.
He often stopped on a journey to bury some stranger lying
dead by the road, and he did this with full and proper ceremony. He himself was buried, as he requested, clothed in the
simple vestments he had worn at his consecration and entombed
in the chapel of St. John the Baptist at the east end of
Lincoln Cathedral (*MV* 2: 191). John the Baptist is specially
revered by the Carthusians, for they share his vocation, as
witnesses of the Lord who live in prayerful seclusion and
ascetic simplicity. In 1280, Hugh's body was translated to a
new shrine. The east end of the church was extended to form
what is known as the Angel Choir (from its beautifully sculp-
tured stone angels). The head came free of Hugh's body when
the earlier tomb was opened, and the head was then placed in
a special reliquary. This rested on a richly carved plinth
that is still standing. In the sixteenth century, agents of
Henry VIII dismantled the shrine and scattered the remains
of Hugh of Avalon.

But he is honored yet at his cathedral. A precious panel
of stained glass of the early thirteenth century is preserved
in the north rose window; it depicts the funeral of St. Hugh.
Archbishops precede the bier, kings follow; a priest kneels
below. John Ruskin suggested in a letter in 1883 that the
Town Council of Lincoln offer a prize for a design to be
painted or frescoed on the Town Hall, depicting "the most
pathetic and significant scene in all British history ... the
funeral procession of Bishop Hugh" (Ruskin, 37: 433). For a
drawing and photographs of the north rose window, see my illustrations of Lincoln Cathedral below, pp. 100-103. In the
St. Hugh medallion, the bier is represented by a block of
brilliant green. Of that color in early glass, R.A.S. Macalister
has this comment, in *Ecclesiastical Vestments: Their Development
and Meaning* (London, 1896), p. 224: "Green, the colour of plants,

was regarded as typifying life, and sacred or beatified persons are sometimes depicted as clothed in this colour in reference to their everlasting life." All life mourns and rejoices with St. Hugh. The stories of Hugh's fondness for animals that Gerald of Wales tells us have a significance beyond their charm. For these incidents show that the created world that Hugh cherished as a miracle cherished him in turn, with miraculous sympathy. His gentleness and innocence attracted animals to him, as those qualities would attract animals to St. Francis of Assisi. Adam adds to Gerald's description of the swan a moving account of how the bird responded to Hugh's death. On his last visit to Stow before embarking on the long journey that would culminate in his death, Hugh found that the swan would not come to meet him as usual. It stayed swimming languidly on the pond, as if ill. Hugh ordered it brought to him, but it took three days for his people to capture the bird, which had hidden itself among the remote rushes. Brought finally to the bishop's presence, the swan hung its head in grief. No one could understand this behavior. Soon afterward, the bishop left, never to return. Following his death six months later, his people perceived that the melancholy swan had been bidding farewell to its friend. The swan lived on there at Stow, Adam remarks, for a long time after Hugh's death (*MV* 1: 109). It was a living sign and memorial. In later times, the swan would become an iconographic emblem of St. Hugh.

"By the holy nut," Hugh would say to those who mourned uncontrollably for someone who had died (using a euphemistic oath that substitutes *nucem* for *crucem*, "cross"), "By the holy nut, it would go very badly for us if we were never allowed to die" (*MV* 2: 223). He hoped that by a penitent death--as the end neared for him, he was laid out in the Carthusian manner on the floor, upon ashes strewn in a cross--and through loving faith in Christ, he would enter into an eternal communion with God. The miracles that occurred at his tomb, together with the holiness of his life, were understood to be evidence that he was indeed with God and that the power of God could be invoked for the grace of imitating Hugh of Avalon. The prayer for St. Hugh's day, November 17, is quoted by Dimock from MS. Bodl. 57 (f. 16) of the Bodleian Library (*Op*. 7: 247, n.2): "Deus, qui beatum Hugonem, confessorem tuum atque pontificem, eminentia meritorum et claritate signorum excellenter ornasti, concede propitius ut ejus exempla nos provocent et virtutes illustrent. Per Dominum nostrum Jhesum Christum" (God, who excellently adorned blessed Hugh, your confessor and bishop, with great merits and glorious signs, mercifully grant that his example may encourage us and his virtues enlighten us. Through our Lord Jesus Christ).

His tomb became a place of rejoicing, as we learn from the
miracles recorded by Gerald of Wales in Parts 2 and 3 of his
Life of St. Hugh: the blind see and clap their hands; the
dumb speak and their friends go shouting the wonder of it
through the streets; the mad cease their shreiks and turn to
tending others who are ill; candles are lit; bells ring; men
and women, girls and boys, priests and people go in procession
to the tomb to which all the unfortunate are given access by
night and day; and in that holy place there is jubilation.

Sources and Influences

Because he sought literary glory, Gerald of Wales was
eager to display learned sources and to manifest distinguished
influences. Consequently, discretion is needed to avoid mis-
taking his pomp for real achievement, or, on the other hand,
to avoid being so offended by his pretensions as not to see
what he has in fact achieved. Citing authorities was an ap-
proved academic method, and Gerald does it often and copiously.
He admits in his *Retractions* (*Op*. 1: 426) that he has plagiarized,
passing off as his own some poems that he had not written. But
he fails to make clear the intermediate sources--the textbooks
and anthologies--from which (most notably in *Gemma Ecclesiastica*)
he sometimes lifts page after page of quotations originally
collected by other scholars. On Gerald's use of the *Verbum
Abbreviatum* of Peter the Cantor, see the articles of Sanford
and Boutémy. For his use of one *florilegium*, see Goddu and
Rouse. In a letter dealing with his works, addressed to Chancellor William de Montibus of Lincoln, Gerald himself expresses a scornful attitude toward the accumulation of learned
citations. This is Letter 3 in *Speculum Duorum* (pp. 168-75).
Gerald had given some of his books to the church of Lincoln.
The donation is recorded on a page of a great medieval Bible
still exhibited at the Lincoln Cathedral Library. Books in
that library began to be listed there under Chancellor Hamo
about the middle of the twelfth century. Gerald's volumes are
entered at the bottom of the first column (see the facsimile
on page 108 below):

> De dono domini Geroldi archid[iaconi] Wall[ensis]
> topographia hýbernica
> et vita sancti remigii et Gemma Sacerdot[alis]

> (Given by Master Gerold, Archdeacon of Wales: *The
> Topography of Ireland*, and *The Life of St. Remigius*,
> and *The Jewel of the Priesthood* [i.e., the work he

later names *Gemma Ecclesiastica*, "The Jewel of the
Church"].)

This donation was presumably made before Gerald left for Rome
in 1199. Subsequently, Gerald heard that Chancellor William
had expressed disapproval of passages in *The Topography of
Ireland* that refer to acts of bestiality. In his response,
written sometime before the death of William de Montibus in
1213, Gerald defends the work as historically accurate and
couched in decent language; and he makes the usual defense
that there is also obscene material in the Bible (*SD* 168).
    William recommended that Gerald write theology rather
than history, as a subject more suited to his mature years.
Gerald's answer is twofold: first, he has written theology,
as in the *Gemma Ecclesiastica* and the *Life of St. Remigius*;
and second, what's wrong with history? Those who write saints'
lives are writing history; Jerome and Augustine wrote history.
Nowadays, there are more than enough books of theology, and
these are only compilations of what others have already said,
newly arranged as if they were something new. But his books
on Ireland and Wales are new, do break new ground, do bring
to light concealed treasures of the insular Celts (*SD* 172).
This assessment identifies what is precious in all of Gerald's
books: not their store of borrowed learning (whether acknowledged
or not), but what is drawn from his own observations, his ex-
periences, travels, and inquiries--the scenes, the creatures,
the incidents, the people, the customs, the sayings, the
dreams, the legends. The anecdotes that enliven Gerald's
Life of St. Hugh derive from his own observations or from
what he has learned by listening to the recollections of
others, such as Chancellor William de Montibus (*VSH* 46).
Hugh's own comments on his life were doubtless a source for
Gerald as they were for Adam of Eynsham (*MV* 1: 43, 45; 2: 74).
For the miracles, it is likely, as Dimock suggests (*Op.* 7: li),
that Gerald wrote from records kept by the custodians of the
tomb and the cathedral chapter.
    In the *Life of St. Hugh*, Gerald omits two kinds of material
that are common in his other works: the salty anecdote and the
mound of quoted texts. There are anecdotes of many kinds,
pungent ones as well as charming ones, revealing Hugh's rigor
as an administrator, his devotion to the ceremonies of the
church, his humility and compassion toward the poor and the
sick, his political tact--all these, in addition to the
often-praised animal stories. But there is no impropriety.
In the *Gemma Ecclesiastica*, Gerald reports two remarks of St.
Hugh's that wittily touch on priestly failings. A woman complained to Hugh that her husband was impotent. Let him be
ordained, said Hugh, and his desires will be awakened (*Jewel*

190). Once Hugh witnessed a priest superstitiously reciting extra gospel readings after mass. He has used up all his material today, said Hugh. What will he have left for tomorrow (*Jewel* 99)? These anecdotes from *Gemma Ecclesiastica* (which, as I have noted earlier, Gerald may have been revising during or after the period in which he wrote the *Life of St. Hugh*) show Hugh to be the sophisticated man all knew him to be. But they are included in the *Gemma Ecclesiastica*, not in the *Vita Sancti Hugonis*. Why the difference? The answer seems to lie in genre. The *Gemma* is an expansive professional manual for priests, full of texts and wit. The *Vita*, on the other hand, is a concise, dignified portrait, written to enlighten and move a general audience.

It was probably composed to be read aloud in full or in excerpts, as the lives of the saints had long been incorporated into the liturgy. Evidence that Gerald's *Vita Sancti Hugonis* was designed for recitation appears in the punctuation of the manuscript. In addition to a large rubricated initial letter for paragraphing and a period followed by a capital letter for the division between sentences, two marks of punctuation within a sentence are regularly used: the comma and the mark resembling an inverted semicolon. Of this second mark, R.W. Southern notes in his introduction to his edition of Eadmer's *Life of St. Anselm* (p. xxix) that it appears to be a guide for a person reading the text aloud and indicates a rise in pitch required before the mark. Eadmer uses it, for example, when a dependent clause precedes the main clause. In Gerald's *Life of St. Hugh*, the mark is used similarly after an opening dependent clause. Frequently, it appears before a verb or verb phrase at the end of a sentence. For the modern reader, this is an awkward separation of the verb from the rest of the sentence (and to avoid that awkwardness, I omit the mark in my text). But for a listening audience, a rise in pitch at that point could be a signal for attention to the concluding verb.

There are quotations (scriptural, patristic, literary) scattered through the *Life of St. Hugh*, but they are used as embellishments, not arguments. The actions of saints were understood to be examples in two senses: as models of behavior that should move us to imitation (as expressed in the prayer for Hugh's feast day, *concede propitius ut ejus exempla nos provocent*) and as illustrations of Christian teaching. Thus, Gerald observes that Hugh fulfilled all the duties pertaining to a bishop (*VSH* 14) and then gives many instances of his episcopal behavior. But he does not expound the doctrine that is thereby illustrated. He could have, and indeed did so in other works, such as *Speculum Duorum* or *Gemma Ecclesiastica*. But the *Vita Sancti Hugonis* is an *opusculum*, a little work.

Near the end of his life--about 1219--Gerald wrote a letter
to the canons of Hereford describing and defending his works.
The last titles he discusses are his saints' lives, which he
calls *opuscula minora*.   These slighter works should not be
underrated, he insists (*Op*. 1: 416), for St. Ambrose wrote the
life of St. Agnes with the same style and care he used in com-
menting on scripture; and St. Bernard, with his characteristic
beauty of style, wrote the life of St. Malachy, the Irish monk,
bishop, and reformer who was Bernard's friend and who died at
Clairvaux in 1148.

Gerald wrote his saints' lives, he says, at the urging of
important men of authority (*Op*. 1: 415).   We may infer that
these important men were canons of the cathedrals associated
with the saints whose lives he wrote.   He wrote lives of St.
Ethelbert, martyr of Hereford; St. David of Menevia, patron
saint of the cathedral named for him; St. Caradog, a twelfth-
century saint and priest who settled near St. David's; and
St. Remigius and St. Hugh of Lincoln.   For St. Ethelbert and
St. David, Gerald wrote conventional lives that followed
traditions preserved at Hereford and St. David's.   Gerald's
life of St. Caradog is lost, but he tells some incidents relating to him in *The Journey Through Wales* (*Wales* 144-45).
Of all these five saints, Hugh of Avalon is the only one who
was a contemporary of Gerald's.   Is Gerald's *Life of St. Hugh*
different in any other respects?

R.W. Southern has shown the distinctiveness of Eadmer's
Life of St. Anselm by exploring the relation of Eadmer's work
to medieval traditions of biography (*Saint Anselm*, 320-36).
Southern distinguishes four traditional patterns: the Heroic,
as in the life of St. Martin of Tours by Sulpicius Severus,
which stresses the impact of the supernatural upon the natural
world; the Commemorative, as in the lives of the Cluniac abbots, in which the emphasis is on showing how these men contributed to the growth of their monasteries; the Secular, modeled
on Suetonius' *Lives of the Caesars*, remarkable for an unsparing
disclosure of personal traits; and the Tradition of the Desert,
represented by those lives of the early desert fathers that
preserve the wisdom of the first Christian monks through simply
told incidents and natural conversation.

Eadmer's work began as the record of his personal friendship with Anselm, but over a period of many years it became
a conventional saint's life.   In the conventional saint's life,
summarizes Southern, "the only essential and invariable features
were portents at birth, miracles and prophecies during life,
a death-bed with its attendant signs, and a continuation of
miraculous intervention after death" (*Saint Anselm*, 321).
Eadmer's *Life of St. Anselm* in its final form has these features.   Yet it is more.   Though its record of Anselm's con-

versation resembles the sayings of the desert fathers, it
evolved, without conforming entirely to any of the traditional
patterns, into something new that Southern calls an "intimate
biography."

Southern's analysis is helpful in relating Gerald's work
to medieval traditions of biography. We may first note that
Gerald's *Life of St. David* (*Op.* 3: 377-404) is in the heroic
pattern. The wonder-working power of David is stressed and
the realities of his life are not critically examined. Indeed,
Gerald is only retelling the saint's life as set forth in the
traditional life written by Rhigyfarch in the late eleventh
century. Gerald works reluctantly at the task, he declares
at the outset, being a busy writer occupied with other projects.
Yet, pressed by his brother-canons at St. David's, he dispatches
the work in ten compact lessons or readings and a concluding
prayer, designed for recitation. Among the wonders he retells
is this: an Irish priest named Barre needed swift transport
to Ireland; David blesses his own horse and lends it to Barre,
who rides it at a gallop across the Irish Sea.

In the *Life of St. Remigius*, the brief lives of the bishops
of Lincoln are commemorative accounts of how this one built,
that one negotiated, this one faltered, that one held firm.
Geoffrey Plantagenet, who was elected but not consecrated
bishop of Lincoln, has his story told by Gerald in a separate
life noted above (*Op.* 4: 355-431). That work offers a portrait of Geoffrey's enemy, William Longchamp, which fits the
secular pattern of the lives of Suetonius, in its graphic disclosure of the justiciar's alleged immorality.

The anecdotes in the *Life of St. Hugh*, with their wise
sayings, call to mind the lives of the desert fathers, as do
similar anecdotes in Eadmer's life of Anselm. Yet Gerald's
life of Hugh is not an intimate biography as is Eadmer's.
Gerald did not have the personal closeness with Hugh for that,
nor was his biography the work of a lifetime as was Eadmer's
biography of Anselm. Still, like Eadmer, he tells Hugh's life
and conversation with some of the naturalness and directness
of the ancient desert lives.

Care was being taken in the twelfth and thirteenth centuries that the lives of saints be told with truth. The process
of canonization was subjected to a stricter discipline, and
the papacy began to require sworn testimony regarding the
holiness and miracles credited to a candidate for canonization
(see Lawrence, 10-14, 27). Gerald's life of Hugh does not
achieve that standard of proof, although he alludes to sworn
statements regarding the miracles. But it seems a reflection
of more critical attitudes that his biography has none of the
features Southern identifies as essential to the conventional
saint's life: no portents at birth, no miracles or prophecies

during life, no death-bed scene with signs. It is true that
Hugh's swan is said to be like a sign, but the bird is first
described as a real bird that responds to a quality in Hugh
that animals could sense. Throughout, Gerald's focus is on
Hugh's character and observable deeds.

The miracles of Parts 2 and 3 of Gerald's *Life of St.
Hugh* extend the scene to the human community at the shrine.
Gerald's accounts may be only a transcript from cathedral
records, yet they have embellishments in Gerald's style. The
original roll of miracles kept at the tomb has not survived,
and the summaries in the canonization report are not so de-
tailed as Gerald's reports. He presents the miracles in
chronological sequence, from one that occurred while Hugh's
body was still being venerated on the funeral bier, in the
presence of the assembled archbishops and bishops, to a double
reporting of miracles in the chapter house that may have occurred in the later months of 1213 (see my note to Paragraph
106). He reports a total of seventeen miraculous cures. Of
these, five are gradual, twelve are instantaneous or virtually
so. Seven cures are effected during sleep at the tomb (Paragraphs 78, 80, 83, 84, 85, 93, 101). Two of the cures--that
of the woman from Beverley with dropsy (*VSH* 77) and that of
the boy who could not speak or chew solid foods because his
tongue was attached to his palate (*VSH* 83)--involve sudden
physical transformations observed by witnesses. Both of
these are among the seven miracles described by Gerald that
are included in the papal commissioners' report. *VSH* 68
corresponds to the second of the two miracles listed by the
papal commissioners as occurring after Hugh's death but before his burial (Farmer 99). Six others recounted by Gerald
are listed by the commissioners among miracles after Hugh's
burial: *VSH* 73-76 is No. xiv in the commissioners' list;
VSH 77 in No. xi; *VSH* 78 is No. iii; *VSH* 83 and 84 are given
together in No. xxii; *VSH* 101 is No. xxiii (Farmer 99-103).

All of the cures reported by Gerald involve some approach
to the body of the saint, an indication that his principal
source was the record kept by the custodians of the tomb.
In some cases, the visit to the tomb was made after the cure,
as a form of thanksgiving to the saint whose intercession had
been successfully invoked. But in most of the cases noted
by Gerald the cure results after the patient has physically
touched or been near the tomb. In *St. Hugh of Lincoln*, p. 179,
R.M. Woolley observes of the tomb: "It had in its base orifices
large enough to enable one to put one's head inside. These
were doubtless made for that purpose, so that those who sought
a cure might be able to get as near the saint's body as possible
and were quite usual in shrines." The knight Milo is cured
immediately upon praying to St. Hugh; but he goes to Lincoln

to express his thanks and there places a wax image of his
healed arm on the tomb (*VSH* 100). The Dean of Marnam has no
sooner begun to make a wax image of his swollen head than he
feels relief (*VSH* 70).

In evaluating medieval miracle accounts, an initial difficulty is posed by vagueness or uncertainty as to the diagnosis
of a patient's condition. For example, Stanley Rubin observes
that what the Middle Ages called leprosy may not always have
been that disease. The wasting away of lips--as described in
VSH 45 in connection with St. Hugh's readiness to embrace
lepers--is, says Rubin, characteristic rather of lupus or
skin cancer than of leprosy, which causes facial skin to
thicken and grow coarse instead of waste away (Rubin 154).
Dr. Manuel delCerro of the Center for Brain Research of the
University of Rochester Medical Center has given me this comment on the miracles reported by Gerald: "St. Hugh's miracles
are of different kinds. One group can be dismissed, rightly
or wrongly, as happy accidents or coincidences, as in the case
of the Dean of Marnam (*VSH* 69-72). Acute abscesses, even
serious ones such as his, may heal by themselves. The paralysis of the girl of Wigford (*VSH* 81) reminds me of the case reports of Jean Charcot--and of Freudian dreams. Charcot (1825-
1893) made brilliant studies of hysterical paralysis and could
either induce or cure an episode of such paralysis by mere
suggestion. He was often called a demigod, but a saint, never!
One may wonder what profound somatic changes occurred in these
deeply faithful individuals during their vigils by a holy tomb
in the lonely darkness of the immense cathedral. We are just
beginning to learn how the mind may influence our immune de-
fenses, and it is likely that the clinicians of the coming
century will better understand some of what happened at Lincoln in the early 1200s."

Gerald records certain features of medical care of the day.
There were hospitals for lepers in Hugh's diocese, and Gerald
mentions the one in Newark (*VSH* 46). There was also one just
south of Lincoln, called Holy Innocents or *la Malanderie*,
across the road from the Gilbertine Priory of St. Katherine's.
There was a second hospital there, Holy Sepulchre, incorporated
with St. Katherine's. This was probably the Lincoln hospital
referred to by Gerald where a paralyzed youth had been a
patient for four and a half years (*VSH* 101). Perhaps it was
also the hospital where Dean Roger of Rolleston placed the
girl cured of madness and where she devotedly served the sick
(*VSH* 85). The mad were chained but were given access to the
tomb (*VSH* 79). The crippled were transported to the shrine in
wagons (*VSH* 98, 104). Gerald often refers to the practice of
foster care for disabled persons, as by canons of the cathedral
(*VSH* 78, 102) or matrons and leading citizens of the city (*VSH*

83, 84, 85). He speaks acidly of the high cost of medical care and the frequent ineffectiveness of it. Some methods he mentions were violent interferences more likely to harm than heal: blood-letting (*VSH* 100) and painful plasters applied to the feet (*VSH* 70). Hugh of Avalon himself practiced what we could call geriatric care. At Villarbenoît, he cared for his father during his last years (*MV* 15). At the Grande Chartreuse, he attended an elderly monk whose infirmities confined him to his cell (*MV* 34), and he also waited on the aged St. Peter of Tarentaise, a Cistercian monk and bishop who often made long visits to the Grande Chartreuse (*MV* 38-40). Adam tells how Hugh frequently washed Peter's feet, a treatment far gentler than plasters that Peter found most helpful for his frail body.

The frequency of dreams in Gerald's miracle accounts may reflect his own interest in dreams, though dreams are a commonplace of medieval literature. The papal commissioners note four dreams, none of which is among those related by Gerald. Gerald writes of the dreams with a care for particularity that suggests he may have sought out information he wanted. He was there in Lincoln, at least for the miracles after the interdict was imposed in 1208. He could have asked for details from the dean and canons or even from some of the cured persons themselves. Some scenes, such as the concluding event in the chapter house when one miracle is topped with another and Gerald tells the names of notable persons who were present as witnesses, suggest that Gerald was there too. Thanks to his narratives, we have knowledge of how Hugh lived on in the dreaming minds of his people, of how they could see him after his death, like the blind woman sleeping with her head in an opening of the marble tomb who dreamed she saw a bishop noble in figure and vested in white going in procession past her, saw him fan her eyes with an altar cloth and pour drops from his chalice upon her eyes. She dreamed that he said "Arise." She woke, and she could see (*VSH* 96).

For Gerald's *Life of St. Hugh* is both a biographical portrait and a record of the beginnings of the cult of St. Hugh. The saint is present at his tomb as an invisible friend who can exercise supernatural power to help those who visit the tomb. Such terms as "invisible friend," "power," "presence," are central to Peter Brown's analysis in *The Cult of the Saints*. Brown's focus is on the evolving cults of late antiquity in the Latin West, when ancient fears were replaced by a new veneration for the holy dead and their tombs (Brown 9). The testimony of St. Augustine indicates that this was no mere popular aberration but an affirmation of central Christian faith in the resurrection of the body (Brown 77). Brown demonstrates that the shrines of such saints as Hugh's hero, St.

Martin of Tours, were outposts of an urban Christianity that
displaced more primitive ways of life. Hugh's world, some
eight centuries later, was different, though Hugh's learning
and sophistication did make of him a civilizer as well as a man
of God. The saints impart a sense of human community to religion, and their shrines were built to be--in the eloquent
words of Peter Brown--"places where men could stand in the
searching and merciful presence of a fellow human being" (Brown
127). Gerald's biography has a similar purpose. He writes of
Hugh as a revered friend whose human affections assume power
in the shrine at Lincoln, and his biography brings the reader
into Hugh's "searching and merciful presence."

Editorial Policy for This Text and Translation

There is one extant manuscript of the *Vita Sancti Hugonis*
by Gerald of Wales. It is contained in an octavo volume numbered 425 at the library of Corpus Christi College, Cambridge.
A late fourteenth- or fifteenth-century manuscript of the letters of Peter of Blois is bound with Gerald's work as the
second part of the volume. The *Vita Sancti Hugonis* (pp. 91-
159) follows Gerald's *Vita Sancti Remigii* in the manuscript,
and the two lives are dedicated to Stephen Langston, archbishop of Canterbury. In his preface, Gerald hopes that his
work will meet the archbishop's eye or ear (through being
read aloud) and that then the archbishop will return it to
Lincoln to be a guide and inspiration to Bishop Hugh of Wells,
so that he may imitate his worthy predecessors at Lincoln.
The manuscript is described by M.R. James (2: 330-32). James
dates the manuscript of Gerald's two lives as early thirteenth
century. They are written on seventy-nine sheets of vellum,
measuring 7 7/10 x 5 2/5 inches. The text is in narrow double
columns of twenty-five lines. James gives this collation:

$$1^8(\text{wants } 1)\ 2^8\ 3^8\ (+ \text{ slip})\ 4^8\text{-}6^8\ (+ \text{ slip})\ 7^8\text{-}10^8$$

The pages of the manuscript are numbered in red chalk, a mark
of its having been owned by Matthew Parker. Underlinings in
red chalk are also evidently in his hand (see facsimile, p.
xii). Parker's extensive manuscript collection is preserved
at the library named for him at Corpus Christi College, of
which Parker was a graduate, fellow, and master. From 1552
to 1554, he was dean of Lincoln Cathedral. During the con-
servative reaction under Queen Mary, he was deprived of the
deanship and lived out her reign in quiet retirement, and then
was consecrated archbishop of Canterbury in 1559. Parker might

ħave brought the manuscript of Gerald's *Lives* with him from
Lincoln (as he did material from the archives of Lincoln
Cathedral). But on the evidence of a "TW" in Parker's hand
on the first leaf of the manuscript, James suggests that it
came to him as a gift from an official with access to manuscripts at Canterbury, either John Twyne, mayor of Canterbury,
or Thomas Wotton, dean of Canterbury Cathedral.

James characterizes the scribe's work thus: "The hand is a
good clear pointed one of cent. xiii early." Dimock describes
the manuscript as written in "a hand of the early part of the
thirteenth century—written, it would seem, and added to in
the margin or otherwise, at different times, but always it
would seem, by the same hand ... the hand is a beautifully
clear and legible one, and remarkably free from scribal blun-
ders.... Of all the early manuscripts of Giraldus's different
works which I have had to study, this C.C.C. 425 seems to me
to have the best claim to be looked upon, if not as his own
autograph copy, yet as written and revised and added to under
his own eye. At any rate, it was, in all likelihood, written
before Giraldus's death; it certainly gives us a most correct
text; and the text, probably, of Giraldus's last revision"
(*Op.* 7: ix-x).

Julia Crick of Gonville and Caius College, Cambridge, has
given me this description of the manuscript: "The manuscript
is now fragile, having a weak binding. The 79 folios are arranged in ten quires of eight leaves in a regular pattern: hair-
sides are outermost in each quire; and within, like sides face
like (hair, flesh, flesh, hair, etc.). Fo. 1 is lacking. There
are two intercalated slips. The first is placed at the end of
quire III, after fo. 24, and is incorporated into the hair-
flesh arrangement. The recto of the slip is written by the
scribe in the usual format. The verso is blank. The second
intercalated slip is an insertion made by the scribe into capitula after the sixth leaf of quire VI (fo. 46). The recto of the
slip is blank but the verso is written, maintaining the capitula
format of alternating red and blue initials. The first half of
quire I is completely blank. Fo. 5 is ruled on the recto and
verso and the text begins on fo. 6. Fo. 45 is completely blank
as are fos. 79ᵛ and 80—the texts end on fos. 44ᵛ and 79ʳ. The
manuscript is ruled in brown pencil in a standard thirteenth-
century layout—double columns with double outer boundary-
lines and a vertical subdivision of the central margin. The top
line of the ruling is not written on, and the top and bottom lines
are ruled to the edges of the page. There are 25 lines on each
page. There is a hierarchy of decoration. There are small
squares of drawn and painted background in strong colours which

enclose gold capitals. The more usual type of capitals occur—
red or blue ink with delicate scroll-type outlining in the contrasting colour. Small plain capitals in red and blue are set
into the text. The manuscript was written by one scribe. The
script is compressed and angular but well-proportioned and of a
type consistent with a date in the first half of the thirteenth
century. There is some influence from chancery-style practice
in the extended ascenders which occur at the top of some folios
and in the tendency for the tops of ascenders to be split and
curled which is evident in places. Some letterforms are beginning to show features which became more common in the middle
of the century (*i*, *o*, *v* are angular, *g* is sometimes crank-tailed,
the haft of *t* is pierced occasionally, *a* takes on its two-
compartment form), but their unevenness of distribution and
other features (like the prevalence of the uncrossed e̲t̲-nota)
argue against placing the hand later than the first half of the
thirteenth century."

The script shows similarities to that in Figure 3 of the
introduction to *Speculum Duorum* (*SD* lxii), and it is possible
that the same scribe copied this portion of the *Speculum
Duorum* (folio 69 recto) and the *Vita Sancti Hugonis*. The
third part of the *Vita Sancti Hugonis*, which recounts miracles
after the interdict was imposed, was an addition, as is shown
by the fact that the table of contents for Part 3 appears on
a half-leaf of vellum inserted between the pages that Parker
numbers 92 and 95.

The manuscript of *Vita Sancti Hugonis* provides the following
evidence as to date of composition. The table of contents
begins with a reference to St. Hugh as "Hugh the First," that
is, the first bishop of Lincoln named Hugh. This was therefore
written after 1209, when the second Hugh, Hugh of Wells, became
bishop. Paragraph 91 alludes to King John's expedition into
Poitou, and the scribe has added *primo* to this allusion.
John's first expedition took place in 1206, and he made a
second expedition into Poitou in February 1214. The added
"primo," consequently, would have been entered after the
second date (see Dimock's comment, *Op*. 7: 137, n. 3). The
interdict, which was not removed until July 1214, is referred
to, as in Paragraph 90, without indicating that it has yet
been lifted. In the dedicatory preface to Stephen Langton,
Hugh of Wells is spoken of as the only bishop Langton has so
far consecrated; this had to be written before October 5,
1214, when Langton consecrated two more bishops (*Op*. 7: 5,
n. 2). Hence, as Dimock concludes, the polishing and presentation of the manuscript to Archbishop Langton probably occurred in the spring of 1214 (*Op*. 7: xiii).

In presenting the Latin text, I have expanded the scribal
abbreviations, rendered *u* and *v* as in modern printing, and
modernized the punctuation; but I have preserved the spelling

and paragraphing of the manuscript. I italicize corrections
and additions entered in the manuscript by the scribe. My own
additions are enclosed in brackets; these consist chiefly of
some chapter titles and a few letters omitted through scribal
oversight. I have also bracketed occasional brief glosses of
mine.

In Paragraph 15, I correct *coniesta* to *congesta*. At the
end of Paragraph 26, I correct the manuscript reading *itenerandum*
to *itinerandum*. In the title of Chapter 13 of Part 2, I correct *exercitatio* to *exercitio*. These corrections appear in
Dimock's edition. In Paragraph 37, I emend *absque mare* to
absque mora (see my note on that paragraph).

Dimock, a thorough and discriminating scholar who edited
three volumes of the Rolls Series edition of the works of
Gerald of Wales as well as two other medieval lives of St.
Hugh, the *Magna Vita* and the *Metrical Life*, did not live to
see his Rolls Series edition of Gerald's lives of Remigius and
Hugh through the press (see *Op.* 7: liii, civ). The following
list shows corrections of his text that he might have noted
himself as *corrigenda*. I give the page and line number of the
Rolls Series edition, Dimock's reading, and the correct reading
of the manuscript:

	Dimock	*CCCC 425*
87.6	amplectanda	amplectenda
88.7	accendatur	accenditur
93.9	solum	sola
93.25/6	principum	principis
102.5	regis	regio
105.5	utrumque	utrumque *vel varium* [scribal
		addition in the margin not
		recorded by Dimock]
110.13	longam	largam
115.15	nobile	nobilem
121.22	opere	operi
133.23	convenerunt	concurrerunt

The page numbers of the manuscript (as chalked in by
Parker) are given in the righthand margins of my edition of
the Latin text. I number the paragraphs, and all my references
to my edition of the *Vita Sancti Hugonis* are by numbered paragraphs. The sources of quotations are given in footnotes to
the Latin text, by paragraph and line number. Explanatory
notes are at the back of the book; an asterisk in my translation
indicates that such a note is provided.

Although some passages, such as the description of the
swan or the encounter with the leper at Newark, have been ex-
cerpted and translated by historians and biographers, this is
the first published translation of the complete text of
Gerald's *Life of St. Hugh*. Dimock doubted that Gerald's heart
was in the project of writing this life, which Dimock describes
as "a simple compilation of what he was told and found recorded at Lincoln" (*Op.* 7: liii). But the simplicity of the

Vita Sancti Hugonis is not artless, nor does its brevity denote indifference on the part of the author. Gerald made a
genuine contribution to the public recognition of Hugh as "a
man such as few men are" (*VSH* 5). When the evidence is
assembled, his testimony proves to have been early, intelligent,
and generous. The succinct paragraphs of his *Vita Sancti
Hugonis* have inspired other artists to fashion tributes to St.
Hugh and can still touch a reader's heart. In translating the
work, I have striven for clarity and naturalness and have had
to depart from the involved syntax and balanced periods of
the Latin original. I keep what I can of Gerald's dignity
and polish, though no translation can reproduce his elegant
puns or consonance. In the substance of what he says, as
Dimock points out, Gerald is straightforward, and in that especially I have tried to imitate him.

The faculty and administration of Nazareth College of
Rochester have supported my work on this book with a sabbatical
leave and travel funds. I am grateful to the staff of the
Nazareth College Library for bibliographic services and tech-
nical assistance in preparing the illustrations for printing.
James Wilhelm, General Editor of this series, has shown helpful
interest in my work on Gerald of Wales from its earliest
stages. The Master and Fellows of Corpus Christi College,
Cambridge, have permitted me to examine the manuscript of the
Vita Sancti Hugonis, MS 425 in their collection, and to use
facsimiles of pages 73 and 97 of that manuscript as illustrations for the present edition, the photographs being made at
the Cambridge University Library. I am grateful to the Librarian at Corpus Christi College, Dr. R.I. Page, for coordinating
these arrangements. The Rev. Joseph Brennan, Dean of St.
Edmund's House, Cambridge, gave me hospitality and orientation
for my research at Cambridge. The Dean and Chapter of Lincoln
Cathedral granted me access to the cathedral and its library
and permitted me to photograph the cathedral and to reproduce
some of the photographs in this volume, together with the
Cathedral Library's facsimile shown on page 108. P.R. Hill,
Clerk of the Works at Lincoln Cathedral, kindly verified my
description of the choir vault. Dr. Kathleen Major has assisted
me generously, from a conference with her on my first morning
in Lincoln, through her reading of this book in typescript.
I am grateful to her for permission to quote from her letters
to me. Lowry Nelson, Jr., Director of Medieval Studies at
Yale University and Latin editor for this series, read the
typescript and offered many valuable suggestions for revision.
Others who read it and provided comments and counsel are
Russell Peck, James Carley, and Dr. Manuel delCerro of the
University of Rochester. David Townsend of the University of
Toronto contributed a note on the *Metrical Life of St. Hugh*.

Julia Crick of Gonville and Caius College, Cambridge, contributed a description of CCCC MS 425. Geraint Gruffydd,
Librarian of the National Library of Wales, has guided me to
relevant publications. At the Vatican Library, I was permitted to examine *Cod. Reg. Lat.* 470, the manuscript containing
Speculum Duorum, and was aided by the Jesuit historian Fr.
Ernest Burrus in searching the Vatican's manuscript catalogs.
We found no record of other manuscripts of Gerald of Wales
there, the copies of his works that he gave to Innocent III
having, it appears, long been lost. But during our visit to
Rome, my wife and I stayed in a hospice near the English College that was founded by Innocent III and of which Gerald became
a member. "Though much is taken, much abides." Gerald was
confident that his works would live, as he was sure of the
sanctity of the great bishop he was privileged to know and por-
tray. Eight centuries after Hugh of Avalon came to Lincoln,
one must be grateful to Gerald of Wales for those yet abiding
words of his that impart warmth and edge to our perception of
Saint Hugh.

R.M.L.
Rochester, New York

SELECT BIBLIOGRAPHY

Abbreviations

Autobiography   *The Autobiography of Giraldus Cambrensis*, ed.
                   and trans. H.E. Butler (London, 1937).

BBL   *The Black Book of Lincoln*, Vol. 1 of *Statutes
                   of Lincoln Cathedral*, ed. Henry Bradshaw and
                   Christopher Wordsworth (Cambridge, 1892).

Farmer   Hugh Farmer, "The Canonization of St. Hugh
                   of Lincoln," *The Lincolnshire Architectural
                   and Archaeological Society: Reports and Papers*
                   6, Part 2 (1956): 86-117.

Jewel   Gerald of Wales, *The Jewel of the Church*
                   (*Gemma Ecclesiastica*), trans. John J. Hagen
                   (Leiden, 1979).

MV   Adam of Eynsham, *Magna Vita Sancti Hugonis:
                   The Life of St. Hugh of Lincoln*, ed. and
                   trans. Decima Douie and Hugh Farmer, 2 vols.
                   (London, 1961-62).

Op.   Giraldus Cambrensis, *Opera*, Rolls Series No.
                   21, 8 vols. (1861-91).

SD   Giraldus Cambrensis, *Speculum Duorum, or A
                   Mirror of Two Men*, ed. Yves Lefèvre, R.B.C.
                   Huygens, and Michael Richter, and trans.
                   Brian Dawson (Cardiff, 1974).

Thurston   Herbert Thurston, *The Life of St. Hugh of
                   Lincoln* (London, 1898).

VSH   Gerald of Wales, *Vita Sancti Hugonis: The
                   Life of St. Hugh*. I cite this work by numbered
                   paragraphs of the present edition.

Wales   Gerald of Wales, *The Journey Through Wales
                   and The Description of Wales*, trans. Lewis
                   Thorpe (Harmondsworth, 1978).

[A comprehensive bibliography through April 1960 is given in
Eileen A. Williams, "A Bibliography of Giraldus Cambrensis,"
The National Library of Wales Journal 12 (Winter 1961): 97-
140. This is supplemented by select bibliographies in the
later editions and studies listed below.]

I. Editions

A. *Works of Gerald of Wales*

Giraldus Cambrensis. *Opera*. Edited by J.S. Brewer, James F.
  Dimock, George F. Warner. Rolls Series, No. 21. 8 vols.
  London, 1861-91. The major works contained in these volumes
  are:

  Vol. 1. *De Rebus a Se Gestis; De Invectionibus* (Parts 5
    and 6). Edited by J.S. Brewer, 1861.

  Vol. 2. *Gemma Ecclesiastica*. Edited by J.S. Brewer, 1862.

  Vol. 3. *De Invectionibus* (Parts 1-4); *De Iure et Statu
    Menevensis Ecclesiae*; *Vita Sancti Davidis*. Edited by
    J.S. Brewer, 1863.

  Vol. 4. *Speculum Ecclesiae*; *Vita Galfridi Archiepiscopi
    Eboracensis*. Edited by J.S. Brewer, 1873.

  Vol. 5. *Topographia Hibernica*; *Expugnatio Hibernica*. Edited
    by James F. Dimock, 1867.

  Vol. 6. *Itinerarium Kambriae*; *Descriptio Kambriae*. Edited
    by James F. Dimock, 1868.

  Vol. 7. *Vita Sancti Remigii*; *Vita Sancti Hugonis*. Edited
    by James F. Dimock (preface completed by Edward A. Free-
    man), 1877.

  Vol. 8. *De Principis Instructione*. Edited by George F.
    Warner, 1891.

Twentieth-century editions of Giraldus are the following, in
chronological order:

  De Invectionibus. Edited by W.S. Davies. *Y Cymmrodor* 30
    (1920).

  "Giraldus Cambrensis in Topographia Hibernie. Text of the
    first recension." Edited by John J. O'Meara. *Proceedings
    of the Royal Irish Academy* 52, Section C (1948-50): 113-
    78.

Speculum Duorum, or A Mirror of Two Men. Edited by Yves
  Lefèvre and R.B.C. Huygens; translated by Brian Dawson;
  general editor, Michael Richter. Cardiff: University of
  Wales Press, 1974.

Expugnatio Hibernica: The Conquest of Ireland. Edited and
  translated by A.B. Scott and F.X. Martin. Dublin: Royal
  Irish Academy, 1978.

B. Medieval Lives of St. Hugh of Avalon

[Adam of Eynsham.] *Magna Vita S. Hugonis Episcopi Lincolniensis.*
  Edited by James F. Dimock. Rolls Series, No. 37. London,
  1864.

[————.] *Magna Vita Sancti Hugonis: The Life of St. Hugh of
  Lincoln.* Edited and translated by Decima L. Douie and Hugh
  Farmer. 2 vols. London: Thomas Nelson, 1961-62.

[Henry of Avranches.] *Metrical Life of St. Hugh, Bishop of
  Lincoln.* Edited by J.F. Dimock. Lincoln: W. and B. Brooke,
  1860.

II. Translations

A translation is included with the Douie/Farmer edition of the
Vita Sancti Hugonis. Translations are also included in the
1974 edition of Gerald's *Speculum Duorum* and the 1978 edition
of his *Expugnatio Hibernica.* The following are other recent
translations of works by Gerald of Wales, in chronological
order:

The Autobiography of Giraldus Cambrensis. Edited and translated by H.E. Butler (principally from *De Rebus a Se
  Gestis* and *De Iure et Statu Menevensis Ecclesiae*). London: Jonathan Cape, 1937.

The Journey Through Wales and The Description of Wales.
  Translated by Lewis Thorpe. Harmondsworth: Penguin Books,
  1978.

*The Jewel of the Church: A Translation of Gemma Ecclesias-
  tica.* Translated by John J. Hagen. Davis Medieval Texts
  and Studies, No. 2. Leiden: E.J. Brill, 1979.

Topographia Hibernica: The History and Topography of Ireland.
  Translated by John J. O'Meara. Harmondsworth: Penguin
  Books, 1982.

III. Critical Studies and Related Works

Ahl, Frederick M. "Amber, Avallon, and Apollo's Singing
    Swan." *American Journal of Philology* 103 (Winter 1982):
    373-411.

Appleby, John T. *England Without Richard, 1189-1199*. Ithaca:
    Cornell University Press, 1965.

Arnold, Hugh. *Stained Glass of the Middle Ages in England and
    France*. Rev. ed. London: Adam and Charles Black, 1939; rpt.
    1955.

Bartlett, Robert. *Gerald of Wales, 1146-1223*. Oxford: Claren-
    don Press, 1982.

Bate, A.K. "Walter Map and Giraldus Cambrensis." *Latomus* 31
    (1972): 860-75.

Benson, Robert L., and Giles Constable, eds., with Carol D.
    Lanham. *Renaissance and Renewal in the Twelfth Century*.
    Cambridge: Harvard University Press, 1982.

Boutémy, André. "Giraud de Barri et Pierre le Chantre: une
    source de la Gemma Ecclesiastica." *Revue du Moyen Âge Latin*
    2 (1946): 45-62.

Bradshaw, Henry, and Christopher Wordsworth, eds. *Statutes of
    Lincoln Cathedral*. Vol. 1, containing the complete text of
    "Liber Niger." Cambridge: Cambridge University Press, 1892.

Brooke, Christopher. *The Monastic World, 1000-1300*. Photo-
    graphs by Wim Swaan. New York: Random House, 1974.

Brown, Peter. *The Cult of the Saints: Its Rise and Function
    in Latin Christianity*. Chicago: University of Chicago Press,
    1981.

Butler, H.E. "Some New Pages of Giraldus Cambrensis." *Medium
    Aevum* 4 (1935): 143-52. Presents improved readings of *De
    Iure et Statu Menevensis Ecclesiae*, based on MS 400 in the
    library of Corpus Christi College, Cambridge.

Cheney, C.R. *From Becket to Langton: English Church Govern-
    ment, 1170-1213*. Manchester: Manchester University Press,
    1956.

————. "King John and the Papal Interdict." *Bulletin of the
    John Rylands Library* 31 (1948): 295-317. Reprinted as No. 9
    in *The Papacy and England, 12th-14th Centuries: Historical
    and Legal Studies*. London: Variorum Reprints, 1982.

Coulton, G.C. *Social Life in Britain from the Conquest to
    the Reformation*. Cambridge: Cambridge University Press,
    1918.

Davies, J.C. "Giraldus Cambrensis, 1146-1946." *Archaeologia Cambrensis* 99 (1946-47): 85-108, 256-80.

Doney, R.J. "Giraldus Cambrensis and the Carthusian Order." *Journal of English and Germanic Philology* 53 (1954): 334-46.

Durandus, William. *The Symbolism of Churches and Church Ornaments.* Book I of *Rationale Divinorum Officiorum.* Translated by J.M. Neale and Benjamin Webb. Leeds, 1843; rpt. New York: AMS Press, 1973.

Eadmer. *The Life of St. Anselm, Archbishop of Canterbury.* Edited and translated by R.W. Southern. Oxford: Clarendon Press, 1962.

Ekwall, Eilert. *The Concise Oxford Dictionary of English Place Names.* 4th ed. Oxford: Clarendon Press, 1960.

Farmer, D.H. "The Canonization of St. Hugh of Lincoln." *Lincolnshire Architectural and Archaeological Society: Reports and Papers*, n.s., 6, Part 2 (1955-56): 86-117.

————. *The Oxford Dictionary of Saints.* Oxford: Clarendon Press, 1978.

Frankl, Paul. *Gothic Architecture.* Baltimore: Penguin Books, 1962.

Froude, James Anthony. "A Bishop of the Twelfth Century." In *Saint Hugh of Lincoln*, with an introduction by Sir Maurice Powicke. Lincoln Minster Pamphlets, 2nd series, No. 1. Lincoln, 1959.

Geoffrey of Vinsauf. *Poetria Nova.* Translated by Margaret F. Nims. Toronto: Pontifical Institute of Mediaeval Studies, 1967.

Gillingham, John. *Richard the Lionheart.* London: Weidenfeld and Nicolson, 1978.

Goddu, A.A., and R.H. Rouse. "Gerald of Wales and the *Florilegium Angelicum.*" *Speculum* 52 (1977): 488-521.

Grandsen, Antonia. "Realistic Observation in Twelfth Century England." *Speculum* 47 (1972): 29-51.

Harvey, John. *English Mediaeval Architects: A Biographical Dictionary down to 1550.* London: Batsford, 1954.

————. *The Master Builders: Architecture in the Middle Ages.* New York: McGraw-Hill, 1971.

Haskins, Charles Homer. *The Renaissance of the Twelfth Century.* Cambridge: Harvard University Press, 1927.

Hill, J.W.F. *Medieval Lincoln.* Cambridge: Cambridge University Press, 1948.

Holmes, U.T., Jr. "Gerald the Naturalist." *Speculum* 11
    (1936): 110-21.

Hunt, R.W. "The Preface to the *Speculum Ecclesiae* of Giraldus
    Cambrensis." *Viator* 8 (1977): 189-213.

Huygens, R.B.C. "Deux sermonnaires médiévaux: Tétère de
    Nevers et Giraud de Barri. Textes inédits." *Studi Medievali*
    10, 3 (1969): 271-96.

————. "Une lettre de Giraud de Cambrien à propos de ses
    ouvrages historiques." *Latomus* 26 (1965): 90-100.

James, M.R. *A Descriptive Catalogue of the Manscuripts in
    the Library of Corpus Christi College, Cambridge.* 2 vols.
    Cambridge: Cambridge University Press, 1912.

Jones, Stanley R. *Four Minster Houses.* Lincoln: Friends of
    Lincoln Cathedral, 1974.

Kealey, Edward J. *Medieval Medicus: A Social History of Anglo-
    Norman Medicine.* Baltimore: Johns Hopkins University Press,
    1981.

Kelly, Amy. *Eleanor of Aquitaine and the Four Kings.* Cam-
    bridge: Harvard University Press, 1950.

Knowles, David. "The Charterhouse of Witham and Hugh of Avalon."
    In *The Monastic Order in England, 940-1216*, 2nd ed. Cambridge:
    Cambridge University Press, 1963, pp. 375-91.

————. "Gerald of Wales." In *Saints and Scholars.* Cambridge:
    Cambridge University Press, 1962, pp. 76-85.

Knowles, David, and R. Neville Hadcock. *Medieval Religious
    Houses: England and Wales.* London: Longmans, 1971.

Lafond, Jean. "The Stained Glass Decoration of Lincoln
    Cathedral in the Thirteenth Century." *Archaeological Journal*
    103 (1946): 119-56.

Latham, R.E. *Dictionary of Medieval Latin from British
    Sources.* Fascicule 1 (A-B); Fascicule 2 (C). London:
    British Academy, 1975-81.

————. *Revised Medieval Latin Word-List from British and
    Irish Sources.* London: British Academy, 1965.

Lawrence, C.H. *St. Edmund of Abingdon: A Study in Hagiography
    and History.* Oxford: Clarendon Press, 1960.

Lefèvre, Yves. "Un brouillon du XIIe siècle: le manuscrit 470
    du fonds de la reine Christine. Étude sur quelques inédits
    de Giraud de Barri." *Mélanges d'archéologie et d'histoire*
    58 (1941-46): 145-77.

Lloyd, John Edward. *A History of Wales from the Earliest Times to the Edwardian Conquest.* 2 vols. 3rd ed. London: Longmans, Green, 1939.

Major, Kathleen. "The Finances of the Dean and Chapter of Lincoln." *Journal of Ecclesiastical History* 5 (1954): 149-67.

————. *Minster Yard.* Lincoln Minster Pamphlets, 2nd series, No. 7. Lincoln, 1974.

————. Review of the Douie/Farmer edition of *Magna Vita Sancti Hugonis. Medium Aevum* 32, 3 (1963): 227-28.

Meade, Marion. *Eleanor of Aquitaine.* New York: Hawthorn Books, 1977.

Moorman, John R.H. *Church Life in England in the Thirteenth Century.* Cambridge: Cambridge University Press, 1946.

Niermeyer, J.F. *Mediae Latinitatis Lexicon Minus.* Leiden: E.J. Brill, 1976.

Owens, Dorothy M. *Church and Society in Medieval Lincolnshire.* Vol. 5 of *History of Lincolnshire*, edited by Joan Thirsk. Lincoln: History of Lincolnshire Committee, 1971.

Pernoud, Regine. *Eleanor of Aquitaine.* Translated by Peter Wiles. New York: Coward-McCann, 1968.

Pevsner, Nikolaus, and John Harris. *Lincolnshire.* Buildings of England Series. Harmondsworth: Penguin Books, 1964.

Pollock, F., and F.W. Maitland. *The History of English Law Before the Time of Edward I.* 2 vols. 2nd ed. Cambridge: Cambridge University Press, 1898.

Powicke, F.M. "Gerald of Wales." In *The Christian Life in the Middle Ages.* Oxford: Clarendon Press, 1935, pp. 107-29.

Radford, U. "The Wax Images Found in Exeter Cathedral." *Antiquaries Journal* 29 (1949): 164-68.

Registrum Antiquissimum. Edited by C.W. Foster and Kathleen Major. 10 vols. Lincoln Record Society, 1931-73.

Rhetorica ad Herennium. Edited and translated by Harry Caplan. Loeb Classical Library. Cambridge: Harvard University Press, 1954.

Richardson, H.G. *The English Jewry Under Angevin Kings.* London: Methuen, 1960.

Richter, Michael. *Giraldus Cambrensis: The Growth of the Welsh Nation.* 2nd ed. Aberystwyth: National Library of Wales, 1976.

Roberts, Brynley F. *Gerald of Wales*. Writers of Wales
    Series. Cardiff: University of Wales Press, 1982. With
    select bibliography.

Rubin, Stanley. *Medieval English Medicine*. New York: Barnes
    and Noble, 1974.

Ruskin, John. *Works*. Edited by E.J. Cook and Alexander
    Wedderburn. 39 vols. New York: Longmans, Green, 1909.

Russell, J.C., and J.P. Hieronimus. *The Shorter Latin Poems
    of Henry of Avranches Relating to England*. Cambridge:
    Mediaeval Academy of America, 1935.

Sanford, Eva Matthews. "Giraldus Cambrensis' Debt to Peter
    Cantor." *Medievalia et Humanistica* 3 (1945): 16-32.

Southern, R.W. *The Making of the Middle Ages*. London:
    Hutchinson, 1953.

————. *Saint Anselm and His Biographer: A Study of Monastic
    Life and Thought, 1059-c. 1130*. Cambridge: Cambridge Univer-
    sity Press, 1963.

Srawley, J.H., trans. and ed. *The Book of John de Schalby,
    Canon of Lincoln 1299-1333, Concerning the Bishops of Lincoln
    and Their Acts*. Lincoln Minster Pamphlets, 1st series, no.
    2; rpt. Lincoln: Friends of Lincoln Cathedral, 1966.

Sulpicius Severus. *Writings: Life of St. Martin, Epistles
    1-3, Dialogues 1-3*. Translated by Bernard M. Peebles. New
    York: Fathers of the Church, Inc., 1949. Latin text in
    Migne's *Patrologia Latina* 20: cols. 159-222.

Thurston, Herbert, ed. and trans. *The Life of St. Hugh of
    Lincoln*. London: Burns and Oates, 1898. Translated from the
    French Carthusian life, with additions.

Thompson, E. Margaret. *The Carthusian Order in England*.
    London: Society for Promoting Christian Knowledge, 1930.

Thorpe, Lewis. "Walter Map and Gerald of Wales." *Medium
    Aevum* 47 (1978): 6-21.

Waddell, Helen. *The Desert Fathers*. London: Constable, 1936;
    rpt. Ann Arbor: University of Michigan, Ann Arbor Paperback,
    1957. Translations from the Latin, with introduction.

Walter Map. *De Nugis Curialium*. Edited by M.R. James. Ox-
    ford: Clarendon Press, 1914.

————. *De Nugis Curialium (Courtiers' Trifles)*. Englished
    by Frederick Tupper and Marbury Bladen Ogle. New York:
    Macmillan, 1924.

Ward, Benedicta. *Miracles and the Medieval Mind: Theory, Record and Event, 1000-1215.* Philadelphia: University of Pennsylvania Press, 1982.

————. *The Sayings of the Desert Fathers: The Alphabetical Collection.* Kalamazoo: Cistercian Publications, 1975.

Warren, W.L. *Henry II.* Berkeley and Los Angeles: University of California Press, 1973.

————. *King John.* Berkeley and Los Angeles: University of California Press, 1978.

Webb, Geoffrey. *Architecture in Britain: The Middle Ages.* Harmondsworth: Penguin Books, 1956.

Westlake, N.H.J. *A History of Design in Painted Glass.* Vol. 1. London: James Parker, 1881.

Woolley, R.M. *Catalogue of the Manuscripts of Lincoln Cathedral Chapter Library.* London: H. Milford, 1927.

————. *St. Hugh of Lincoln.* London: Society for Promoting Christian Knowledge, 1927.

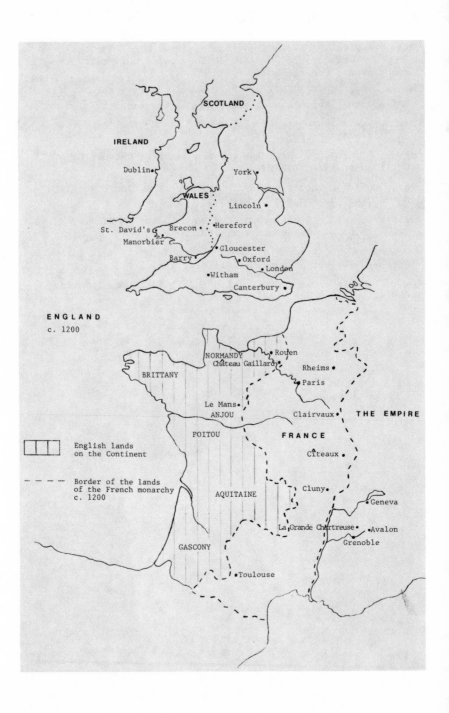

SCOTLAND

IRELAND

Dublin•

York•

WALES

Lincoln•

St. David's•   Brecon•   •Hereford
    Manorbier•
        Barry•   •Gloucester
            •Oxford   •London
            •Witham
                •Canterbury

ENGLAND
c. 1200

NORMANDY   •Rouen
    Château Gaillard•
                    Rheims•
BRITTANY   •Paris

    Le Mans•
    ANJOU   Clairvaux•   THE EMPIRE

    POITOU   FRANCE

                •Cîteaux

            Cluny•

    AQUITAINE   •Geneva

        La Grande Chartreuse•   •Avalon
                    Grenoble•

    GASCONY

□□□ English lands
     on the Continent

- - - Border of the lands
      of the French monarchy
      c. 1200

        •Toulouse

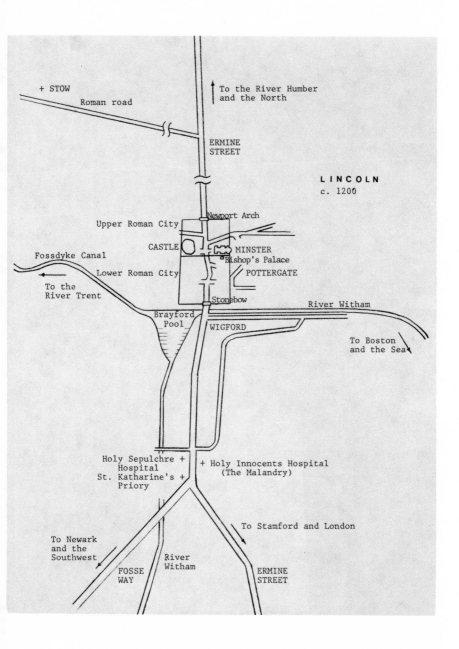

VITA SANCTI HUGONIS:

THE LIFE OF ST. HUGH

[VITA SANCTI HUGONIS]

[THE LIFE OF ST. HUGH]

Here begin the chapter headings to the Life of St. Hugh.

An asterisk in the translation indicates that a note on that passage is provided in the Notes on Text and Translation at the end of the book.

Incipiunt Secunde Distinctionis Capitula.

[Incipiunt Tertiae Distinctionis Capitula.]

Expliciunt Capitula.   [95]

*The chapters of the third part are listed on the verso of a
half-leaf inserted after the page Parker numbers 92.*

Here begin the chapter headings of the second part.

[I] The second part treats of the translation of the saint's
body from London to Lincoln and how it was gloriously
received there and made famous by many wonderful and
virtually miraculous events. *[39]*

II Of the knight of Lindsey who at the saint's tomb recovered from an ulcer the first year after the saint's
death. *[43]*

III Of the Dean of Marnam who was cured of a serious abscess
and whose son was delivered from death. *[45]*

IV Of the woman from Keal with contracted hands who was
cured at the saint's tomb. *[49]*

V Of the woman [from Beverley] with dropsy who was cured
at the saint's tomb. *[51]*

VI Of the youth who at the saint's tomb recovered the sight
he had long been without. *[53]*

VII Of the youth from Ancaster who went mad and who was
restored to sanity at the saint's tomb. *[55]*

VIII Of the man from Stubton who recovered sight at the
saint's tomb. *[57]*

IX Of the girl from Wigford completely paralyzed in the
legs and knees who was cured at the saint's tomb. *[57]*

X Of the mute boy in Wigford who was also cured at the
saint's tomb. *[59]*

XI Of the similarly mute boy from Pottergate who was also
cured at the saint's tomb. *[63]*

XII Of the mad girl from Wigford cured at the saint's tomb. *[63]*

XIII By way of an epilogue, a commission given to new writers,
with a hope for compensation and due reward. *[65]*

[Here begin the chapter headings of the third part.]

I A transition from signs before the interdict to signs
given by God during the interdict itself. *[69]*

II Of John Burdet, knight, cured of paralysis. *[69]*

III Of Matilda, a blind woman, cured at the saint's tomb. *[71]*

IV Of John from Plungar cured of an ulcer. *[73]*

V Of the knight Milo cured of a tumor and pain in the arm. *[75]*

VI Of a paralyzed and contracted youth who was cured at
the saint's tomb. *[77]*

Here end the chapter headings.

Incipit proemium in vitam Sancti Hugonis Lincolniensis
episcopi.

1   Quanto rarius ecclesia senescente quam nascente virtutes
in sanctis et signa clarescunt, tanto carius ea, cum emerser-
int, gracius atque iocundius amplectenda. Quanto nimirum in
cordibus fidelium caritas hodie plus refrixit, tanto fervor
eiusdem ebulliens, in hoc algore repertus, maiori commenda-
cione pariter et admiracione dignis laudum preconiis est
efferendus.
2   Sicut igitur inter metalla conmunia aurum rutilans et
obrizum, sicut inter arenas innumeras preciose virtutis gemma
reperta, sicut inter nubes et nebulas procellosas sol clarius
erumpens et diem irradians, sic sanctus hic noster Lincolniensis antistes, scilicet Hugo primus, quo nostro nunc causam
calamo dedit, insulam Britannicam, continuis more insulari
fluctibus et procellis exagitatam, virtutibus et vite meritis
hiis nostris diebus illustravit. Quanto namque, pertinaciore   96
regni sacerdociique conflictu, Christi ecclesiam gravior de
die in diem urgebat afflictio, tanto, remedio longe uberiore,
solacioque propensiore, rubicundam et odoriferam unguenti
effusi Cancie rosam, precioso sanguine *fuso* rubricatam, lilii-
que Lincolniensis luculentam lampadem mittens, amicus amicam,
et sponsus sponsam, nubil*os*issimis hiis temporibus, oculo
benigniore respexit.
3   O quanta Dei pietas, bonitas, et gracia, quantaque, descendens in terras deorsum, celestis gloria, tam pio benigni-
tatis studio temporis malicie remedia prestans, quod in his
ultimis diebus, quibus mundi tam caritas refrigescit quam etas,
per sanctorum quorumdam merita simul et exempla, fides gelidior
quasi follibus quibusdam et ventilabris excitatur et inflam-
matur, et ex [s]cintilla modica, aut etiam favilla iam fere
totaliter emortua, per hec eadem suffragia quasi rogus igneus
et indeficiens caritatis lampas accenditur.
4   In primis itaque de ortu presulis Hugonis primi et edu-
cacione, erudicione quoque et promocione, laudabilique in
omni statu suo conversacione, deinde de signis et miraculis
que meritis eiusdem gloriose in terris operatus *est* Deus,
noster nunc, divina opitulante clemencia, planis admodum
verbis et non politis, stilus explicare curabit.

Explicit proemium.

Here begins the preface to the Life of St. Hugh, Bishop
of Lincoln.

1   The more rarely that miracles and signs appear in saints
when the church is old than when she is young, the more lov-
ingly, the more gratefully and joyously should they be cherished
when they do appear. The more that love has cooled today in
the hearts of the faithful, the more should love's overflowing
warmth discovered amid this chill be made known by worthy
tributes, with greater praise and wonder.
2   Like shining pure gold among common metals, like a jewel
of precious power found amid numberless grains of sand, like
the sun bursting more brightly from stormy clouds and mists
to light the day, so our saint, the Bishop of Lincoln, Hugh
the First, who has now engaged my pen, in these our days by
his virtues and the merits of his life has been a light to the
island of Britain, beset, as islands are, by constant waves
and storms. While heavy blows every day oppressed the church
of Christ because of constant conflict between royal and
ecclesiastical government,* so with a richer remedy and with
greater comfort, by sending the red rose of Kent--sweet with
ointment poured out and red from the shedding of precious
blood--and the glowing lamp of the lily of Lincoln, the Friend
looked with a kindlier eye on his friend, the Spouse upon his
spouse, in these most clouded times.
3   How great is the affection, goodness, and grace of God!
How great is the heavenly glory that descends to earth! With
what loving zeal for kindness does he offer remedies for the
ill will of the age, that in these last days, when the world's
love has grown as cool as its age, through the merits as well
as the examples of particular saints, cold faith is stirred
and inflamed by such bellows and fans. And the undying lamp
of love, now almost extinguished, from a little spark or even
embers, by these intercessions is lit like a fiery pyre.
4   With the help of God's mercy and in very plain and unpolished words, my pen will first strive to tell of the origins
of Bishop Hugh the First and his education, learning, and promotion, and his admirable dealings in every circumstance,
then of the signs and miracles which by his merits God gloriously performed on earth.

Here ends the preface.

[DISTINCTIO I]

I

De ortu Lincolniensis episcopi, scilicet Hugonis primi,
educatione, conversatione laudabili, et promotione.

5   Vir igitur hic, et vere virorum vir perpaucorum, de remotis imperialis Burgundie finibus, haut procul ab Alpibus,
originem duxit. Qui ā parentibus militaris ordinis, generosi-
tate quoque non infimis, legitime natus, et ad Dei cultum educatus, in etate tenerrima literarum studiis addictus, iuxta
mentis vehemenciam ad hoc applicatam, Deique favorem et graciam
suis et se diligentibus in bonum per omnia cooperantem, iusta-
que suorum vota foventem et promoventem, in brevi quidem tempora multa conplevit. Cum autem iam quasi decennis existeret,
pia patris providencia in loco qui Villa Benedicta vocatur,
cenobio conventuali et canonico, discipline regularis habitum
simul et animum suscepit. Ubi et pater ipsius, paucis postmodum annis, habitu suscepto, secularique milicia pro celibe
et celesti prorsus abiecta, laudabili conversacione vitam
feliciter terminavit. Qui longe ante religionem assumptam,
sicut et post, vinculis ferreis sed occultissimis, una cum
abstinentiis plurimis, Dalilam suam domans, variis et exquisi-
tis modis carnem spiritui servire coegit.
6   Puer autem noster, ā patris puritate et devocione non
degenerans, vitam canonicam viribus totis et nisibus amplex-
atus, ā studiis tamen literalibus, et maxime theologicis,
animum loco et tempore non relaxavit. Preceptor etenim eius,
vir bonus, antiquus, et auctenticus, auctorum loco gentilium
qui fabulis interdum minus honestis animos inficiunt audi-
torum, Prudentium, Sedulium, Fulgencium, ceterosque libellos
similes, sincera solum Christiane religionis dogmata redol-
entes, deinde et Bibliotecam assidue legendam exponebat. Quam
ratione dupplici, tum propter primevam doctrinam, que teneris

5.8-9 *Cf.* Wisdom 4:13, "Consummatus in brevi explevit tempora
multa."

PART ONE

Chapter One

Of the origins of the Bishop of Lincoln, Hugh the First, his education, admirable manner of life, and promotion.

5   This man, truly a man such as few men are,[*] was born on the distant· borders of imperial Burgundy near the Alps.[*] He was the legitimate son of parents of knightly rank, not undistinguished in their nobility, and was trained for the service of God. Devoted to the study of letters at a very early age, he accomplished much in a short time through the energy of mind he applied to this and the favor and grace of God, who in all things cooperates for good with his own and those who love him, fostering and promoting their just desires. When he was about ten, in accordance with the devout plan of his father, he took on the habit and spirit of religious discipline in a place called Villarbenoît, a conventual and canonical monastery.[*] There his father also took the habit, exchanging secular military service for celibate spiritual warfare, and after a few years happily ended his life with honor. Long before he entered the religious life, as afterwards, the father forced his flesh to serve the spirit in various well-considered ways, mastering his sensuality with concealed iron chains and many abstinences.[*]
6   Not departing from his father's purity and devotion, our child embraced the canonical life with all his strength and effort and, whatever the place or time, did not relax from literary and especially theological studies. For instead of the pagan authors who sometimes infect the minds of their audience with less decent tales, his teacher, a good man, old and true, expounded Prudentius, Sedulius, Fulgentius, and similar works fragrant with the teaching of the Christian religion alone; and then the Bible, to be read assiduously.[*] On two accounts, because of the early instruction that sticks to young minds by being more firmly impressed and because of

9

inpressa mentibus tenacius heret, tum etiam propter assiduam
et infatigabilem eiusdem quolibet in statu suo lectionem,
adeo ad manum habebat quod vix ulla ex parte coram ipso legi
posset quin clausulas plurimas, tam precedentes quam sequentes,
fideli et infallibili memoria recitaret. Doctor autem eius,
quociens ipsum propter pueriles excessus aliquos, cum tamen
puer existens parum puerile gessisset in opere, doctrinali
ut moris est virga castigaret, statim, puero plorante, senex
in lacrimas prorumpens dicere consuevit, "Noli, fili mi, flere.
Noli, puer optime et indolis electe, noli, lacrimis tuis,
senilibus ab oculis lacrimas elicere. Ad Deum enim desuper te
mitto, et ad Deum ibis sine dubio."

7   Cum autem etatis sue quintum decimum iam annum ageret,
quia "cani sunt sensus hominis et etas senectutis vita in-   99
maculata," propter maturitatem teneris in annis statim
assu[m]ptam, et scintillancia iam future sanctitatis indicia,
in cella domus sue que Sancti Maximi dicitur prior est effectus ceterisque prefectus. Quam incontinenti tam provide
rexit et tam mature, ut quam pauperem susceperat et exilem,
possessionibus amplis opulentam in brevi redderet et opimam.

8   Videns itaque nimiam mulierum ad locum illum ex antiquo
patrie more frequenciam, qui de facili vel absque scandalo
deleri vel absque periculo gravi sustineri non posset, cum
fugiendus sit hostis huiusmodi, et arte magis quam Marte
vincendus, austerioris vite causa et ar[c]tioris religionis
gracia, Cartusiam non procul inde distantem se felici pro-
posito transferre curavit.

9   Unde et natale solum, quod sui memores innata dulcedine
quadam ab honestis plerumque propositis retrahere solet,
transiens et preteriens, nec amicos ibidem visitandos censuit
nec cognatos. Sed tanquam archam Domini usque Bersames
mugiendo ferens, nec colla reflectens aut respiciens, dicti
duriciam ordinis, qui preter abstinencias ceteras et afflic-
tiones corporis graves, omni loco et tempore carnium esum
abhorret, et iugi cilicio riget, spontanea sanctaque cum
devocione suscepit.

10   Ibi ergo vir Deo datus, virtutibus et vite meritis am-   100
plius de die in diem proficere studens, tam simplicem et be-
nignum se cunctis rebus exhibuit, quod aviculas etiam et
mures silvestres qui vulgari vocabula Scurelli dicuntur, adeo
sibi domesticos efficeret et mansuetos ut de silva exeuntes
et horam cene cotidie observantes, conmensales eos in cellula
sua, et non in mensa solum sed etiam de disco proprio et manu
comedentes, sibique fere iugiter assistentes haberet. Conper-

7.2 Wisdom 4:8-9. 9.1-2 *Cf.* Ovid, *Ex Ponto* 1.3:35-6, "Nescio-
qua natale solum dulcedine cunctos/ ducit et inmemores non
sinit esse sui." 9.4-5 *Cf.* 1 Kings 6:12.

his eager and unwearied reading in every state of life, he
had the Bible so in hand that scarcely any part of it could
be read in his presence but he would recite several of the
preceding and following passages with faithful and exact recollection. Whenever his teacher would in the usual way
chastise him with the school-rod because of some youthful
errors, when he, being a child, had done something immature
in his work, as soon as the boy wept, the old man bursting
into tears would say, "Do not cry, my son! Do not, good boy,
chosen soul, do not by your tears draw tears from an old man's
eyes! For I entrust you to God above, and you will surely go
to God."

7   In his fifteenth year, because of the maturity he attained
in youth and sparkling signs of his future sanctity--since
"a man's wits are white hairs and a spotless life is old age"--
he was made prior and superior in the cell of his house called
St. Maxime's. This he at once ruled with such foresight and
maturity that what he had received impoverished and destitute
he soon made rich and abundant in ample possessions.*

8   Then seeing that women frequented the place by an old
local custom that could not be eliminated easily or without
scandal nor tolerated without serious danger, since such an
enemy should be fled and overcome by art rather than by fighting,
he made the happy decision to move to the Carthusian monastery
nearby for a more austere life and the grace of a stricter
religious profession.*

9   He consequently bypassed his native region, which from an
inborn sweetness often leads those mindful of it away from
noble purposes, and he decided not to visit his friends or
relatives there. He was like [the cows] bearing the ark of
the Lord to Bethsames, lowing and neither turning their necks
nor looking back. With willing and holy devotion he took on
the austerity of that Order which, besides other abstinences
and heavy corporal penances, avoids eating meat everywhere and
at all times and maintains rigor by always wearing haircloth.*

10   Striving there day by day to advance in virtues and merits
of life, the man of God showed himself so simple and kind in
all things that he even tamed little birds and domesticated
the forest rodents commonly called squirrels. He had them in
his cell as table companions. They left the woods and daily
kept the hour of dinner, not only at his table, but even eating from his own dish and hand and almost always attending him.
For the forest creatures too had somehow discovered the natural
kindness and innocence of his soul and so were not afraid to
be tame with the simple and harmless man. At length, the
prior learned of this, and Hugh was told to refrain, lest
these practices please him too much and disturb his prayer.

erant enim ipsa quoque quodammodo sylvestria innatam animi ipsius benignitatem et innocenciam. Ideoque se mansuetas exhibere viro simplici et innocuo non formidabant, donec, hoc â
priore conperto, ne nimis id ipsum delectaret et devocionem
eius inpedire valeret, quod ab hiis de cetero cessaret mandatum suscepit.

11 Cum igitur ordinis austeritati tante rigorem etiam in se
quantum potuit vir Deo ex toto datus adiceret et, tanquam
inter nebulas glorie solare lumen erumpens, Cartusiense ceno-
bium sanctissima conversacione sua iam aliquamdiu feliciter
illustrasset, ad cellam quandam ordinis eiusdem ab Anglorum
rege Henrico secundo nuper in Anglia fundatam, in australibus
scilicet insule partibus, cui loco vel â candore "Witham" vel
â sapiencia "Wittham," littera geminata, barbara quondam lin-
gua nomen inposuit, prior eiusdem et preceptor est trans-   101
missus.

12 Quanta vero maturitate pariter et modestia domum illam
tam doctrina interius et morum venustate quam providencia ex-
terius et vigili per omnia sollicitudine gubernaret, noster
quidem digne explicare stilus non prevaluit. Inter cetera
vero plurima sanctissime sue conversacionis indicia, nec
illud reticendum esse censuimus, quod aviculam quandam que
Burneta vocatur adeo et hic in cellula sua mansuetam habebat
et domesticam, ut cotidie ad mensam suam, tanquam innata viri
benignitate conperta, de manu ipsius et disco pabulum et escam sumptura veniret. Hoc autem omnibus et singulis anni diebus, preterquam solo nidificacionis tempore, faciebat. Per
illud enim tempus totum absens existens, nature licencius
indulgebat. Sed que sola ab ipso recedebat, quasi more diutine conpensacione reddita, tempore conpleto, cum turba redibat et pullos, plena iam pennarum et firma maturitate suscep-
ta, more solito ad mensam veniens domino suo presentabat.
Hec autem viro benigno per triennium integrum tam delectabilis
et admirabilis quoque vicissitudo duravit, donec anno quarto
avicula casu aliquo ut creditur exstincta, non absque viri
sancti et benigni molestia grandi, iam cessavit.   102

13 Quoniam igitur unguentum effusum nomen eius, cum non solum domum suam, sed etiam australem Britanniam totam doctrina
ipsius et moralitas plurimum irradiasset, regisque notitiam,
qui frequenter eum visitabat et libenter ipsum audiebat, fa-
miliaritatem plurimam et dileccionem sibi conparasset, in
Lincolniensem antistitem, cleri et capituli consona et canoni-
ca quidem electione, populique tocius applausu necnon et principis assensu, est sublimatus. Tanquam scilicet super pauca
fidelis inventus, ideoque â Domino supra multa constitutus.

13.1 *Cf.* Song of Songs 1:2.   13.8-9 Matthew 25:21, 23.

11   When the man of God even added what rigor he could to the
Order's great austerity, and like the sun breaking through
clouds of glory, had for some time happily illuminated the
Carthusian monastery by his holy way of life, he was sent to
be prior and master of a cell of his Order recently founded
by King Henry II in England.* It was in the southern part of
the island, at a place named in the people's tongue either
"Witham" for whiteness or, doubling the letter, "Wittham" for
wisdom.*
12   With what great maturity and discretion he governed that
house, both inwardly through instruction and grace of conduct,
and outwardly through foresight and watchful care in all things,
my pen cannot adequately express. But among many signs of his
holy manner of life, this ought not to be passed over, that in
his cell he had a little bird called the hedge sparrow, so
tamed and domesticated that she would come to his table every
day, having learned the man's natural kindness, to take food
and nourishment from his hand and dish. She did this every
day of the year except at the time of nest-building. Absent
during all that period, she freely obeyed her instincts. But
once this was completed, as if making legal restitution, she
who had been alone when she left him returned with a throng.
Approaching the table as usual, fully feathered now and confident in acquired maturity, she presented her chicks to her
master. For three full years this delightful and wonderful
interchange continued for the good man, until in the fourth
year it ended. The bird seems to have died somehow, not without much grief for the gentle holy man.*
13   Since his name was like ointment poured out, his teaching
and character enlightened not only his own house but all of
southern Britain and gained the notice of the king, who often
visited him and gladly listened to him. He won the king's
friendship and favor and consequently was promoted to be Bishop
of Lincoln, by due canonical election of the clergy and chapter, and with the applause of all the people and the sover-
eign's assent.* As one found faithful over a few, he was
therefore set over many by the Lord.

II

De pontificali eiusdem in omnibus conversacione
et contrariorum detestatione.

14 Quanta vero et quam vigili cura, iam in episcopum conse-
cratus et inthronizatus, cuncta que ad episcopum spectabant
complebat officia, precipueque in puerorum confirmacionibus,
ubi Spiritus *amplior* gracia confertur, et ecclesiarum conse-
crationibus, ubi sponso sponsa coniungitur, ceterisque sacramentis ecclesiasticis cunctis ad episcopi officium speci-
aliter assignatis, quam solicitum et quam infatigabilem se
exhibuerit, Lincolniensis novit ecclesia tota.

III

De puerorum confirmationibus, ubi Spiritus gracia datur,
quam infatigabilem se in his exhibere curaverit.

15 Contigit enim et hoc pluries quod cum ecclesiam aliquam
sue diocesis hiemali tempore solempniter consecrando, laborio- 103
sum officium illud usque ad vesperam fere produxisset, col-
lecta ibidem et congesta puerorum crismate sacro signandorum
multitudine magna, ceteris cunctis fatigacione pariter et
fame affectis, solus ipse, qui plus omnibus laboraverat, neutro retardatus nec labore fatigatus, opus operi adiciens et
continuans, pueros per ordinem confirmavit, et non absque
suorum tedio magno, sciens et probans honorem hunc et honus
suum annexum habere, usque ad magnam noctis partem gravi et
operoso huic officio pie et devote indulgere non cessavit.
16 Accidit autem aliquando quod cum, magna hominum multitudine in loco quo ad hoc convocati fuerant ab ipso confir-
mata, iam inde discedens equum ascenderet, quoniam ob sacra-
menti reverenciam semper hoc opus pedes explebat, et versus
locum alium non procul inde distantem, propter id ipsum ubi
coadunati fuerant, cum festinacione transiret, ecce rusticus
quidam ẽ vestigio sequens et currens, magnaque voce clamans,
devote sacre confirmacionis munus expetiit. Cui cum renun-
ciaret episcopus, non semel sed sepius, quatinus ad locum
condicti satis propinquum cum aliis accederet, se rusticus
id facturum omnino negavit, sed a cursu statim in sessionem
versus, defectus illius periculum, celum suspiciens et manus 104
ambas illuc tendens, episcopo inposuit. Quo audito, quoniam
crebro quid acturus esset ille presul respiciebat et lora re-
trahebat, illico reversus et ab equo dilapsus, illum confir-
mare non tardavit. Sed quoniam in senium iam ille vergebat,

Chapter Two

His episcopal behavior in all things and his dislike
for anything inconsistent with that.

14   The entire church of Lincoln knows with what watchful
care, once he was consecrated and enthroned, he fulfilled all
the duties pertaining to a bishop, especially in confirming
children, where a fuller grace of the Spirit is conferred,
and in consecrating churches, by which the spouse is joined
to the Spouse; and how concerned and untiring he showed himself in all the other sacraments of the church that are
specially assigned to the office of bishop.*

Chapter Three

How he strove to be tireless in confirming children,
where the grace of the Spirit is given.

15   It often happened in winter that when the hard task of
solemnly consecrating a church of his diocese had lasted almost till evening and a great number of children had gathered
together to be signed with the holy chrism, everyone else was
fatigued and hungry and he alone, who had worked more than
any of them, was neither slowed nor wearied by the work. Per-
severing and adding one task to another, he confirmed the
children in due order. Through a good part of the night--not
without greatly tiring his people--he did not cease attending
devoutly to this heavy and exacting duty. He knew and affirmed that the episcopal dignity had its accompanying burden
too.
16   Once after he had confirmed many men at a place where
they had been summoned for that purpose, he mounted his horse
to leave--since out of respect for the sacrament he always
fulfilled this function on foot*--and hurried to another place
not far off where they had been gathered for the same purpose.
A peasant followed on foot, running and crying aloud, and
devoutly begged the gift of holy confirmation. The bishop
denied him, not once but often, for he could approach with
the others at the appointed place that was sufficiently nearby. The peasant said he would not do that, but turned from
the procession to a resting place. He looked up to heaven
and, stretching both hands in that direction, charged the
peril of this omission on the bishop. When the prelate heard
that, since he often reconsidered what he was about to do and
drew in the reins, he turned back. He got off his horse and

quia sacramentum hoc saluti necessarium tam diu inpetrare dis-
tulerat, faciei ipsius alapam dextra manu fortiter inflixit.
17   Quadam autem die cum fatigatus plurimum esset et vexatus,
tam opere tali quam itinere, rusticus quidam solus, in collo
suo puerum ferens, ipsum itinerantem est cum grandi clamore
secutus. Episcopus autem, puerum putans ad confirmandum
afferri, statim descendens exspectavit, et cum stolam assumer-
et et crismale paratum esset, dixit ille puerum quidem confir-
matum esse, sed ut felicior et fortunatior esset, nomen ei
per episcopum mutari vellet. Quod audiens episcopus, antiquum
gentilitatis errorem necnon et sortilege vanitatis crimen ab-
horrens, quesivit ab eo quod nomen puer haberet. Et cum res-
ponsum accepisset quod Johannes, ait, "O vere villane, insipi-
ens et vesane, qui melius ei nomen queris quam Johannes, quod
'Dei gracia' sonat." Et protinus ei penitenciam ob hoc in-
iunxit, quatinus per totum scilicet annum illum, omnes sextas
ferias in pane et aqua ieiunaret et in cibo quadragesimali   105
quartas anni eiusdem ferias omnes.

IV

De innata viri pietate ac liberalitate.

18   Item tam pia gestabat hic viscera tamque per omnia rerum
terrenarum minime cupida, ut cum bovem defuncti cuiusdam de
feudo ipsius, tanquam meliorem mortui possessionem iuxta terre
consuetudinem domino debitam, ministri eiusdem abduxissent,
uxor eius statim ad episcopum accedens, quatinus bovem illum
qui solus ei superstes fuerat ad puerorum sustentacionem
misereque familie iam patre private remitti iuberet, cum lacrimis imploravit et inpetravit. Quod videns senescallus loci
eiusdem, ait illi, "Domine, si hec et similia vobis de iure
conpetencia sic remiseritis, terram nequaquam tenere poteri-
tis." Episcopus autem, hoc audito, statim ab equo dilapsus
in terram, valde tunc ibidem et profunde lutosam, ambabus
manibus plenis lutum tenens, "Nunc," inquit, "terram teneo,
et tamen mulieri paupercule bovem suum remitto." Et sic manibus luto proiecto et in altum suspiciendo, subiunxit, "Nec
enim terram tenere deorsum, sed celum potius desuper quero.
Duos tantum laboratores mulier hec habuit. Meliorem ei mors
abstulit, et nos alterum eidem auferemus? Absit á nobis avi-
ditas ista, quoniam consolacione digna magis nunc foret, in
hoc tanti luctus articulo, quam maiori afflictione.   106
19   Item filio quoque militis de feudo suo centum solidos,
post mortem patris more patrie domino quasi pro relevacione
debitos, simili pietate remisit, dicens iniquum esse nimis et

was not slow in confirming the man. But he slapped his face
smartly with his right hand, because he was already approaching old age and had so long postponed asking for this sacrament necessary for salvation.*

17   One day as he journeyed on, when he was very tired and
troubled from such work and travel, a solitary peasant carrying a boy about his neck came after him with a loud cry. The
bishop thought the boy was presented to be confirmed, and he
got off his horse and waited. When he had put on the stole
and the chrismatory* was ready, the peasant said that the boy
had been confirmed, but that he wanted the bishop to change
the boy's name so that he would be happier and luckier. When
he heard this, the bishop, who hated both the old error of
paganism and the crime of vain fortune-telling, asked what
name the boy had. When he got the answer that it was John,
he said, "Foolish and mad peasant, to want a better name for
him than John, which means 'the grace of God.'"* And he
directly imposed as a penance for this that he should fast
every Friday of that year on bread and water and observe the
Lenten fast every Wednesday of the year.

                        Chapter Four

        Of his natural piety and generosity.

18   He had such holy compassion, always so free of coveting
earthly things, that when his officers had brought him the ox
of a certain deceased man as his heriot--being the dead man's
best possession owed to the lord by custom of the land--the
man's wife came to the bishop and begged him with tears to let
the ox go, since only that ox remained to her and her poor
family for the support of her children, now without a father.
The steward of the place saw this and said to him, "My lord,
if you concede these and similar legal claims of yours in this
way, you will not be able to hold land." When he heard this,
the bishop slipped from his horse to the ground, which was
very muddy at the time, and filling both his hands with clay,
said, "I am holding land now, but I concede to the woman her
poor little ox." And he threw the clay from his hands. Looking up, he added, "Because I am seeking not to hold land below,
but rather heaven above. This woman had only two workers.
Death took away the better one, and shall we take the other
from her? Far be that greed from us, for she deserves comfort at a time of so much grief, not more affliction."
19   And with the same kindness, he also conceded to a knight's
son, after his father's death, the heriot of a hundred shill-

iniuriosum, quia patrem amisit, ideo et pecuniam quoque amit-
tere debere. "Per nos utique duplex ei tribulacio non con-
surget."

V

    De ecclesia Lincolniensi ab eodem miro lapideo
    tabulatu constructa, et longe mirifice ac magnifice
    magis ab ipso ex vivis lapidibus adornata.

20   Item Lincolniensem beate Virginis ecclesiam â viro sancto,
loci eiusdem antistite primo, beato scilicet Remigio, iuxta
morem temporis illius egregie constructam, quatinus moderne
novitatis artificio magis exquisito longeque subtilius et in-
geniosius expolito fabricam conformem efficeret, ex Pariis
lapidibus marmoreisque columpn*ell*is alternatim et congrue
dispositis et tanquam picturis variis albo nigroque, naturali
tamen color'um varietate, distinctis, inconparabiliter, sicut
nunc cerni potest, erigere curavit eximiam.
21   Nec solum ex insensibili materia locum illum sic illustravit, verum etiam ex vivis lapidibus, omni marmore omnique
auro, argento,et ebore preciosioribus,longe excellencius et
laudabilius, ex eruditioribus et honestioribus Anglie personis, firmas et fidelissimas ecclesie sue columpnas erexit.
Unde et ad ipsum illud poeticum laudis elegantis eloquium non   107
ineleganter dirigi posse dinoscitur, "Lectos ex omnibus horis/
evehis, et mores, non que cunabula, queris."

VI

    De realibus horis omnibus quas diligenter explebat,
    et precipue septima qua se infatigabilem exhibebat.

22   Ad hec etiam, cum reales horas omnes et singulas devota
mente semper expleret, maxime tamen et precipue in septima,
mortuorum scilicet corporibus sepeliendis, se conmendabilem
et infatigabilem exhibebat. Accidit enim ut quadragesimali
tempore quodam, longa dieta grandique peracta, cum Lincolniensem longe post nonam urbem intraret, in urbis introitu australi audiens corpus humanum inhumatum iacere, statim illuc
accedens et quamquam itineris labore vexatus plurimum et

21.7-8 Claudian, *De Consulatu Stilichonis* 2:122-3; Claudian
has "meritum" rather than "mores."

ings owed to the lord by custom of the country as the relief.*
He said it was quite wrong and oppressive that because he had
lost a father he should lose money too. "In any case, do not
let a double burden come upon him because of us."

Chapter Five

His building of the church of Lincoln with wonderful
stone roofing and his adorning that church far more
wonderfully and magnificently out of living stones.

20 The church of St. Mary at Lincoln which the first bishop
of the place, St. Remigius, built with distinction according
to the style of his age, [Hugh] undertook to make incomparably
fine, as can now be seen.* To bring the building into conformity with the more delicate craftsmanship of modern invention,
far more subtly and ingeniously finished, he used small columns of Parian [i.e., white] stone and [black Purbeck] marble
alternately and harmoniously arranged. They were distinguished
as if by painted contrasts, though actually by a natural variation of white and black.
21 Nor did he brighten the place only with lifeless material
in this way, but from living stones, more precious and far
more excellent and admirable than all marble and all gold,
silver, and ivory, [that is] from the more learned and virtuous persons of England, he constructed sound and reliable pillars for his church. That poetic expression of fine praise
can, it seems, be rightly applied to him: "You promote choice
men from all regions, and you look for virtuous conduct, not
circumstances of birth."

Chapter Six

How he diligently kept all the natural hours and
showed himself especially tireless as to the seventh.

22 In addition, while he always devoutly fulfilled each of
the natural hours, he was most commendable and tireless as to
the seventh, that is, burying the dead.* Once during Lent,
after finishing a great and long day's journey, when he entered the city of Lincoln well after nones [midafternoon], he
heard that a corpse was lying unburied at the southern entrance
to the city. He went there at once and though worn out by the
labor of the journey, religiously buried the body. Then when

fatigatus, nichilominus tamen illud devotissime sepelivit.
Eoque peracto, cum ad partem urbis borealem versus ecclesiam
edesque pontificales accederet, audito et in ulterioribus
finium illorum urbis partibus corpus sepeliendum esse, ilico
et illuc accelerans laborique laborem adiciens et nichil prorsus omittens, sed cuncta pocius plenarie conplens, et illud
quoque sepulture dedit. Et sic tanquam dupplici victoria
palmam reportans, parum ante vesperam, non absque suorum tedio
et murmure magno, ad cenam accessit.   108
23 Cum autem, mandato regis Henrici secundi, in transmarinis quandoque cum ipso Normannie et Aquitannie partibus ageret, apud Cenomanniam existens, cum ā rege vocatus esset quatinus summo mane consiliis eius assisteret, ipse, sicut moris
habebat, nichil ad Deum spectans et ad ordinem suum propter
seculares curas unquam omittens, nocturnis horis et matutinis
expletis necnon et missa debita cum sollempnitate celebrata,
demum versus curiam equitans, quatuor defunctorum corpora
diversis in locis obiter inventa, unum post alterum ordine
quo reperta fuerant, nec cursim et prepropere sed debita cum
maturitate et morositate sepelivit. Et sic ad curiam veniens
et tam archiepiscopos et episcopos quam barones et proceres,
qui sicut vocati fuerant illuc summo mane convenerant, simul
inveniens, cum de negociis regiis nichil actum ab ipsis adhuc
aut tractatum fuisset, nullam omnino more sue tam diutine
mencionem audivit aut indignacionem incurrit.
24 Hoc quoque pretereundum non putavi, quod quociens in loco
ubi erat episcopus mortui sepeliendi rumor ad ipsum non perveniret, elemosinarius eius, cui precipuam inquisicionis huius
curam iniunxerat, tanquam lege data et incurie ipsius ultione
statuta, eo die in pane et aqua ieiunabat.
25 Quodam autem festo confessoris cuiusdam et non pontificis,109
Hugo Conventrensis episcopus mane simul cum Lincolniensi missam
auditurus, eius introitum incepit, scilicet, "Os iusti meditabitur sapienciam," voce rotunda et prosaica pronunciacione,
non melica. Lincolniensis autem, eundem introitum statim alta
voce incipiens, cum melica debitaque modulacione protraxit.
Et cum Coventrensis subiungeret, "Properandum pocius nobis
esse propter regem, qui nos cum festinacione vocavit," respondit Lincolniensis, "Quinimmo propter Regem regum, cui potis-
[s]ime est obsequendum et cuius obsequiis propter seculares
curas nil subtrahendum, festive pocius hoc festo et non festine est agendum." Et sic missa demum ad finem usque debita
cum solempnitate producta, Lincolniensis ad curiam solita cum
gravitate et maturitate perveniens, quamquam ceteri vocati
longe ante venissent, cunctis rebus agendis integris adhuc et
illibatis, nullus omnino more ipsius potuit defectus imputari.

25.3-4 Psalm 36:30.

he came to the northern part of the city, near the church and
the bishop's palace, he heard that there was also a body to
be buried in the outlying district at that end of the city.
He hurried there immediately and added one labor to another.
Neglecting nothing, but completing everything fully, he gave
that body to the grave, too. And so, as if bearing the palm
back in a twofold victory, he went to dinner a little before
vespers, not without annoyance and great complaining among his
people.

23   One day when he was overseas by the command of King
Henry II, accompanying the king in Normandy and Aquitaine,
he was summoned by him to be present early in the morning at
his council at Le Mans. As was his custom, he omitted nothing
having to do with God and his order because of secular responsibilities. He completed the night and morning liturgical
hours and celebrated mass with proper solemnity. When he was
finally riding to the court, four dead bodies were encountered
in various places on the way. He buried these one after the
other in the order in which they had been found, not hastily
and hurriedly, but with suitable time and care. Coming then
to the court, he found archbishops and bishops assembled, with
the barons and princes who had arrived there early in the morning as they had been summoned. Since no royal business had
yet been transacted by them, he heard not a word about his
long delay nor did he incur any reproof.

24   This too I thought should not be neglected: that in
whatever district the bishop was, if report failed to reach
him of some dead person to be buried there, his almoner, to
whom he had assigned responsibility for this sort of inquiry,
would fast that day on bread and water, as by established law
and as the appointed penalty for his carelessness.

25   On the feast of a certain confessor not a bishop, Bishop
Hugh of Coventry was about to celebrate mass in the morning
with the Bishop of Lincoln. He began his introit, namely,
"Os justi meditabitur sapientiam," in a smooth spoken voice,
not singing. But the Bishop of Lincoln immediately began the
same introit loudly, in a musical chant of the required rhythm.
Coventry commented, "We ought to be quick, for the king's sake,
who has called us in haste." Lincoln answered, "No. For the
sake of the King of Kings, who should be honored most of all
and whose services ought not to be shortened because of worldly
business, the services on this feast should be conducted in
the manner of a feast and not in haste." And so the mass was
prolonged to the end with due solemnity, and Lincoln came to
the court with his usual gravity and composure. Although the
others who had been summoned had arrived long before, no fault
could be imputed to his delay, since the matters at hand were
still not finished.

26   Hoc etiam inter cetera notabile censui quod estate illa
qua rex Henricus quem sequebantur in transmarinis partibus
occubuit, cum pluries acciderit quod propter dies arduis ne-
gotiis eius agendis â principe prefixos, festa valde solempnia,
scilicet Ascensionis, Pentecostes, Sancte Trinitatis, cetera-
que similia, debita cum solempnitate peragi non possent, ce-   110
teris tam archiepiscopis quam episcopis iter hiis diebus agen-
tibus et versus curiam accelerantibus, solus Lincolniensis
episcopus, tam festivis diebus festive se habendo et moram
faciendo, modis omnibus summo Deo sanctisque suis morem gerere
sathagebat, tantisque solempnitatibus solempnizandum pocius
et festivandum quam itinerandum et festinandum dignum esse
ducebat.
27   Unde et Deo, cuius obsequiis et honori tantis nisibus indulgebat, actus ipsius prosperante et tanquam honorem eiusdem
vice versa conservante, contigit ut dicti dies omnes concili-
orum tractatibus prestituti, variis ut fieri plerumque solet
casibus emersis, mutati forent et in ulteriora tempora proter-
minati.
28   Hoc etenim fixum in animo ferebat et inmutabile, quod
cunctis secularibus negociis semper essent divina preponenda,
quibus expletis et debita cum devocione premissis, secularia
subsequenter comode prosperanda fide firmissima, Domino dis-
ponente, credebat. Noverat enim ex evangelio minora bona pro
utilitate maiorum esse pretermittenda, et ut ait Ieronimus,
"Non mediocriter errat qui magno bono prefert mediocre bonum."
29   Ad hoc etiam, quod regi tam acceptus in omnibus et tam
placabilis erat, multum id facere potuit. Sciens enim et non   111
ignorans rex tam intensam erga Deum viri sancti intencionem,
plurima eius facta tolerabilia duxit, plurimaque sub dissimu-
lacione pertransiit, que forsan ab alio gesta gravem ei gignere
possent indignacionem.
30   Quoniam igitur divinis omnino mancipatus obsequiis, quasi
pro nichilo in eorum respectu reputabat secularia cuncta.
Sic ei fere per omnia Domino favorem et graciam inperciente,
ad vota successit ut et summo Regi in nullo defuerit et ter-
reno principi in suis agendis nusquam defecerit. Tanquam Deo
duce Deoque rectore, sic actus suos librans ac moderans ut
ordine conpetenti semper divina preponens, que Cesaris erant
Cesari redderet, et que Dei Deo.

28.7 *Source not identified.*

26   I have also thought noteworthy what happened when they
were attending King Henry during the summer he died overseas.*
Often major feasts such as Ascension, Pentecost, and Holy
Trinity could not be observed with proper solemnity because
the prince had scheduled the days for transacting his own
urgent business. On those days, while the other archbishops
and bishops made the trip and hurried to the court, the Bishop
of Lincoln alone, by observing the ritual of a feast on such
feasts and by taking his time, was completely occupied with
the supreme God and his saints, according to his custom, and
thought it right on such religious occasions rather to celebrate and keep the feast than to travel and rush about.
27   For this reason, God, whose services and honor he cherished with such effort, made his works succeed and, as it were,
guarded his honor in turn. All those days appointed for councils to deliberate were changed and prorogued on account of
new circumstances, as so often happens.
28   Firmly and unalterably, he bore in mind that divine things
were always to be put before secular things. Once the former
were cared for with the devotion they deserved, he strongly
believed that secular business would get done easily afterward,
through the Lord's managing. For he knew from the Gospel that
lesser goods should be passed over for the sake of greater
goods; and as Jerome says, "He does not go slightly astray who
prefers a slight good to a great good."
29   It was also because he was so acceptable to the king in
everything and so pleasing to him that he could do this so
much. For the king knew and was not unaware of the holy man's
intense concern for God. He regarded many actions of his as
permissible and privately winked at several things that if
done by another might have provoked great indignation in him.
30   Because he was devoted to sacred observances, the saint
counted all worldly things nothing in comparison. The Lord
therefore bestowed favor and grace on him in virtually everything. He kept as personal commitments that he would withhold
nothing from the supreme King nor ever fail in his duties to
the earthly prince. With God guiding and ruling him, he
weighed and regulated his actions so that he always rightly
preferred what was holy and rendered to Caesar the things that
were Caesar's and to God the things that were God's.

VII

De his que in coronatione regis Ricardi ab ipso
Londoniis laudabiliter gesta sunt.

31 Accidit autem ut coronato Londoniis post patris obitum
rege Ricardo, cum die quodam solempni mane convenissent episcopi regio mandato ad pollicendum ei iuxta regni consuetudinem
fidelitatis obsequium, solus Lincolniensis noster in hospicio
suo solita gravitate et maturitate cuncta disponens, post
horas nocturnas pariter et matutinas, sole iam excelsa lus-
trante, missam debita cum solempnitate celebravit. Quamquam
sepius tamen ā suis, morositatem eius moleste ferentibus, ut   112
ad curiam accelraret commonitus fuisset. Demum igitur, equis
adductis, versus Westmonasterium proficiscens cum parumper
processisset, corpore humano inhumato in platea reperto, protinus inquiri fecit utrum Iudeus an Christianus fuisset, et
hoc propter stragem pridie de Iudeis, die scilicet corona-
cionis, factam, et audito quod Christianus esset, statim ab
equo descendens, et sui cum eo, panno novo quem emi iussit
corpus insui fecit. Ipse quoque manus apponendo et diligenciam adhibendo, suosque maiores tam clericos quam laicos manus
apponere conpellendo, duos etiam milites de familia sua corpus effere et in cimiterio sepulcrum effodere fecit. Et sic
corpus cum exequiis debitis et obsequiis, nichil omittendo,
sepelivit.
32 Hiis itaque seriatim sic conpletis, ad curiam veniens,
coepiscopos suos, qui summo mane convenerant, una cum archi-
episcopo in camera quadam invenit, maiore iam parte diei in-
utiliter eis et tediose consumpta. Nec mora post eius adventum, in cameras peniciores ad regem adducti, negocium incontinenti propter quod advenerant conpleverunt.
33 Hic itaque vir sanctus in cunctis agendis semper ea que
Dei sunt anteponens et hiis que Cesaris erant secundo loco et
subsequenter intendens, et summum Principem principaliter ac
precipue placare curavit et terrenum tamen nunquam, nisi   113
facili et frivola forsan offensa ubi etiam Deus in causa,
molestavit.

Chapter Seven

His admirable deeds in London at the time of King
Richard's coronation.

31   After King Richard had been crowned at London following
his father's death, the bishops assembled at the king's command
on the morning of a certain feast day to pledge their loyalty
according to the custom of the realm. Only our Bishop of Lincoln conducted everything in his residence with his usual
gravity and composure.* After the night and morning office,
when the sun had risen and was already shining, he celebrated
mass with due solemnity. Yet he had often been pressed by
his own people, who endured his delay with annoyance, to hurry
to the court. At length, horses were brought, and he set out
for Westminster. When he had gone a little way, an unburied
human body was found in the street. He inquired immediately
whether the dead man was a Jew or a Christian, because of the
massacre of the Jews the day before.* When he heard it was a
Christian, he dismounted at once with his men and had the
corpse sewn up in a new cloth that he ordered to be purchased.
Exerting himself with all diligence, he compelled his senior
staff, clerical and lay, to apply themselves. He also had two
knights of his episcopal household carry the body and dig a
grave in a cemetery, and he thus buried the body with due
rites and ceremonies, omitting nothing.
32   When these services were completed in order, he came to
the court and found his fellow bishops in a certain room.
They had gathered early in the morning, together with the
archbishop; the greater part of the day had already passed,
quite uselessly and tediously for them. Promptly upon his
arrival, they were conducted to the king in more private rooms
and soon completed the business for which they had assembled.
33   Thus, in all things to be done, this holy man always put
first the things that are God's and attended to those that
were Caesar's afterward, in second place. He both strove
chiefly to please the supreme Prince and yet never annoyed
the earthly [prince] save by some simple and perhaps slight
opposition, where God also was concerned.*

VIII

De rege Ricardo ab Alemannia reverso, graviter in
episcopum causam Dei tuentem exacerbato.

34   Accidit enim quod rex Ricardus, post iniuriosam ipsius
in Alemannia capcionem et gravissimam eiusdem postea, transmarinis Normannice et Aquitannice Gallie partibus, guerris
fortissimis et pertinacibus inquietudinem, in Anglicanam cepit
ecclesiam duris exactionibus debaccari. Unde collecto in unum
regni clero, habitoque contra insolitum et tam urgens incomodum districtiore consilio, verbum ad inportunas pariter et
inportabiles imposiciones contradictionis et cleri totius pro
ecclesiastica libertate responsionis in ore Lincolniensis,
tanquam persone pre ceteris approbate religionis et autentice
magis, conmuni omnium desiderio est assignatum.
35   Quo facto, cum ocius ut mos est interpretacione sinistra
regiis id auribus insonuisset, tantam ergo virum sanctum
subito concepit indignacionem quod baronia sua tota, quam
"Regalia" regales appellant, ipsum ilico destitui iussit, et
familiares suos omnes per officiales regios modis omnibus
molestari, quosdam etiam â regno perturbari, publico precepit
edicto.
36   Soli namque Lincolniensi, quia solus pre ceteris et pro
ceteris cunctis ecclesiasticam extulit in publico libertatem,   114
totam iniuriose nimis iniuriam pariter atque repulsam inputa-
vit.
37   Sed quoniam quod lima ferro, quod fornax auro, quod
flagellum grano, quod prelum acino, quod tritura tritico, hoc
tribulacio iusto, vir fidelis et constans hiis auditis contra
familiarium suorum monita fere cunctorum, iusta solius animi
sui motum et Spiritus inpetum, quia qui Spiritu Dei ducitur
securus incedit, versus regem Ricardum, in transmarinis tunc
agentem, iter incunctanter arripuit et mare Gallicum absque
mora transfretavit. Et quamquam illud poeticum non ignoraver-
it, "Da spacium tenuemque moram, male cuncta ministrat/ inpetus."
Et illud, "Dum furor in cursu est, currenti cede furori." Et
illud quoque sapientis eloquium ei â mente non exciderit, "Ira
principis rugitus leonis." Ad regem tamen apud rupem de
Andeleiea confidenter accessit.
38   Sciens quippe causam suam iustissimam, et conscienciam
per omnia gerens serenissimam, firmato ad utrumque *vel varium*
fortune eventum equanimiter animo, adoptanda quidem duxit
obprobria ubi Christus in causa, felicissimum quoque se repu-
tans si dignus habeatur pro Christi ecclesia contumeliam pati.

37.9 Statius, *Thebaid* 10:704.   37.10 Ovid, *Remedium Amoris* 119.
37.11-12 Proverbs 19:12.

Chapter Eight

How King Richard after his return from Germany was
gravely provoked against the Bishop in his defense
of God's cause.

34   After King Richard's unjust captivity in Germany and his
great trouble afterward from hard and constant wars overseas
in Normandy and Aquitaine, he began to rage against the English
church with harsh demands. The clergy of the kingdom therefore met and held an angry council against this unusual and
oppressive imposition. By common choice, the expression of
resistance to the severe and intolerable demands and of all
the clergy's defense of the liberty of the church was entrusted to the mouth of the Bishop of Lincoln, as one surpas-
sing the rest in proven and authentic religion.*
35   When this quickly came to the king's ears with an un-
favorable interpretation, as often happens, he conceived such
indignation towards the holy man that at once he ordered him
deprived of his whole barony (which the royal party call
"temporalities") and by public edict ordered all the members
of his episcopal household to be harassed in every way by the
royal officials, some even to be driven from the kingdom.
36   For most unfairly he blamed only the Bishop of Lincoln
for all the offense and resistance, since he alone, before
and on behalf of the others, publicly upheld the liberty of
the church.
37   But as suffering is to the just man what the file is to
iron, what the furnace is to gold, the flail to grain, the
winepress to the grape, or threshing to wheat, when the faithful and steadfast man heard these things, against the warnings
of almost all his attendants, by the impulse of his soul alone
and the impetus of the Spirit, since one who is led by the
Spirit of God goes safely, he journeyed quickly to King Richard,
who was active abroad at that time, and crossed the channel
without delay.* He knew the poetic line, "Allow time and some
delay; impulse manages everything badly." And this, "While
fury is on its course, let it race on." Nor did that saying
of the Wise Man slip his mind, "A prince's wrath is the roar-
ing of a lion." Nonetheless, he confidently approached the
king at Roche d'Andeli [Château Gaillard at Les Andelys].*
38   Knowing his cause to be most just and keeping a serene
conscience throughout, his soul was calmly strengthened for
better or worse fortune or alternating fortune. He believed
that reproaches should be endured where Christ is in question,
even thinking himself happy to be held worthy to suffer con-
tumely for the church of Christ.

39   Ad regem itaque mane in capella apud Andeleiam veniens,
ipso salutato et ad osculum tam verbo quam vultu provocato,
cum rex inprimis aliquantulum se retraheret, episcopus pro-   115
sequens et propius accedens, iterum ipsum ad osculum efficaci-
ter invitavit. Rex autem, episcopo mox ut decuit in osculo
suscepto, sub risus modici significancia, salva querela sua,
se illud ei fecisse subiecit. Episcopus autem respondit
nichil esse revera, quod et ei pro certo cum ipsi placeret
erat ostensurus, unde iuste de ipso conqueri posset.
40   Post hec autem ad missam quam capellanus regis celebrabat,
cum archiepiscopus quidam extraneus curie tunc forte sequela,
de corpore Christi et ore presbiteri pacem regi portasset,
ipse statim de stallo suo descendens et ad episcopum in choro
veniens, pacis osculum ei, cunctis admirantibus, ipse portavit.
Et eodem die ante prandium lucium grandem episcopo, quem a̅
carnibus abstinere noverat, presentavit. Priusquam tamen a̅
capella discederent, episcopus regem secreto conveniens, super
excessibus quibusdam gravibus et enormibus ipsum corripuit et
paterno filium affectu ad emendacionem invitavit. Ipse vero
paternam conmonicionem et castigacionem valde pacienter et
benigne suscepit et emendacionem in omnibus humiliter et devote
promisit. Inter ultima vero verba tunc inter eos ibi conserta,
rex episcopum obnixe rogavit quatinus negocia sua in Anglia
de cetero non inpediret. Ipse vero se pocius ea respondit   116
ubique pro viribus suis expediturum, dum tamen contra Deum
aperta fronte non fuerint et ecclesiastice libertatis honorem.
41   Dicebat etiam Rex se id non ignorare, sed magis absque
dubio certum habere quod archiepiscopi et episcopi ceteri ea,
quorum ipsi auctores extiterant et contra ipsum machinatores,
ei tanquam magis autentico, quatinus maliciam suam quasi sub
eius auctoritate velare possent, proponenda suggerebant.
42   Mira Dei virtus et mira viri gracia, quod principis ani-
mus, tam effrenis et efferus et fere tirannicus, necnon et
paulo ante graviter offensus, in ipso viri graciosi adventu,
primoque ipsius propemodum aspectu, adeo incontinenti mites-
cere cepit et mansuescere quod statim rex ipsum in osculo
susceperit et digno debitoque cum honore tractaverit. Et quod
ipsum etiam ad propria, contra spem omnium, cum gracia plena
remiserit.
43   Verumtamen, sicut in vita sancti cuiusdam legitur, "Ne-
cesse erat ut quem gracia perfuderat ab omnibus diligeretur."
44   Fere enim semper hilaritatem et iocunditatem in vultu ex
consciencie securitate et sinceritate preferebat. Familiamque
suam totam, tam clericos scilicet quam milites ac servientes,
decenter et honeste vestiri et in mensa sua tam ipsos quam
hospites, eosque precipue, laute ac splendide exhiberi vole-

43.1-2 Source not identified.

39   In the morning, then, coming to the king in the chapel
at Les Andelys, he greeted him and by word and look invited
him to kiss.   When the king at first drew back a little, the
bishop pressed on and drew nearer and once more invited him
to kiss, [this time] with success.   After the bishop was soon
properly embraced, the king commented that he had embraced
him as something of a sport, since his complaint was still
intact.   But the bishop answered that there was nothing the
king could justly complain of regarding him and this would be
demonstrated when the king pleased.

40   Afterward, at the mass which the king's chaplain was
celebrating, when a foreign archbishop who then happened to
be following the court had brought the king the kiss of peace,
from the Body of Christ and the mouth of the priest, the king
immediately descended from his stall.   He came to the bishop
in the choir and gave him the kiss of peace, while all mar-
veled.*   And that day before dinner he gave a large pike to
the bishop whom he knew to abstain from meat.   But before they
left the chapel the bishop met the king in private.   He accused
him of certain serious and irregular excesses and with a
father's affection invited the son to amendment.*   This fa-
therly reproof and correction the king accepted very patiently
and gently, and he humbly, devoutly promised amendment in everything.   Among the last words exchanged between them, the king
in his persistent way asked the bishop not to thwart his
affairs in England from then on.   The bishop said he would
rather promote them everywhere so far as he could, provided
they were not obviously opposed to God and respect for the
liberty of the church.

41   The king said he realized that, but he was sure the archbishops and the other bishops were suggesting that the Bishop
of Lincoln--as one who was more forthright, that they might
hide their ill will under his authority--should promote the
policies they themselves had planned and worked out against
the king.

42   Wonderful is the power of God, and wonderful the grace
of this man, that the spirit of a prince so unbridled and
fierce, almost a tyrant, and deeply offended just now at the
gracious man's mere approach and at the very sight of him,
should so quickly soften and grow mild that on the spot the
king received him with a kiss and treated him with appropriate honor, and that he also restored him to his possessions
with full favor, contrary to everyone's expectation.

43   But as we read in the life of a certain saint, "He whom
grace had filled had to be loved by all."

44   For almost always there was cheerfulness and happiness
in his face, from repose and sincerity of conscience.   He
wanted his whole episcopal household, clerks, knights, and

bat. Unde suis plerumque dicere consuevit, "Bene comedatis,   117
et bene bibatis, et bene ac devote Deo serviatis."
45   Ad hec etiam devotissimus erat et frequentissimus in
visitando infirmos, et maxime leprosos, eisque benefaciendo
et tam rebus quam verbis solacium eis prestando, ipsosque
in discessu suo per ordinem osculando, â quo nulla eum lepre
deformitas, ubi nec *etiam* oris seu labiorum forma apparuit
ulla, sed tantum dentes extabant et prominebant, absterreri
valebat, nec rei monstruose magis quam forme humane osculum
inprimere ob nimiam devocionis humilitatem et caritatis ar-
dorem abhorrebat.
46   Testatus est autem magister Willelmus, quem prefatus
pontifex in ecclesia sua Lincolniensi canonicum instituit et
cancellarium, quod in villa Newerc quemdam leprosum osculatus
est episcopus sanctus Hugo, et ne magnum quid se in hoc egisse
reputaret episcopus, immo pocius defectum suum in hoc attend-
eret, quod leprosum deosculando non curaret, dixit ei predictus Willelmus, familiaris eius admodum et dilectus, "Martinus osculo leprosum mundavit." Et respondit episcopus,
dicti causam intelligens, "Martinus osculando leprosum curavit
eum in corpore. Leprosus autem osculo sanavit me in anima."
47   Quicquid ad officium pontificale, quicquid ad ordinis et
dignitatis episcopalis spectabat honorem, totis exequi viribus 118
totoque conamine effectui mancipare curabat.
48   Vix etiam nostris diebus visus est homo in potestate simul et sub potestate constitutus qui aut minus hominem timeret
aut plus Deum, filiali timore scilicet et non servili.

                              IX

        De regia palii exactione, per discrecionem eiusdem
        et sollertiam, unica pecuniae largitione cassata.

49   Inter multa quoque gesta eiusdem laudabilia et collata
ecclesie sue beneficia, detestabilem illam exactionem pallii
centum librarum, quod semel incaute prestitum, personali de-
licto redundante nimis ad onus simile successorum, â sede sua
scandalum omne removens et maculam abstergens, in perpetuum
unica pecunie largicione sedavit.

servants, to be fittingly and respectably dressed, and at his
table he wanted them and especially guests to be served sump-
tuously and abundantly. Therefore, he often used to say to
his people, "Eat well, and drink well, and serve God well and
faithfully!"

45   He was also loyal and constant in visiting the sick, especially lepers. He gave them assistance and comfort, both
in words and material things, and at his departure he kissed
them one by one. No deformity of leprosy, where there was no
shape of mouth or lips, but only the teeth projecting outward,
could frighten him away from them. Through the great humility
of his devotion and the warmth of his charity, he had no horror of imprinting a kiss on a form more monstrous than human.

46   Master William [de Montibus], whom the bishop installed
in his church at Lincoln as canon and chancellor, testified
that in the town of Newark the holy Bishop Hugh kissed a certain leper. Lest the bishop think he had done something great
in this, rather to make him conscious of his limitation in not
curing the leper with a kiss, William (who was very much his
friend and favorite) said to him, "Martin cleansed a leper
with a kiss." Understanding what prompted the remark, the
bishop answered, "Martin, by kissing the leper, cured him in
body, but the leper with a kiss has healed me in soul."*

47   He was careful to do with all his strength whatever belonged to the pontifical office, whatever pertained to the
honor of the episcopal order and dignity.

48   Scarcely was there seen in our days a person holding power and subject to power who feared man less or God more, that
is, with a son's not a slave's fear.

Chapter Nine

How through his discretion and skill the royal tribute
of the mantle was canceled by a single payment of money.

49   Among many worthy acts of his benefiting his church, he
settled finally by a single payment of money that offensive
tax of the mantle worth a hundred pounds. The mantle had been
contributed once, imprudently. Then one person's fault had
extended to become an equivalent obligation for his successors.
Bishop Hugh's action removed all the scandal and cleared away
the stain from his see.*

X

De olore aput Stowan iuxta Lincolniam in primo episcopi
adventu tanquam obviam ei venienti et miro modo, vel
etiam miraculoso, se mansuetissimum ei statim reddente.

50   Illud etiam inter cetera eiusdem preconia silendum esse
non censui quod, sicut tam apud Wittham quam Carthusiam ab
aviculis, sic statim et in statu pontificali non ab avicula,
sed ab ave grandi et regia, pia et innocua quodammodo viri
benignitas est conperta, propter quod et animo miti ac man-
suetissimo se mansuetas et quasi domesticas exhibuerunt. Unde
quod et hic contigit et in signum aliquod ac pronosticalis
eventus indicium absque dubio datum videtur sub silencio   119
[quidem] pretereundum non putavi. Eo namque die, vel circiter
illum proximo, quo apud Lincolniam primo susceptus fuit episcopus Hugo et incathedratus, apud manerium ipsius quasi per
octo milliaria ab urbe Lincolniensi distans, iuxta Stowan,
silvis et stagnis delectabiliter obsitum, olor [novus et]
numquam ibi antea visus advolavit. Qui intra paucos cignos
quos ibidem plures repperit mole sue magnitudinis omnes op-
pressit et interemit, uno tamen feminei sexus ad societatis
solacium, non fecunditatis augmentum, reservato. Erat enim
tanto fere cigno robustior quanto cignus ansere maior, cigno
tamen in omnibus et precipue in colore et candore simillimus,
preter quantitatem etiam hoc distante, quod tumorem in rostro
atque nigredinem more cignorum non preferebat, quinimo locum
eundem rostri planum croceoque decenter colore, una cum capite
et colli parte superiore, distinctum habebat.
51   Avis autem hec regia et tam qualitate quam quantitate
conspicua in primo ad locum illum presulis adventu quasi
sponte et absque difficultate domestica facta, ad ipsum in
camera sua propter admiracionem *est* adducta. Que statim â
manu ipsius panem sumens et comedens eique quam familiariter
adherens omnem silvestrem interim ut videbatur exuta naturam,
nec eius attactus nec astancium undique turbarum et intueun-
cium accessus sive tumultus abhorrebat. Consueverat etiam
interdum, cum ab episcopo pascebatur, capud cum colli longi-   120
tudine tota in manicam ipsius largam et peramplam inque sinum
interiorem avis extendere. Ibique aliquamdiu cum sollicitudine quadam modo suo domino congratulans atque preludens,
tanquam aliquid queritando musitare. [Item, sicut asserebant
ministri et custodes manerii, contra presulis adventum ad
locum illum, cum forte aliquamdiu absens fuisset, tribus die-

50.9, 13 *The words in brackets in this paragraph and the next
are from the account of the swan in* The Life of St. Remigius
(*Op.* 7: 73-5), *here transcribed from the manuscript.*

Chapter Ten

How at the Bishop's first visit to Stow near Lincoln,
a swan came as if to meet him and in a remarkable, even
miraculous way, at once became very tame with him.

50   Among his other praises, I think this should not go
unmentioned, that as by small birds at both Witham and the
Grande Chartreuse, so too when he became a bishop, his com-
passionate and innocent kindness was somehow quickly recognized,
not by a small bird but by a large and royal bird. Because of
this, birds were quiet and tame with the gentle and peaceful
soul. Consequently I must not omit what happened, which seems
without doubt to have been given as a sign and prophetic mark
of what was to come. For about the day or the day after Bishop
Hugh was welcomed and enthroned at Lincoln, a [new] swan not
seen there before flew in at the bishop's manor near Stow,
some eight miles from Lincoln, a place delightfully covered
with woods and ponds. By its greater size, the bird over-
powered and killed all the many small swans it found there,
except one female which it spared for the pleasure of companionship, not procreation. For it was almost as much stronger
than a [mute] swan as a [mute] swan is larger than a goose.
Yet it was quite like a [mute] swan in everything, especially
in color and whiteness. Apart from the difference in size,
it differed also in this, that it did not have the same swelling
or black marking in the beak as [mute] swans, but instead that
part of the beak was level and handsomely marked with yellow,
and there was a difference, too, in the head and upper part
of the neck.*
51   When the bishop first visited there, this royal bird,
remarkable in feature as in size, was brought to him in his
chamber to marvel at. It had been tamed without difficulty,
as if by its own will. Immediately, the bird took and ate
bread from his hand and stayed with him so like a pet that
for the time being it seemed to have shed all its wildness.
It did not shrink from the bishop's touch* nor the approach
or the commotion of the crowd standing all around and gaping.
Sometimes when it was being fed by the bishop, the bird would
stretch its head and its whole neck into his large and roomy
sleeve, right to the breast. And there with marked attention,
it would favor and admire its master, making low sounds as if
asking for something. [And whenever the bishop had been away
for a long time, the attendants and custodians of the manor
said that the bird would move about more quickly than usual
for three or four days before he returned. It would fly along
the surface of the streams, striking the water with its wings
and crying loudly. And it would sometimes leave the pond and

bus vel quatuor solebat se solito alacrius avis agitare, voli-
tando videlicet in amnis superficie et aquas alis verberando,
altaque voce clamando. Interdum etiam ā stagno exeundo, nunc
ad aulam, nunc etiam ad portam ulteriorem, tanquam advenienti
domino obviam pergens, magnis passibus deambulabat. Credibile
satis est quod imminente apparatu et instante servorum frequencia maiore atque discursu, cum subtilis sint et aerēe
volucres nature, ā quarum etiam gestibus prognostica temporum
multa sumuntur, et ista forsan ex eadem natura avis hec per-
pendere potuit.] Mirum hoc etiam quod nemini preterquam episcopo soli se familiarem vel ex toto tractabilem exhibebat,
quin pocius astans domino ab aliorum eundem accessu, sicut
aliquociens cum admiracione conspexi, clamando, alis et rostro
minando, voceque altisona iuxta nature sue modulos crocitando,
defendere solet, tanquam se propriam eius esse demonstrans
eique soli in signum fuisse transmissam manifeste declarans.
52   Non enim misterio carere potuit quod avis candida, immi-
nentis interitus cantu nuncia, viro innocenti, pio, ac puro,
mortisque minas, quia sancti mortem habent in desiderio et
vitam in paciencia, nil formidanti, divino tanquam oraculo
destinata transmittitur. Quemadmodum enim avis ista, candore
spectabilis, mortis discrimina docet non dolenda, et imminente
letali articulo, tanquam de necessitate virtutem faciens,
funebria fata canendo contempnit. Sic viri virtutum meritis
candidati ab erumpnis huius seculi leti discedunt, solumque
Deum fontem vivum sicientes, ā corpore mortis huius liberari
dissolvique cupiunt et esse cum Christo.
53   De avibus autem istis, tam maioribus quam minutis, sic   121
viro sancto mansuetis effectis et quasi miraculo quodam domes-
ticatis, minus admirari debet quisquis apud Torneholm in Lindeseia minutas aviculas que vulgari vocabulo "Mesenges" vocan-
tur, de silvis et pomeriis passim prodeuntes, canonicorum
loci eiusdem manibus extensis, humeris, et capiti, escam peti-
turas aut quesituras insidere conspexerit nil formidantes.

                                   XI

       Qualiter demum in urbe Londoniensi gravi morbo correptus,
       peracto vie et vite istius cursu, rebus humanis feliciter
       est exemptus.

54   Cum igitur hiis et similibus moribus et actibus vir sanctus gloriose in terris vitam ornaret et venustaret, in brevi
rapiendus ē medio ne posset in deterius forte mutari. In urbe

52.10 *Cf.* Psalm 41:3; Romans 7:24.   52:11 Philippians 1:23.
54.3 *Cf.* Wisdom 4:11.

walk about with great steps, now to the hall, now even to the
outer gate, as if going to meet its master. With preparations
being made and the servants crowding more and running about,
the bird could probably judge what was going on. Birds are
gifted in that way, since they are naturally sensitive and
like the air, and seasonal forecasts are made from their move-
ments.]* Also wonderful is that only with the bishop was it
friendly or at all tractable. Indeed, it would stand beside
its lord to defend him against the approach of others, as I
have often seen with amazement. It would cry out, threatening
with its wings and beak and trumpeting loudly with a high voice
in its natural song, as if declaring that it belonged to the
bishop and was entrusted to him alone, as a sign.

52   For it could not lack mystery that a white bird that
announces its impending death by song should, as if by God's
design, be given to that pure and holy innocent man who had
no fear of the threats of death. For the saints cherish and
desire death and only endure life with patience. This bird of
wonderful whiteness teaches that the agonies of death are not
to be lamented. When the last moment is near, making a virtue
of necessity, it scorns its fated death by singing. Thus men
who shine with the merits of their virtues are happy to leave
this world's strife. Thirsting for God alone, the living
fountain, they long to be delivered from the body of this
death and to be dissolved and be with Christ.*

53   The saint's subduing and nearly miraculous taming of these
large and small birds should seem less extraordinary to anyone
who at Thornholm in Lindsey has seen the small birds called
titmice that emerge here and there from woods and parkways and,
afraid of nothing, sit on the outstretched hands, shoulders,
and heads of the canons of that place.

Chapter Eleven

How at last he was seized with a critical illness at
London and having completed the course of his life and
pilgrimage, was blessedly delivered from human concerns.

54   Although the saint gloriously adorned and enhanced life
on earth by such character and deeds, he was taken suddenly
from our midst, lest by chance he decline in virtue.* About
November he became very sick in his residence at the Old
Temple in London and was racked with fevers. When the illness worsened from day to day and he was confined to his sick
bed, he would not remove for an hour the haircloth that he
always wore. From the force of the disease and his great
fever and sweat, it had eaten into his sides, almost to the

Londoniensi apud Vetus Templum in hospicio suo quasi mense
Novembri graviter infirmatus et febribus exagitatus, cum in
lecto egritudinis, morbo de die in diem aggravescente, iam
accubuisset, nec cilicium quo iugiter utebatur et quo iam, ex
morbi vehemencia et tam calore nimio quam sudore, latera ipsius usque ad intestina fere corrosa fuerant, ad horam depon-
ere volebat. Nec carneis vel ad modicum uti sustinuit nutri-
mentis, in neutro scilicet medicis ad hoc instantibus et in
hoc concordantibus obtemperare volens, sed usque ad mortem
magis ordinis Cartusiensis austeritatem atque rigorem obser-   122
vans.
55   Clericis autem suis et canonicis tunc dicebat quod contra
adventum regis et archiepiscopi et coepiscoporum suorum apud
Lincolniam, scilicet in festo Sancti Eadmundi, illuc ire non
postponerent. Et ut de facultatibus suis tam regi quam singulis ordinis utriusque magnatibus honor debitus et dignus ex-
hiberetur, operam et diligenciam exhiberent. Nonnullis quoque
suorum qui vix et inviti ab ipso in tali articulo discedebant,
se quoque Lincolnie tunc affuturum quasi spiritu vaticinali
confidenter asseverabat.
56   Nec mora, morbo urgencius invalescente, vir sanctitate
conspicuus, rebus humanis exemptus, feliciter ab hac vita
migravit ad Dominum. Anno scilicet etatis sue quasi quinqua-
gesimo, anno ab incarnacione Domini M⁰CC⁰., presidente Rome
papa Innocencio tercio, regnantibus in Francia Philippo, in
Anglia Iohanne.

Explicit Distinctio prima.

intestines. Nor would he take even a little meat, choosing
to obey neither the physicians who urged him to do so nor
others who gave the same advice, but he observed till death
the austere regimen of the Carthusian Order.*
55   He told his clerks and canons not to put off going to
Lincoln to meet the king, the archbishop, and his fellow
bishops on the feast of St. Edmund.* As their means permitted
them, they were to see that full honor be shown to the king
and every lord of church and state. Some of his people could
hardly bring themselves to leave him at a time like this. He
assured them with confidence, as if prophesying, that he would
be in Lincoln then, too.
56   The illness soon grew much worse, and the man of remarkable holiness, freed from human concerns, passed happily from
this life to the Lord. He was in about his fiftieth year, in
the year of Our Lord 1200, Pope Innocent III then presiding at
Rome, King Philip reigning in France and King John in England.*

Here ends the first part.

[DISTINCTIO II]

Incipit proemium in sechundam [distinctionem].

57 Quoniam autem de vita viri sancti et ipsius in terris
conversacione, que pocius tamen in celis dici potuit quo totis
affectibus hanelabat totisque desideriis aspirabat, hucusque
tractavimus, non totis tamen conprehensis vite ipsius preconiis, sed amplius notis et maiori certitudine conprobatis,
amodo de signis et virtutibus quibus sanctum suum Dominus *post
transitum eiusdem* mirificavit in terris plantamque suam eate-
nus irrigavit donec firmissime radices fixerit et donec fir-
mitas eius et sanctitas omnibus amussim et indubitanter inno-   123
tuerit, tractatu dilucido, Deo dante, declarabimus.

I

Secunda distinctio continet de corpore viri sancti ab
urbe Londoniensi Lincolniam usque translato et ibidem
gloriose suscepto multisque mirificis actibus et
tanquam miraculosis declarato.

58 Cum itaque corpus sanctissimum, conditum ut decuit et in
feretro reconditum, de Londoniis versus Lincolniam deferretur,
eadem die quo magnates Anglie cum principe suo Lincolniam convenerant, iuxta vaticinale verbum ipsius super hoc emissum
quod falli nec decuit nec debuit, illuc Deo sic ordinante
pervenit.
59 Aderant autem et ibi tunc, tanquam *ex condicto*, Rex
Anglie Iohannes et Rex Scotie Willelmus, et qui nominis inter
ceteros erat non modici, Regulus Galwethie Rollandus, et archiepiscopi tres, Hubertus Cantuariensis et Iohannes Dublinensis
et *Anselmus* Sclavonensis. Item et episcopi novem, et preter
comites et barones regni plurimos, abbates et priores con-
ventuales multi, cum ceteris personis ecclesiasticis variis
certo numero non conprehensis. Fuerunt enim ut perhibent
preter ceteros, baculis pastoralibus prediti valde plurimi.

[PART TWO]

Here begins the preface to the second [part].

57   So far I have treated the saint's life and conduct on
earth, though one might rather say "in heaven," toward which
he bent every affection and lifted every desire. I have not
included all the glories of his life, but only those that are
better known and more surely confirmed. Now with God's help
I will give a straightforward account of the signs and miracles
by which the Lord glorified his saint on earth after his death.
With these, the Lord watered his plant till he was firmly
rooted and till his constancy and sanctity were known to all,
exactly and beyond doubt.

Chapter One

    The second part treats [in chapter one] of the trans-
    lation of the saint's body from London to Lincoln and
    how it was gloriously received there and made famous
    by many remarkable and virtually miraculous events.

58   The holy body, honorably embalmed and placed upon a bier,
was carried from London to Lincoln. On the same day that the
lords of England met with their prince in Lincoln, it arrived
there by God's design, in accord with the saint's own prophetic statement on the matter which should not and could not
be in error.*
59   There were present at the time, as agreed, King John of
England, King William of Scotland, and--of no little rank
among the rest--Prince Roland of Galloway; and three archbishops,
Hubert of Canterbury, John of Dublin, and Anselm the Slav*;
also nine bishops and numerous courtiers and barons of the
kingdom; many abbots and priors of religious houses, with
various other people of the church not counted precisely.
For it is said that beside the others, there were a great many
endowed with croziers.

60   Hii autem fere cuncti quos pretaxavimus et alii multi
extra urbem obviam corpori procedentes exequiarum obsequium
devotis ei mentibus impenderunt. Et per plateam urbis longam
et tunc temporis valde lutosam, maiores regni proceres, per-   124
sonis ad hoc ecclesiasticis vix admissis, feretrum apud cathedralem ecclesiam detulerunt. Reges etiam ipsi, archiepiscopi,
et episcopi, humeros et colla submittentes, usque in ecclesiam
ipsam et ecclesie chorum tam nobilem thesaurum intulerunt.
61   Quis autem exprimere posset quanta virorum et mulierum
ad corpus in ecclesia iam positum catervatim accedencium et
feretrum osculancium et ad corpus sacrum, pia et laudabili
presumpcione pariter et devocione, nondum tumulatum, nondum
signis aut miraculis clarificatum aut canonicatum, aurum et
argentum offerencium multitudo concurrit? Unde et tanta tamque conserta, utriusque sexus, hominum ad hoc in ipso choro
turba confluxit quod vix etiam in stallis suis canonici con-
pressi stare valerent.
62   Hoc etiam notabile duximus quod sicut si apud Cartusiam
vel Wittam decessisset tantum duodecim fratres tertiidecimi
exequiis assisterent, cum numerum istum ordinis illius conventus non excedat, sic et nunc duodecim fratres ipsius, scilicet episcopi, exequiis eius qui tertiusdecimus extiterat
astiterunt.
63   Ubi et hoc quoque notabile censui quod in exequiarum eius
celebracione lectiones libri Iob funeri conpetentes soli pro-
nunciavere pontifices.
64   Nec hoc est sub silencio pretereundum quod, iuxta numerum episcoporum, duodecim marce argenti ad corpus eodem die   125
sunt oblate, et tantum auri in anulis et monilibus, necnon et
bizanciis, quasi pro terciodecimo, scilicet defuncto, tanquam
pre ceteris aureo, non deaurato quidem, immo et auro purissimo
igne probato, quod marcam argenteam aut amplius etiam ad ple-
num equiparare valeret.
65   [I]tem inter eventus quoque notabiles et illud adicimus
quod duo reges aliquantum antea discordes, tunc ibidem ad
pacem et concordiam sunt revocati. Abbates etiam, qui propter exactiones regias illuc convocati fuerant, et maxime Cis-
terciensis ordinis, leti abinde et in nullo gravati recesser-
unt. Quinimmo rex ibidem ex insperato abbatiam ordinis eiusdem in australi Anglie parte non procul a mari, qui Bellus
Locus nomen accepit, construere fiscalibusque sumptibus erigere firmiter disposuit, locumque simul cum prediis et pas-
cuis amplis assignavit.
66   Domino quippe totum ordinante, dignum et hoc fuit quatinus in tanti thesauri adventu et tanquam sponsi ad thalamum
et quietis locum, cuncta cum gaudio et letitia, cuncta cum
pace et condordia provenirent.
67   Hos igitur eventus omnes tam notabiles et conventus in

60 Almost all those I have mentioned and many others went outside the city to meet the body and devoutly joined the funeral procession. Down the long central street of the city, which was very muddy at the time, the principal noblemen of the kingdom carried the bier to the cathedral church, allowing scarcely any churchmen to share in the task. The kings themselves, the archbishops and bishops, bending their shoulders and necks, brought the noble treasure into the church and to the choir.*

61 Who can describe how many men and women crowded together, thronging to the body now placed in the church? They kissed the bier and with loving and admirable readiness and devotion offered gold and silver to the sacred body, which was not yet entombed nor yet made famous or canonized through signs and miracles. Thus, so large and mixed a crowd of people, both men and women, thronged into the choir that the canons were squeezed together and could hardly stand in their stalls.

62 I think it also noteworthy that, just as if he had died at the Grande Chartreuse or at Witham with only twelve brothers attending the funeral of the thirteenth (since a convent of that Order does not exceed this number), so now twelve of his brothers, that is, the bishops, attended the funeral of him who was the thirteenth.*

63 Besides, I thought it deserving notice that in the celebration of his exequies only bishops recited the readings from the Book of Job that are appointed for a funeral.

64 And I would not pass over in silence that, equaling the number of bishops, twelve marks of silver were offered to the body that day, and enough gold--in rings, necklaces, and bezants [gold coins from Byzantium]--as would fully equal the value of a silver mark or more. This was as a gift for the thirteenth [bishop], that is, the dead man, as one more golden than the others, not gilded, but rather of the purest gold, proven by fire.

65 Also among the important events I include this, that two kings [John of England and William of Scotland] who for some time had been in disagreement were restored then and there to peace and friendship. And abbots who had been summoned there because of royal exactions, especially abbots of the Cistercian Order, went away happy and not taxed at all. Quite the contrary, the king unexpectedly decided to build and securely endow with public funds a monastery of that Order in southern England, near the sea, which took the name of Beaulieu, and at the same time he granted it a site with ample estates and pastures.

66 In truth, the Lord arranged all of this worthily, so that on the arrival of such a treasure, like a bridegroom coming to the bridal chamber and to a place of rest, all things might be

hoc articulo sic concurrentes, et quod eius exequiis qui
ceterorum exequias tantopere curabat tantum honorem dedit
Deus, et qui sepeliendis corporibus tanquam Tobias alter tam
infatigabili studio opus et operam inpendebat, ipsum quoque   126
sepeliri tam magnifice voluit, tanquam non anime solum vic-
toriose in celis, verum etiam corpori gloriose in terris tam
pie devocionis mercede soluta, totum revera pro grandi miraculo est reputandum et inter signa insignia quasi primum et
precipuum hoc admirandum et annotandum.

II

De milite de Lindeseia quem ad tumbam sancti viri
[primo transitus eiusdem anno] gutta festra reliquit.

68   Cum in Lindeseia miles quidam, tribus annis ante transitum viri sancti, gravi egritudinis incomodo laborasset, morbum quem vulgares guttam festram vocant habens in brachio
sinistro, quo nulla medicorum opera curari potuit, aut etiam
alleviari, crebrescente iam fama de episcopo defuncto, et de
corpore ipsius Lincolniam advecto et tam gloriose suscepto,
tum amicorum consilio, tum propria quoque devocione et quasi
spe certa sanctitatis illius, cuius vitam et conversacionem
tam sinceram in terris et sine macula non ignoraverat, peni-
tentia purgatus inprimis et confessione, devotas fundens
preces, ad corpus sacrum accessit. Et cum aliquamdiu sub
feretro prostratus in oracionibus et lacrimis perseverasset,
tandem exurgens coram archiepiscopis et episcopis, ceterisque
magnis viris assistentibus, brachio nudato et morbo cunctis
ostenso ubi, carne fere tota consumpta, ossa eminencia con-
parebant, flens et gemens humiliter inploravit quatinus manu   127
dextra viri sancti brachium sua dicta infirmitate corrosum,
facto crucis signaculo, contingere liceret. Cuius precibus
tam lacrimosis pium prestantes assensum, tanteque miserie ipsius moti atque miserti conpassionis affectu, desiderium eius
impleri conmuniter indulserunt. Nec mora, vulnera brachii,
seu pocius ulcera, que sanie insanabili et insaciabili paulo
ante defluebant, tam meritis viri sancti quam fide quoque propria et devocione, tam graviter afflicti mox arescere ceperunt,
et caro corrosa nervique contracti et inbecilles effecti paulatim ad pristinum robuste valetudinis statum redierunt.
Sanitate vero in brevi plene secuta, Lincolniam ilico miles
accessit, cum amicorum quoque sequela congratulancium et con-
testancium, et coram venerabilibus viris, R. Decano, ceteris-

67.4 *Cf.* Tobias 1:20-1; 2:1-9.

done with joy and gladness, all in peace and friendship.
67   These unusual events and the concurrent meetings at that
time and the fact that God honored the funeral of one who was
so concerned for the funerals of others and who with such constant zeal, like another Tobias, spent toil and care in the
burial of bodies--all this should be judged a great miracle,
admired and recognized as the first and foremost among [the
saint's] remarkable signs. God willed that he be buried so
magnificently as if paying a reward for such devotion, not only
triumphantly to the soul in heaven, but also gloriously to the
body on earth.

Chapter Two

Of the knight of Lindsey who at the saint's tomb
recovered from an ulcer [the first year after the
saint's death].

68   A certain knight in Lindsey had been very ill for three
years before the saint's death. In his left arm, he had the
disease commonly called an ulcer. No effort of the physicians
could cure it or even relieve it. Then the fame of the dead
bishop spread, both as to how his body was carried to Lincoln
and how it was gloriously received there. The knight had
near-certain confidence in the sanctity of the bishop, whose
life and sincere and unstained conduct on earth were not unknown to him. On the advice of his friends and moved by his
own piety, he was first purified by penance and confession,
and then, offering devout prayers, he approached the holy body.
He lay prostrate for some time before the bier, not ceasing to
pray and weep. Finally, he stood up in the presence of the
archbishops and bishops and other great persons in attendance.
His arm was bare, and the disease was evident to them all,
with the flesh nearly eaten away and the bones exposed. With
tears and sighs he humbly begged that after making the sign
of the cross he might touch the arm, ravaged with that disease of his, to the saint's right hand. Responding kindly to
his tearful prayers and moved to compassion for his great suffering, they joined in granting his request. Soon, by the
saint's merits and the knight's own faith and devotion, the
wounds of the terribly diseased arm, or rather the sores,
which just before were running with incurable pus that could
not be stopped, began to dry up. The wasted flesh and the
cramped and weakened sinews little by little returned to their
original vigor. When full health followed soon afterward, the
knight went straight to Lincoln with friends who rejoiced with

que personis cathedralis ecclesie cum canonicis in capitulo
convocatis, brachium suum quod paulo ante tam invalidum viderant, tamque horrendum aspectu et tam informe, nudum exposuit
et episcopi sancti meritis integre sanitati sic restitutum,
cum gaudio magno lacrimisque quas gaudium educit, propalavit,
magnificans Deum tam admirabilem in sanctis suis et tam gloriosum.

III

De decano de Marnam â gravi apostemate curato, et filio
ipsius â morte liberato.

69 Accidit eodem anno quo vir sanctus ab hac vita migravit
quod cum decanus de Marnam â domo militis cuiusdam cuius eo   128
die coepulator extiterat versus domum suam rediret, non procul inde sed quasi per miliare distanti, apostema subito in
ore ipsius excrevit quod crescendo nimis invalescens et inflacione turgescens, priusquam ad domum suam perveniret, fac-
tum est pomo silvestri in quantitate conforme. Morbo vero
ingravescente, sequenti diluculo vix verbum proferre potuit,
adeo ut pre nimia pestis vehemencia videretur morti proximus
et ex toto fere desperanter afflictus. Senciens autem se
tanquam in extremo iam articulo constitutum, convocatis amicis
Christique sacerdotibus et iuris discretis, sano eorumdem et
salubri consilio, domui sue disponere et testamentum condere
curavit, et de legitimis agendis, iuxta doctrinam ecclesiasticam, nichil omisit. Nocte vero sequente morbi malicia for-
cius urgente, capud eius adeo mane inflatum extiterat quod
pocius ibi monstrum informe quam humana figura cunctis intu-
entibus appareret.
70 Tercio vero die postquam morbus incepit, ei quasi laboranti in extremo et iam in extasi posito, videbatur quod cum
super eligendo pontifice Lincolniensi tractatui cum aliis
interesset, miles quidam, nuncius regis, capitulo breve regium
palam porrexit quo pro clerico quodam, proprio nomine tunc
nominato, non autem hic nominando, rogavit quatinus ipsum in
episcopum suum eligere modis omnibus non postponerent. Et   129
incontinenti quandam vocem audivit, quasi de sublimi dicentem
et intonantem, nominatum illum nimis indignum esse tanto viro
in episcopalem succedere dignitatem. Et eadem vox eidem, ut
videbatur, propius accedens, ait, "Et tu quare non inprimis
ẏmaginem ad honorem sacri pontificis Hugonis, unde sanitatem
valeas recuperare?" Ille autem, hoc audito, quoad sinebat
nimia debilitatis et infirmitatis anxietas, experrectus,
astantes et quasi iam moribundum lacrimis et lamentis prose-

him and confirmed his account. The dean, R[oger of Rolleston], and other officials of the cathedral, with the canons, were assembled in chapter. In the presence of these venerable persons, he showed his bare arm, which not long before they had seen so diseased and so dreadful to look at and so disfigured. With great joy and with the tears that joy draws forth, he displayed the arm restored thus to full health by the merits of the holy bishop, and he magnified God who is so wonderful in his saints and so glorious.

Chapter Three

Of the Dean of Marnam who was cured of a serious abscess and whose son was delivered from death.

69   The year the saint passed from this life it happened that the dean of Marnam was returning home from the house of a certain knight with whom he had dined that day. Not far from there, about a mile away, an abscess suddenly developed in his face, and it did not heal but grew large and swollen. Before he got home it had become as big as a crab apple. The condition got worse, and the next morning he could hardly say a word, so that from the virulence of the infection he seemed near death and utterly afflicted, almost beyond hope. Thinking he was in his last hour, he called together his friends, as well as priests of Christ and competent lawyers. With their sound and reasonable advice he undertook to settle his household and to write his testament. He omitted nothing that the church teaches should lawfully be done. The following night the illness was even more oppressive, and by morning his head was so swollen that to all who saw it, it seemed a monstrous growth rather than a human form.
70   The third day after the onset of the disease, when he was evidently in his last throes and already out of his right mind, it seemed to him that he was involved in a discussion with others on the election of the bishop of Lincoln.* A knight who was a messenger of the king publicly offered the chapter a royal brief. In this, he petitioned in favor of a certain cleric who was then named (but is not to be named here), that by all means they should not postpone electing him their bishop. At once the dean heard a voice speaking and thundering as if from on high that this candidate was quite unworthy to succeed such a man [as Saint Hugh] in the episcopal dignity. And the same voice, seeming to draw nearer, said to him, "And you, why do you not mould an image in honor of the holy Bishop Hugh whereby you could regain your health?" When he heard

quentes et conplangentes, nutu convocavit et voce tenui prout
potuit notificavit quatinus ceram ei calefactam ocius affer-
ent. Qua continenter allata, vix capite ẏmaginis ab ipso for-
mato, totum ilico morbum illum quo gravabatur in capite subito per corpus sensit ad pedes descendere, et statim, tumore
sedato pariter et dolore, facies ipsius totumque capud ad pris-
tinam formam et sanitatem integram est restitutum. Unde cum
dolor ille totus ac tumor ad partes pedum inferiores iam
descendisset, pre nimiis quas ibi sensit angustiis, ad amicorum
instanciam, medici cuiusdam quamquam vix et invitus apponi
tandem emplastra permisit. Quibus appo[s]itis, protinus incepit tam vehementi parcium illarum dolore torqueri quod ipse,
medico non exspectato set ferro mox arrepto, vincula pedum
propria manu scidit et totum incunctanter emplastrum abiecit,   130
coniectans secum et dicens quoniam hec non inmerito patieba-
tur, quando medicum alium ad inferiores partes admisit quam
illum qui superiores tam efficaci curacione sanavit.

71   Quo facto, preces pias et devotas fudit ad Dominum, postulans et cum lacrimis inplorans quatinus integra sibi, per merita beati presulis Hugonis, tam pedum scilicet quam capitis
sanitate reddita, filio quoque suo in extremis tunc laboranti,
quem pre cunctis creaturis plus diligebat, dupplicato beneficio
seu pocius multiplicato, multiplici nimirum pietate preditus
et inconprehensibili, vite metas protelaret et tam inportunos
quam intempestivos iamiam urgentes et miserum ā corpore spiri-
tum extorquentes mortis aculeos proterminaret.

72   Porro, quoniam "mirabilis Deus in sanctis suis," qui
etiam habundancia pietatis sue et merita supplicum excedit et
vota, vir ille, voti statim conpos utriusque, misericorditer
est exauditus. Quapropter et pater, una cum filio quasi vite
restituto, necnon et amicorum multitudine, quibus habundabant,
et vicinorum eis congratulancium Deumque collaudancium, ad
tumbam viri sancti Lincolniam accesserunt, communiter omnes
quod actum utrique fuerat testificantes et Deum in sancto suo
magnificantes.

IV

De muliere de Keles, manibus contracta, ad tumbam   131
viri sancti curata.

73   Accidit in villa de Keles quod mulier quedam, incredula
nimis et indevota, die quadam sabbati post nonam operi servili indulsit, filum scilicet in glomellum convertendo. Cum

72.1 Psalm 67:36 (Vulgate).

that, so far as the torment of his exhaustion and illness
allowed, he awoke and with a nod summoned those who were
standing about. They were attending him with tears and laments
and mourning as if he were already dead. In the weak voice he
was able to muster, he told them quickly to bring him warm wax.
They brought him some at once. Scarcely had he shaped the head
of the image than he instantly felt the sickness that afflicted
him in the head descend through his body to the feet, the
swelling and the pain being relieved at once. His face and
entire head were restored to their original form and full
health. Then, since all the pain and swelling had moved to
the lower parts of the feet, because of the intense pains he
felt there, at his friends' urging, though himself reluctant,
he finally allowed the plasters of a certain physician to be
applied. As soon as the plasters were applied, he began to be
tortured with such extreme pain in his feet that, without
waiting for the physician, he quickly took the knife and with
his own hands cut the bindings on his feet and immediately
threw off the whole plaster. On reflection, he said that he
deserved to suffer that pain, since he let a different physician treat the lower parts of his body from the one who cured
the upper parts so effectively.

71   After that he prayed fervently to the Lord. Full health
was restored to him through the merits of the blessed Bishop
Hugh, in both his feet and his head, and therefore he petitioned for his son also, whom he loved above all creatures and
who was then suffering on the verge of death. With tears he
implored the Lord, whose mercy is truly great and incomprehensible, to double or multiply his kindness and extend the
limits of his son's life, postponing the savage and untimely
stings of death that were already upon him and tearing the
poor spirit from the body.

72   Since God is wonderful in his saints and by his abundant
compassion surpasses both the merits and the desires of those
who pray to him, the man was mercifully heard and gained both
of his petitions immediately. The father, together with the
son who had been virtually restored to life, and a crowd of
their many friends, and neighbors who rejoiced and praised God
with them, came to the saint's tomb at Lincoln, all testifying
what had been done for the two men and magnifying God in his
saint.

tamen vir venerabilis abbas de Flai, ex transmarinis partibus
in Angliam veniens et predicacionis officio fungens, inter
cetera laudabilia duo predicando monuit et suasit, ut diebus
dominicis ā publicis foris et mercaturis cuncti cessarent et
omni die sabbati post nonam ā quolibet opere servili feriarent,
multos etiam utriusque sexus homines ad votorum induxerat
emissionem. Quorum hec omnium vota deridens et dicti viri
boni predicacionem parvipendens, necnon et tam viri sui quam
vicinorum hoc audiencium et videncium vituperacionem et correp-
cionem omnino contempnens, operi incepto nichilominus insiste-
bat. Nec mora, mulier illa miserrima, videntibus qui ibi tunc
aderant cunctis, clausis ambabus firmiter tanquam in pugnum
manibus, subito in terram corruit, velud exanimis aut amens
effecta. Omnes autem hoc videntes et ulcionem divinam tam
manifestam attendentes, stupefacti valde et consternati, ad
ecclesiam concurrerunt et tam persone quam clericis ecclesie
quod acciderat intimarunt. Et illi statim decano suo plebano   132
et postea simul cum illo loci illius archidiacono miraculum
hoc significarunt. Quod etiam non solum in ecclesiis, verum
et in foris publicis et conventibus, quatinus unius punicio
multorum sit municio, quatinus unius fletus multorum sit metus,
quatinus unius error multorum sit terror et horror, quia
"cum feriunt unum, non unum fulmina terrent," per provinciam
totam est publicatum.

74   Processu vero temporis mulier illa dicto incomodo fatigata plurimum et afflicta, sibique suisque prorsus inutilis
effecta, demum amicorum consilio, Lincolniam ad tumbam viri
sancti, tremulis et lassis passibus, debilis et inbecilla
transivit. In primis igitur ad penitencialem, subdecanum
scilicet Willelmum, virum eruditum et discretum, confessione
purganda devote profecta.

75   Hoc inter cetera quod ei infortunium istud, sicuti credebat, pro peccatis suis acciderat, et exprimens maxime quibus,
est professa. Penitencialis autem, putans quod audiebat tru-
tannicum et ficticium esse, manum mulieris manibus ambabus
arripuit eamque, vires apponens omnes, vi voluit aperire et
extendere, nec profecit. Penetrans igitur et vagis urbem
totam circu[i]ens passibus et tanquam amens effecta, pugnos
ambos pariter collisit, et quandoque capud, quandoque cetera
membra que attingere poterat, pugnis cedere non cessavit.
Demum autem Cantuariam transiens, sanctum Thomam adivit. Ad   133
cuius tumbam cum fessa dormiret, vocem ei dicentem audivit
quatinus Lincolniam quam cicius rediret, ad tumbam beati
Hugonis sanitatem procul dubio receptura. Que statim exurgens et versus Lincolniam iter accelerans, dominica palmarum

73.26 Ovid, *Ex Ponto* 3.2.9; *Ovid has* feriant *instead of*
feriunt.

Chapter Four

Of the woman from Keal with contracted hands who was
cured at the saint's tomb.

73   A very skeptical and irreligious woman in the village of
Keal was engaged in menial work one Saturday after nones [mid-
afternoon], spinning thread into a ball.* But when the venerable Abbot of Flay had come to England from abroad and conducted a mission of preaching, he urged and stressed two
points among other good counsel in his sermons: ˙that on Sun-
days everyone should avoid public markets and shops and that
every Saturday after nones they should rest from any kind of
menial work. He also persuaded many men and women to pledge
this observance. The woman from Keal mocked the pledges of
all these people and dismissed the good man's preaching. She
also quite scorned the reproach and criticism of her own husband and the neighbors who heard and saw what she was doing.
She simply kept at the work she had begun. All at once, in
the sight of everyone there, the unfortunate woman fell to the
ground with both hands closed tight in a fist, as if she had
died or gone insane. All who saw this and observed the divine
vengeance made so plain were stupefied and dismayed. They ran
to the church and informed the parson and the parish clerks
of what had happened. And they promptly reported the miracle
to the local dean and then, with him, to the archdeacon of
that place. It was publicized throughout the district, not
only in churches but in public squares and assemblies, so that
the punishment of one might be a safeguard for many; the weeping of one, an alarm for many; the error of one, a terror and
horror for many--since when thunderbolts strike one person,
it is not just one person that they terrify.
74   As time went on, the woman became altogether exhausted
and tormented by that burden and quite useless to herself and
her family. Finally, on the advice of friends, she journeyed
crippled and weak, with weary and trembling steps, to the
saint's tomb at Lincoln. She first devoutly approached the
penitentiary and subdean, William [of Bramfeld], a learned
and discreet man, to be purified by confession.
75   Among other things she confessed that she believed this
calamity had happened to her because of her sins, and she told
what those principally were. But the penitentiary thought
what he heard was a dishonest piece of make-believe. He took
the woman's hand in both his own and tried with all his
strength to open her hand and forcibly stretch it out, but he
could not. With wandering steps, then, she went here and
there about the whole city. As if gone mad, she beat her
fists together and kept hitting them against her head and the

ad tumbam sanctam accessit, et inter pugnos candelam tenens,
pro sanitate recuperanda lacrimosas ad Dominum et ad sanctum
suum preces effudit. Et cum dictus W[illelmus] subdecanus ad
altare sancti Johannis Baptiste, quod tumbam viri sancti col-
lateralem ā sinistris et proximam habet, missam de die tunc
celebraret, dum passio legeretur, una manus mulieris super
tumbam erecta est et extensa, et altera similiter paulo post,
priusquam missa celebrata fuisset. Videntes autem hii qui
aderant et contractam manibus antea noverant, tam clerici quam
laici, Dei virtutem tantam et signum insigne, mirabilem Deum
in sanctis suis collaudarunt.
76   Ad maiorem quoque rei geste probacionem et miraculi certitudinem, milites quidam de Lindeseia et viri fide dignissimi,
qui eam ab inicio sic contractam viderant et inutilem diucius
et invalidam, Lincolniense capitulum intrantes, tactis sacrosanctis evangeliis, palam et publice iuraverunt hanc eandem
esse revera quam antea viderant in Lindeseia, vindicta divina
manus ambas in pugnum clausas et contractas habere. Unde et
precentor W[illelmus] qui paulo post episcopus Lincolniensis   134
effectus est, eodem palmarum die in sermone suo ad populum
solempniter hoc miraculum promulgavit.

                                V

        De muliere de Beverlaco idropica ad tumbam viri sancti
        curata.

77   Mulier quedam de Beverlaco ẏdropico per triennium morbo
vexata graviter fuit et occupata, adeo ut non solum faciem et
tibias, verum etiam ventrem et corpus totum in modum vesice
perlucidum haberet et luridum, distentum enormiter et inflatum. Cum autem vir eius multum in medicis inaniter consump-
sisset, adeo ut apporiatus iam plurimum fuisset et tedio quoque nimis affectus, mulier pre verecundia pariter et morbi
angustia solum natale relinquens et Lincolniam adiens, ibique
per mensem moram faciens, victumque ut potuit nendo perquir-
ens, viri sancti suffragia pro sanitate recuperanda precibus
assiduis efflagitavit. Tandem vero tanquam desperans effecta,
se sanctum martirem Cantuariensem Thomam causa sanitatis vel
ibi optinende firmiter adire proposuit. Et cum ad tumbam
presulis Hugonis, quasi licenciam ā sancto prius acceptura
veniret, et devotis ibidem precibus diucius perseverasset,
tandem sopore correpta, vocem hanc tanquam ā tumba proveni-
entem audivit, "Surge, mulier, quia curata es." Illa vero
statim, hoc audito, tam stupefacta plurimum quam etiam gavisa
surrexit, et incontinenti zona ipsius qua cincta fuerat,   135

other parts of her body she could touch. But at last, she
journeyed to Canterbury and approached Saint Thomas. While
she slept exhausted at his tomb, she heard a voice saying to
her that she should return to Lincoln as soon as possible with
confidence that she would recover her health at the tomb of
the blessed Hugh. She got up at once and hurried to Lincoln.
She approached the saint's tomb on Palm Sunday. Holding a
candle between her fists, she poured out tearful prayers to the
Lord and his saint for recovery of her health. The saint's
tomb is near the altar of St. John the Baptist, to the left.
The subdean William [of Bramfeld] was then celebrating the
mass of the day at that altar. While he read the Passion,
one of the woman's hands was raised and stretched out over the
tomb, and a little after, before the mass was over, the other
hand likewise. Those who were present and who had known her
to have contracted hands, clerics as well as layfolk, seeing
God's great power and the extraordinary sign, praised God
who is wonderful in his saints.

76 For greater proof of the event and assurance of the miracle, certain knights of Lindsey who were well deserving of
trust and who had seen her from the start, helpless and weak
for so long with that contracture, entered the chapter house
at Lincoln. With their hands on the holy Gospels they openly
and publicly swore that this was indeed the very woman they
had previously seen in Lindsey who by God's punishment had
both hands rigidly closed and contracted into a fist. William
[of Blois] the precentor, who was shortly afterward made Bishop
of Lincoln, therefore solemnly proclaimed the miracle that same
Palm Sunday in his sermon to the people.

Chapter Five

Of the woman from Beverley with dropsy who was cured
at the saint's tomb.

77 A woman from Beverley was seriously troubled with the
disease of dropsy for three years. It had so filled her that
not only her face and legs but also her stomach and her whole
body, like a bladder, were transparent and pale yellow, enor-
mously swollen and inflated. After her husband had spent a
great deal on physicians with no improvement, so that he was
now quite impoverished and exhausted too, the woman left her
native region because of shame as well as the torment of the
disease and went to Lincoln. There she stayed for a month,
getting a living as she could by spinning. With constant
prayers she earnestly sought the saint's intercession to

cuius ambitus ob ventrem turgidum nimis et tumidum amplus
erat valde, circa pedes eius clausa deorsum subito corruit,
et gracilis ilico, absque ulla inclusi liquoris infusione,
iuxta pristinum sanitatis statum reperta fuit. Et cum custos
tumbe cum ceteris qui aderant quesissent ab ipsa quenam esset
et unde illuc advecta et quo morbo laborasset, totumque per
ordinem ab ore ipsius audissent, totumque capitulo canonicorum id notificassent, convocatis hiis cum quibus illa per
mensem in urbe moram fecerat, et ab illis quoque rei geste
veritas et inquisita est diligenter et patefacta. Capitulum
vero Lincolniense, cupiens etiam super hiis amplius cercior-
ari, literas suas et nuncios fideles ad capitulum Beverlacense
destinavit, rogans et monens quatinus et ipsi veritatem diligentissime super hiis inquisitam ipsis renunciarent. Illi
vero, ad mandatum et preces capituli Lincolniensis, convocatis hominibus fide dignioribus de tribus vicis proximis ubi
nata fuit mulier et nutrita, per sacramentum ipsorum tam
super evangelia quam super corpus beati Johannis de Beverlaco
corporaliter prestitum, veritatem quam mulier ipsa professa
fuerat ab eis inquisitam et patefactam literis suis sigillo
beati Johannis signatis capitulo Lincolniensi rescripserunt.
Quo demum testimonio plene certificati pariter et exhilarati,
canonici et clerici Lincolnienses, facta processione ut de-   136
cuit, pulsatisque campanis, dictamque mulierem ad tumbam beati Hugonis ducentes Deoque gracias conmuniter agentes, miraculum hoc solempniter populo predicandum et publice propalan-
dum tunc denique dignum duxerunt.

VI

     De iuvene qui visum, quo diu iam caruerat, ad
     tumbam viri sancti recuperavit.

78   Adolescens quidam inter canonicos et cives Lincolnienses
nutritus tempore iam multo visu caruerat, nubecula quadam
pupillam eius obtegente, adeo ut cilia claudere vix potuisset.
Hic ad tumbam viri sancti vigilia Pentecostes devotus accessit, noctemque per illam totam in lacrimis ibidem et oracionibus perseveravit. Mane vero, circa horam primam, cum eum
dormientem ad tumbam inventum ã sompno excitassent, ne ab
hominum frequencia circiter horam illam ad tumbam confluenci-
um conprimeretur, statim illi exurgenti ab oculis eius undique tanquam albumen ovi defluebat. Nec mora, se visum rece-
pisse proclamavit, Deo et beato Hugoni gracias referens. Hoc
itaque sepius iterando et vociferando, pre gaudio quoque proclamans et palmas ad insimul percuciens, clamore tali simul

restore her health. At last, having grown desperate, she made
up her mind to go to the martyr St. Thomas of Canterbury to
try to gain her health there instead. She came to the tomb
of Bishop Hugh, as if to obtain the saint's permission first,
and had long continued there in devout prayers when at last
she fell asleep. She heard a voice that seemed to come from
the tomb, saying, "Arise, woman, for you are cured." On hearing this, she got up, as surprised as she was happy, and at
once the belt she was wearing, which was a very full one because her belly was so swollen and distended, dropped still
fastened to her feet. She was found to be suddenly slender
and in her former health, though none of the enclosed fluid
had flowed out. A custodian of the tomb, with others who were
present, asked her who she was and where she came from and
what illness she had suffered. When they heard the whole
story in sequence from her own lips, they met with the canons
and reported it all to the chapter. Those with whom she had
stayed for the month in the city were summoned and from them
too the truth of what happened was carefully sought out and
made known. But since the chapter at Lincoln wanted to be
even more sure of this, they sent their own letter with reliable messengers to the chapter at Beverley, asking and advis-
ing that they closely inquire and report to them the truth
of the matter. Responding to the instruction and petition of
the chapter at Lincoln, they assembled men worthy of trust
from three places near where the woman was born and reared.
These men confirmed the truth of what the woman had claimed,
by an oath on the Gospels and before the body of St. John of
Beverley. The Beverley chapter reported their inquiry to the
chapter at Lincoln, in their own letter, sealed with the seal
of St. John.* Fully convinced and overjoyed at this testimony,
the canons and clerks of Lincoln went in customary procession
and rang the cathedral bells. They conducted the woman to the
tomb of Saint Hugh, all thanking God together. Then at last
they concluded that this miracle should be solemnly preached
to the people and publicly proclaimed.

Chapter Six

Of the youth who at the saint's tomb recovered the
sight he had long been without.

78   A youth who had been a ward of the canons and citizens
of Lincoln had been without sight for some time.* A certain
cloudy substance covered his pupil so that he could hardly
shut his lids. On the vigil of Pentecost he approached the

et gestu multos ad se intuendum et admirandum convocavit.
Plurimi vero qui cecum illum satis antea noverant, tam clerici
quam laici, Deum conmuniter et sanctum Hugonem laudaverunt,   137
statimque, simul cum tumbe custodibus, miraculum istud tam
manifestum decano et subdecano necnon et universo capitulo
tunc presenti ex ordine propalarunt. Iuvenis autem qui visum
susceperat, ad iussionem illorum eis in capitulo est presenta-
tus, ubi non solum civium qui bene eum noverant testimonio,
sed etiam decani ipsius, de cuius elemosina iam diu fuerat
sustentatus, et aliorum quoque quorundam de capitulo, declar-
atum est hoc miraculum et approbatum. Et eodem Pentecostes
die in sermone ad populum facto dignis preconiis est pro-
palatum.

VII

De iuvene quodam de Hanecastro in amenciam verso,
ad tumbam viri sancti sanitati restituto.

79   Iuvenis quidam de Anecastro in frenesim versus et amens
effectus, â parentibus et amicis ad plurima loca sanctorum
causa sanitatis recuperande frustra circumductus, tandem Lincolniam ad tumbam sancti Hugonis astrictus vinculis et ligatus
est adductus. Ubi cum septem diebus continuis moram iuxta
tumbam fecisset cum precibus et lamentis, et de die in diem
melius habere cepisset, die dominica divinis auditis et ad
altare beati Iohannis Baptiste, iuxta tumbam, sacramentis
Dominici corporis debita devocione perceptis, iuvenis ille,
tam viri sancti meritis quam suorum quoque devocionibus, integre sanitati est restitutus. Unde et paulo post domum per
se regreditur, cathenas manibus deferens quibus ligatus fuer-   138
at, dicens se meritis beati presulis Hugonis solutum esse et
integre sanitati restitutum. Pater autem eius, cum eadem
hora ab agro revertens filium suum iuxta matrem sane et discrete in verbis et gestibus se gerentem invenisset, admiratus
est plurimum et ultra quam credi possit exhilaratus. Nec
mora, parens uterque cum amicis et vicinis suis plurimis quibus miraculum istud notum extiterat, Lincolniam venientes et
Deum in sanctis suis collaudantes, decano et capitulo conmuniter istud declararunt.

saint's tomb with faith and stayed there the whole night weeping and praying. In the morning, about the hour of prime,
they found him asleep at the tomb and woke him, lest he be
pressed by the crowd of people thronging to the tomb at that
time. As soon as he got up, something like the albumen of an
egg flowed from every part of his eyes. Immediately he declared that he had recovered his sight and gave thanks to God
and blessed Hugh. He repeated this several times and cried
out, exclaiming for joy and clapping his hands. With such an
outcry and gesture he provoked many people to look at him and
marvel. Most of these, both clerics and layfolk, had known
him to be blind for some time. They too praised God and Saint
Hugh, and at once, with the custodians of the tomb, they duly
reported the evident miracle to the dean and subdean, as well
as to the whole chapter which was then meeting. At their request the youth who had gained his sight was presented to them
in chapter. There the miracle was recounted and confirmed by
the testimony of not only the citizens who had known him well,
but the dean himself, by whose alms the boy had long been supported, and other members of the chapter. That same Pentecost
Sunday the miracle was announced with fitting praises in the
sermon to the people.

Chapter Seven

Of the youth from Ancaster who went mad and who was
restored to sanity at the saint's tomb.

79   A youth from Ancaster became delirious and went out of
his mind. He was taken by his parents and friends to many
shrines to be healed, but with no effect. At length, he was
brought, bound and tied with chains, to the tomb of Saint Hugh
at Lincoln. He stayed at the tomb for seven days continuously,
praying and sorrowing, and day by day he began to improve. On
Sunday, after hearing mass at the altar of St. John the Baptist, next to the tomb, and devoutly receiving the sacrament
of the Lord's body, the young man was fully restored to sanity
by the merits of the saint as well as the prayers of his
family. Soon afterward, he went home on his own, carrying in
his hands the chains by which he had been bound and saying
that he had been freed and completely restored to sanity by
the merits of the blessed Bishop Hugh. His father was returning from the field just at that time and found his son at his
mother's side acting sanely and reasonably in both words and
gestures. The father was very astonished and unbelievably
happy. Both parents, with their friends and many neighbors

VIII

De viro quodam de Stubetre qui ad tumbam viri
sancti visum recuperavit.

80   Vir quidam in villa de Stubetre oculorum lumine privatus,
ad tumbam beati Hugonis adductus, cum feria sexta post ves-
peras illuc pervenisset ibique in lacrimis et precibus devotissime pernoctasset, diluculo post matutinas meritis viri
sancti desiderati luminis gaudia recuperavit. Inventus autem
ibidem mane ā clericis ecclesie et custodibus tumbe, gaudens
et videns, Deumque laudans et sanctum Hugonem, coram ecclesie
canonicis est adductus. Capitulum vero amplius super hoc cer-
tiorari cupiens, capellano de Stubetre literis suis et nunciis
significarunt quatinus ille veritatem diligenter inquisitam
ipsis indubitanter explicaret. Ille vero, die nativitatis
beate Marie, cum pluribus et maioribus ac melioribus ville
sue de Stubetre, ad ecclesiam Lincolniensem accedentes, coram   139
episcopo Willelmo et capitulo ad hoc congregato, sacramentis
coram omnibus corporaliter prestitis, rem ita in veritate se
habere sicut vir ille predixerat, affirmarunt. Episcopus autem, de veritate tam evidenti securus effectus, solempniter
hoc miraculum eodem die in sermone suo ad populum pronuncia-
vit.

IX

De puella de Wicford tibiis totis et poplitibus
contracta, ad tumbam viri sancti curata.

81   Puella quedam in vico de Wikeford, cui nomen Aliz, nocte
visionem vidit quod vir quidam eam in aera sustulit et diu
super aquam magnam toto corpore suspenso tenuit, et quod tandem illam in aquam eandem precipitavit, ubi nichil aliud nisi
certissimum mortis periculum expectavit. Mane vero facto,
cum domina sua diem conperit, mirata est ancillam suam preter
solitum sompno diutino detineri. Que multocies eam clammose
vociferando, tandem ipsam ā sompnis excitavit. Que cum primo
tibias et crura flectere et ad surgendum sibi attrahere vellet
totisque nisibus hoc attemptaret, quia totum corpus ā zona
inferius tanquam emortuum habebat, non profecit. Domina vero
ipsius, cui revelaverat illa ut potuit incomodum suum, anxia
nimis et dolens, inque Deum et sanctum Hugonem certam fiduciam
figens, mulierem illam ad tumbam beati Hugonis deferri fecit.   140
Cui, feria tercia post diem palmarum, circa horam primam,
nervi tibiarum et crurium stridorem facere grandem et strepi-

who knew of the miracle, came at once to Lincoln, praising
God in his saints, and together reported the miracle to the
dean and chapter.

Chapter Eight

Of the man from Stubton who recovered sight at
the saint's tomb.

80   A man in the village of Stubton who could not see was
brought to the tomb of blessed Hugh. He stayed there on Friday after vespers and devoutly spent the night in tears and
prayers. At dawn, after matins, he recovered by the saint's
merits the joys of sight that he desired. He was found in
the morning by clerks of the church and custodians of the
tomb, rejoicing and seeing, and as he praised God and Saint
Hugh he was led before the canons of the church. The chapter
wanted to substantiate what had occurred and by their letter
and messengers notified the chaplain at Stubton that he should
carefully investigate and report the truth of this case to
them exactly. On the feast of the Nativity of Blessed Mary
[September 8], the priest came to the church at Lincoln with
many of the leading worthy people of his village of Stubton.
In the presence of Bishop William [of Blois] and the chapter
assembled for the purpose they took oaths before all of them
and affirmed that the case was just as the man had earlier
reported. The bishop was convinced of the evident truth and
solemnly announced this miracle the same day in his sermon to
the people.

Chapter Nine

Of the girl from Wigford completely paralyzed in the
legs and knees who was cured at the saint's tomb.

81   A girl in the suburb of Wigford whose name was Alice saw
a vision at night in which a man carried her in the air and
for a long time held her whole body suspended over a great
body of water; finally he threw her into the water, where she
expected nothing but the surest peril of death. When morning
came and her mistress saw it was day, she was surprised that
her servant-girl was late because of over-sleeping, which was
most unlike her. She finally wakened her by shouting to her
loudly many times. When the girl wanted at first to bend her

tum, cunctis audientibus qui aderant, tunc ceperunt. Illa
nimirum paulo post unam týbiam ad se traxit, et post aliam,
et deinde surrexit, Deoque et sancto Hugoni devotas gracias
agens. Cum autem fama miraculi istius ad dominam suam cicius
pervenisset, illa exhilarata plurimum et stupefacta, vicinos
suos quam plurimos et vicinas qui famulam suam contractam
viderant ad tumbam secum adduxit, rem quam viderant et optime
noverant conmuniter contestantes, et sacramento corporaliter
prestito confirmantes. Hec autem conprobacio facta fuit feria tercia septimane paschalis, anno sexto postquam beatus
Hugo ab hac vita migravit.

82   Ad hoc autem miraculum plenius conprobandum, narravit
magister Philippus, Lincolniensis ecclesie tunc subdecanus,
R. decano et universo capitulo visionem quam viderat nocte
dominica subsequente post matutinas. Hanc scilicet: cum
lecto dormiret, vir quidam venerabilis ei apparuit, dicens
semel et iterum ut surgeret et ad ecclesiam quamcicius per-
geret. Ille vero respondit se paulo antea ab ecclesia venis-
se. Predictus autem vir ille denuo dixit ei quatinus surgeret
velociter et ecclesiam incunctanter adiret, quia gloria Dei
descendit de celo in ecclesiam et maxime super tumbam sancti   141
episcopi Hugonis. Ad hanc autem vocem expergefactus ã somno,
sicut ei videbatur, et exurgens, ecclesiam ingrediebatur, et
accedens ante altare sancti Iohannis Baptiste et circa tumbam
viri sancti, visus est sibi tantam claritatem videre quantam
antea numquam viderat. Hanc quoque visionem, sicut ipse as-
seruit, ostendit ei Deus quia prius de beati viri sanctitate
parumque hesitaverat. Set post hanc visionem, sanctitatis
ipsius publicus predicator effectus est et assertor.

                                   X

       De puero in Wicford muto et ad tumbam viri sancti
       curato.

83   Puer quidam in urbe Lincolniensi, vico scilicet de Wike-
forde, nutritus erat mutus per tres annos existens, et adeo
linguam palato firmiter herentem habens quod escas solidas
masticare non potuit, nec cibis aliquibus vesci nisi tantum
mollibus et sorbilibus consuevit. Et quoniam hic educatus
erat in domibus Ade maioris et Reimbaldi divitis, aliorumque
maiorum de vico illo, procurantibus ipsis in vigilia assumpcionis beate Virginis et caritative conmotis, ad ecclesiam
cathedralem beate Marie et ad tumbam beati Hugonis est adductus. Ubi cum nocte tota pervigil in oracionibus et devocione,
qua sola potuit pro sanitate recuperanda, Dei sanctique sui

legs and pull them towards her to get up, she tried with all
her strength but could not do so, because from the waist down
her body seemed dead. She explained the trouble as well as
she could to her mistress. Anxious and sad, but having strong
faith in God and Saint Hugh, her mistress had the girl carried
to the tomb of blessed Hugh. On the Tuesday after Palm Sunday, about the hour of prime, the sinews of her legs began to
make a loud wrenching noise which was heard by all who were
there. Soon after she drew one leg toward her and then the
other, and then she got up, giving devout thanks to God and
Saint Hugh. As soon as word of the miracle came to her mistress, she was surprised and overjoyed. She brought with her
to the tomb as many of her neighbors as possible, men and
women, together testifying what they had seen and knew well,
and they confirmed their testimony with an oath. This confirmation of the miracle was made on the Tuesday of Easter Week
in the sixth year after blessed Hugh passed from this life.
82   To confirm the miracle all the more, Master Philip, then
subdean of the church of Lincoln, told R[oger of Rolleston],
the dean, and the whole chapter a vision he had after matins
on the night of the following Sunday. It happened thus.
While he slept in bed, a venerable man appeared to him saying
once and once again that he should rise and go to the church
as quickly as possible. He replied that he had come from the
church a little before. But the man said he should rise quickly and go to the church without delay, since the glory of God
had descended from heaven into the church, especially at the
tomb of the holy Bishop Hugh. At these words, it seemed to
him that he woke from sleep, got up, and entered the church.
As he drew near, he seemed to see such brightness in front of
the altar of St. John the Baptist and around the saint's tomb
as he had never seen before. And God showed him this vision,
he declared, because earlier he rather doubted the blessed
man's sanctity. But after this vision he became a public
preacher and defender of his sanctity.

Chapter Ten

Of the mute boy in Wigford who was also cured
at the saint's tomb.

83   In the Lincoln suburb of Wigford, a boy was brought up
as a foster child who was dumb for three years.* His tongue
was so firmly attached to the palate that he could not chew
solid food nor eat any food but that which was soft and could
be sucked down. Because he had been brought up in the homes

suffragium inplorasset, in matutinarum hora cepit per pavi-   142
mentum iuxta tumbam se volutare et voces clamosas emittere.
Adeoque tanquam rabie frenetica se undique proripuit quod vix
â duobus hominibus teneri posset. Nec mora, cum post graves
hos et miserandos labores ad tumbam parum obdormisset, visum
erat ei in sompnis quod domina quedam inconparabilis excellen-
cie et episcopus venerande reverencie sustulerunt eum ad locum amenum et preclarum, ubi et episcopus domine humiliter et
devote supplicavit quatinus illius vinculum solita solvere
benignitate ac pietate dignaretur. Cui domina piissima precibus obnixis clementer obtemperans, et digito linguam eius,
ut ei videbatur, paulatim sublevans, vinculum illud quo lin-
gua ligabatur totum abrupit. Quo viso, statim expergefactus
ille prosiliit, exclamans Anglice, Deoque gracias et sancte
Marie et sancto Hugoni de sanitate recuperata, semel et iterum, immo et multipliciter, tumbam deosculando, devocius egit.
Matrone vero civitatis, quarum circa tumbam vigilancium cum
luminaribus suis grandis copia fuit, que mutum optime noverant, miraculum hoc tam insigne videntes, maritos suos, quibus
similiter non ignotus fuerat, utpote de quorum elemosinis
diucius extiterat sustentatus, ad hoc miraculum videndum
nunciis ocius missis invitarunt. Quibus ad hoc confluentibus   143
cum aliis multis idem audientibus, factus est concursus popu-
lorum magnus, adeo ut, sole orto, repleta promiscui sexus
hominibus fere fuerit ecclesia tota, Deum et sanctum Hugonem
glorificancium et pre gaudio miraculi tanti, quod oculis suis
videre meruerunt, collaudancium. Mane vero circa primam,
capitulum super hoc ad unguem adeoque ut nichil supra certificari volens, Adam prelacione maiorem, et R. agnomine divi-
tem, aliosque quam plures de civibus illis circiter quos et
de quorum elemosinis diucius fuerat sustentatus, convocaver-
unt, et veritate rei ipsius diligencius ab ipsis inquisita,
cognoverunt et cum gaudio susceperunt, sacramento quoque ab
ipsis corporaliter prestito, ita revera fuisse, sicut mutus
eloquio restitutus fuerat protestatus. Et tunc demum qui
mutus fuerat, cum processione dignoque tripudio, ad tumbam
sancti Hugonis est transductus et inter ceteros ibi mirifice
et magnifice curatos annumeratus.

of Adam the Mayor and Reimbald the Rich and other elders of
the town, they arranged on the vigil of the Assumption of the
Blessed Virgin, moved by charity, to bring him to the cathedral church of Blessed Mary and to the tomb of blessed Hugh.
He spent the whole night awake in prayers and devotion, the
only means by which he could recover health, and begged the
favor of God and his saint. Then at the hour of matins he
began to roll around on the pavement beside the tomb and
uttered loud cries. He thrashed so in a wild frenzy that two
men could barely hold him down. After these grievous and
pitiful exertions he slept awhile beside the tomb. Soon it
appeared to him in his sleep that a lady of incomparable excel-
lence and a bishop of great dignity carried him to a bright
and pleasant place. There the bishop humbly and devoutly
implored the lady with her accustomed kindness and love to
loosen the boy's bond. The affectionate lady gently complied
with these urgent prayers. By lifting his tongue, so it
seemed, little by little with her finger, she succeeded in
severing the bond that had held it. After this vision, he
immediately woke up and sprang to his feet, exclaiming in
English, and devoutly gave thanks to God and Saint Mary and
Saint Hugh for his restored health, kissing the tomb once,
then again, and yes, many times. A great number of married
women of the city were keeping the vigil with their lamps.
They were well aware that he had been dumb, and when they saw
the amazing miracle they quickly sent messengers to summon
their husbands, who had also known this boy who was long supported by their alms, that they might see it. When the husbands came crowding to see, with many others who had heard
the same news, a great throng gathered. By sunrise, the
church was almost filled with men and women glorifying and
praising God and Saint Hugh, for joy at so great a miracle
which they had merited to see with their own eyes. That
morning about the hour of prime, the chapter, wishing to be
apprised of this in detail, omitting nothing, summoned Adam
the elected Mayor and R[eimbald] called "the Rich" and as
many as possible of the other citizens in whose homes and by
whose alms the boy had long been supported. After diligent
inquiry into the truth of the matter, to which these citizens
took an oath, the chapter knew and acknowledged with joy that
the facts were as the now articulate boy had declared. And
then at last the once mute boy was led to the tomb of Saint
Hugh in procession and with appropriate jubilation, and he
was enrolled among the others who had been cured there in a
great and extraordinary way.

XI

De puero de Potteregate similiter muto et ad
tumbam viri sancti curato.

84   Circiter id ipsum tempus puer quidam mutus nutritus erat
in vico de Poteregate bonorum virorum elemosinis qui, audito
miraculo de muto de Wikeford, destinaverunt eum in festo
sequenti nativitatis beate Virginis ad tumbam sancti Hugonis,   144
innuentes ei quatinus mente devota sanctumHugonem pro sanitate
sua recuperanda deprecaretur. Qui cum ibidem cum lacrimis et
lamentis pernoctasset, circa finem matutinarum fessus ad
tumbam obdormivit. Qui cum ā confluentibus illuc populis
orandi gracia, sicut ea hora fieri solet, premeretur, evigilans clamavit, "Deo gracias et beato Hugoni refero, quia nunc
incontinenti mihi loquela est restituta." Clerici vero in
Poteregate manentes qui mutum optime noverant et matrone vici
eiusdem ad tumbam tunc vigilantes que eum nutriverant, viso
miraculo, exilientes per vicos clamabant quia mutus ille ad
tumbam sancti Hugonis iam recte et expedite loquebatur. Clerici vero, chorum ingredientes, illis qui in choro fuerant
miraculum hoc nunciaverunt. Canonici vero, volentes super
hoc certificari, vocari ad se fecerunt capellanum et maiores
parochie illius. Quibus accedentibus, tam iuvenes quam senes
utriusque sexus, ut mos est in tante et tam prodigiose novitatis ostento, cum eis concurrerunt. Capellanus autem, in-
spectis sacrosanctis evangeliis, iuravit se vidisse eum mutum,
et quod viderat eum lingulam habentem tanquam esset avicule
in confinio gutturis, ita quod vix eam videre potuit. Simili-   145
ter et alii hoc idem iuraverunt. Canonici autem, hiis auditis, cum gaudio ad tumbam accedentes, pulsatis campanis omnibus, Deum et sanctum suum Hugonem dignis debitisque preconiis
glorificaverunt.

XII

De puella de Wicford furibunda, ad tumbam
sancti viri curata.

85   Modico post tempore, quoniam ad festum sancti Michaelis
proximo subsequens, quedam puella de Wikeford in frenesim
rapta fuit, adeo ut vincta diucius et graviter vexata, tandem
ad tumbam beati Hugonis circa festum apostolorum Simonis et
Iude adducta fuit. Que iuxta tumbam usque ad festum Omnium
Sanctorum conmorans assidue fuit, cuius nocte fere tota clam-
mosis plus solito vocibus ecclesiam et chorum valde turbavit,

Chapter Eleven

Of the similarly mute boy from Pottergate who was
also cured at the saint's tomb.

84 About the same time, in the suburb of Pottergate, some
good men who had fostered a mute boy by their alms heard about
the miracle of the mute boy from Wigford.* They sent him to
the tomb of Saint Hugh on the following feast of the Nativity
of the Blessed Virgin [September 8], indicating to him that he
should devoutly beg Saint Hugh to restore his health. He
spent the night there weeping and sorrowing. About the end
of matins, he grew tired and fell asleep at the tomb. When he
was pressed by the people thronging there to pray, as happens
at that hour, he woke up and cried out, "I thank God and Saint
Hugh, for now all of a sudden speech has been given back to
me!" Clerics living in Pottergate who were well acquainted
with him as being dumb, as well as married women of that suburb
who had fostered him and were then keeping vigil at the tomb,
leaped to their feet once they saw the miracle. They went
shouting through the neighborhood that this mute boy was now
speaking correctly and easily at the tomb of Saint Hugh. As
they entered the choir, the clerics announced the miracle to
those who had been in the choir. The canons wanted to be
assured of this and had the local priest called to them, along
with the elders of that parish. When they arrived, people
young and old of both sexes rushed together with them, as is
usual at a marvel of such great and unusual rarity. Before
the holy Gospels, the priest swore that he had seen him dumb
and also that he had seen that he had a little tongue, as in
the tiny space of a small bird's throat, so that one could
scarcely see it; and others also swore the same thing. After
hearing this, the canons went to the tomb with joy. All the
cathedral bells were rung, and they glorified God and his
Saint Hugh with worthy and fitting praises.

Chapter Twelve

Of the mad girl from Wigford cured at the saint's tomb.

85 Soon after, near the following feast of St. Michael
[September 29], a girl from Wigford was so taken with delirium
that she was fettered for a long time and seriously afflicted.
She was finally brought to the tomb of blessed Hugh, about the
feast of the Apostles Simon and Jude [October 28]. She stayed
constantly at the tomb till the feast of All Saints [Nov. 1].

adeo etiam quod ad altare sancti Iohannis Baptiste, quod tumbe
preminet, missa celebrari non potuerit. Omnes siquidem ecclesiam intrantes, eamque tanta rabie vexatam esse videntes et
miserie sue misericorditer condolentes, Deum pro sanitate sibi
restituenda devotissime deprecabantur. In diluculo vero vexata nimium, iuxta tumbam obdormivit, usque dum turbarum frequencia eam conculcancium excitata resedit. Que statim surgens, sapienter et discrete tam in opere se gerens quam sermone, peplo quod ei donatum fuerat recte satis et discrete   146
capud suum involvit. Et sic surgens et ad tumbam accedens,
flexis genibus Deo et sancto suo Hugoni sapienter et devote
preces effudit, dicens astantibus et alta voce proclamans
meritis sancti Hugonis sibi sanitatem esse restitutam. Matrone vero civitatis, que et ipsam de elemosinis suis educaverant
et de tanta morbi sui vehementia nimium lamentate fuerant,
letabunde nunc exultantes, Deo sanctoque Hugoni gracias ob hoc
miraculum agere non cessarunt. Illa vero, sanitati restituta,
in brevi postea psalterium didicit, bonisque moribus et honestis ex toto inherere cepit. Unde et vir bonus, Decanus Lincolniensis ecclesie Rogerus, ipsam in hospitali Lincolnie
caritatis intuitu collocavit, ubi morbidis et egrotis nocte
dieque diligenter obsequitur et devote.

86   Que sicut ad tumbam viri sancti sanitatis optinuit graciam, sic et meritis eiusdem caritatis perseveranciam, necnon
et finalem auream sive aureolam, cum ceteris cunctis tam hic
sanitati restitutis quam et ibidem pia suffragia sincera devocione postulantibus, valeant et gaudeant optinere quam op-
tant. Prestante Domino nostro Ihesu Christo, qui cum Patre
et Spiritu Sancto vivit et regnat Deus in secula seculorum.
Amen.

XIII

De finali tanquam epilogo novisque scriptoribus, spe   147
remunerationis et condigne retributionis, exercitio
dato.

87   Hiis itaque signis et virtutibus aliisque plurimis sub
hoc conpendio non conprehensis, priusquam interdicto tam inopinato et tam diuturno Anglicane ecclesie organa suspensa
fuerunt, Dominus sanctum suum in terris clarificavit. Ad ea
vero tractanda que postea contigerunt et cotidie fere adhuc
contingunt per viri sancti merita Christi magnalia, novo al-
terius studio novoque beneficio, quia "non omnia possumus omnes,"

87.7 Virgil, *Eclogues* 8.63.

Nearly all night she greatly disturbed the church and the
choir with her cries, which were louder than usual, so that
it was impossible even to celebrate mass at the altar of St.
John the Baptist which rises above the tomb. Everyone who
entered the church and saw her troubled with such madness felt
tender pity for her grief and begged God to restore her to
sanity. Much afflicted, she slept near the tomb that morning
until, wakened by the press of crowds closing in on her, she
sat up again. She rose at once and behaved wisely and dis-
creetly both in act and speech. Correctly and modestly, she
covered her head with a cape that had been given to her, and
rising thus and approaching the tomb, she knelt and wisely and
devoutly poured out prayers to God and to his Saint Hugh. She
said and proclaimed aloud to those standing there that by the
merits of Saint Hugh sanity had been restored to her. Matrons
of the city who had fostered her with their alms and who had
grieved at the violence of her illness now rejoiced and were
glad and did not cease thanking God and Saint Hugh for this
miracle. Soon after she had regained sanity, she learned the
Psalms and in every way began to practice good and decent
habits. Therefore that good man, the dean of the church of
Lincoln, Roger [of Rolleston] placed her in the hospital of
Lincoln for reasons of charity. There night and day she
served the sick and diseased with care and devotion.
86   As she won the grace of health at the saint's tomb, so
also may she win perseverance in charity and the final golden
halo or aureole, and may she and all others who have here
regained health and those who sincerely seek merciful favors
in this place prosper and rejoice in gaining their desire.
May our Lord Jesus Christ grant this, who with the Father and
the Holy Spirit lives and reigns, God for ever and ever. Amen.

Chapter Thirteen

By way of an epilogue, a commission given to new
writers, with a hope for compensation and due reward.

87   Before the operations of the English church were suspended by the interdict (as unexpected as it has been long-
lasting), the Lord glorified his saint on earth by these signs
and miracles and many others not included in this brief summary. Since we all cannot do all things, I yield to the new
zeal and new service of another in dealing with the great
works of Christ that later occurred through the saint's
merits and that occur almost daily to the present time.
Though I had a hundred tongues and a hundred mouths and a

locum damus. Quoniam "non mihi si lingue centum sint oraque
centum,/ ferrea vox," digne promere cuncta queam.
88   Porro scriptores novos novis studiis, tam sua quam coepiscoporum suorum gesta declarantes et scriptis egregiis
Lincolniensem ecclesiam illustrantes, Hugo, successor Hugonis
iure succedaneo, literatos promovendo viros et studiosos re-
munerando labores, ad scribendum per ampla beneficia provo-
cabit. Qui utinam tam hiis quam aliis preconialibus eiusdem
titulis eius expressa vestigia sequi. Et sicut nominis et
dignitatis, sic et ominis et felicitatis, mereatur Hugo
secundus Hugonis primi plene per omnia, vel saltem pene,
successor haberi.   .
89   Quatinus tercia Lincolniensis ecclesie lampas perlucida,
eandem ecclesiam triplici fortiter patrono suffultam, et sic   148
iam terque quaterque beatam, multiplici virtutum lumine
reddat illustrem.

87.8-9 Virgil, *Georgics* 2.43; *Aeneid* 6.625.

voice of iron, I could not adequately tell them all.
88   Besides, Hugh [of Wells], by lawful succession the successor of Hugh [of Avalon], will through generous patronage
encourage new writers to write, promoting learned men and
rewarding their studious labors, and by new works these writers
will proclaim his deeds as well as those of his fellow bishops,
and with distinguished books they will make the church of
Lincoln famous. Would that he might follow St. Hugh's well-
marked footsteps in these and other of his titles of honor!
May he fully merit to be recognized as the successor of Hugh
the First, in all or nearly all respects of divine favor and
fortune as well as name and rank.*
89   So may he, as the third shining lamp of the church of
Lincoln, cause that church to be strongly sustained by three
patrons and as it is already three and four times blessed,
make it bright with a multiple light of virtues.

[DISTINCTIO III]

I

Transitus de signis ante interdictum ad signa
divinitus in ipso interdicto data.

90   Quamquam autem huic operi et delicioso labori finem hic
ponere promiserimus, cum tamen nichil honestum vere valeat aut
debeat amicicie denegari, ad instanciam viri venerabilis
Rogeri Decani Lincolniensis et ea miracula quibus nubiloso
nichilominus interdicti tempore divina bonitas, tanquam luculentam in tenebris lucernam accendens, sanctum suum clarifi-
cari in terris voluit et magnificari, scolastico quoque digerere stilo ceterisque non inconpetenter adicere, dignum
duximus.

II

De Iohanne Burdet, milite, â paralitico morbo curato.

91   Tempore quo rex Iohannes cum exercitu Anglicano *primo* in
Pictaviam transfretavit et expedicionem in Gasconiam duxit,
miles quidam de Lindeseia oriundus, cui nomen Iohannes Burdet,
in castellum Montis-Albani cum ceteris insultum faciens, subito et inopinato paralisis incomodo brachio dextro percussus
obstupuit. Adeo nempe morbi malicia statim invalescere cepit
quod nullatenus aut in modico brachium erigere, aut vultum
suum crucis signaculo consignare, aut etiam cibum ori suo   149
dextra porrigere manu prevaleret. Cum ergo nec medicorum
opera sumptuosa sanitate secuta, nec per sanctorum terre
illius merita quos fere per anni circulum circueundo devote
requisierat, demum nec curatus nec etiam alleviatus in quoquam repatriasset, ilico matrem ecclesiam suam et matricem,
Lincolniensem scilicet, cum summa devocione requisivit.
92   [A]ccedensque statim ad desideratam beati Hugonis tumbam,

PART THREE

Chapter One

A transition from signs before the interdict to signs
given by God during the interdict itself.

90   Although I intended to conclude this work and this
delightful effort at this point, I have decided at the urging
of the venerable Roger [of Rolleston], dean of Lincoln--since
nothing honorable can or should be denied to friendship--to
summarize also the miracles by which God's goodness willed
that his saint be glorified and magnified on earth even in
the clouded period of the interdict, as if kindling a bright
lamp in the darkness.*   I shall give a digest in the style of
the schools and add some additional relevant material.

Chapter Two

Of John Burdet, knight, cured of paralysis.

91   When King John sailed for the first time with an English
army to Poitou [in 1206] and led an expedition into Gascony,*
a knight of Lindsey named John Burdet, making an assault on
the castle of Montauban with the others, was hit and stunned
with sudden and unanticipated paralysis in his right arm.
Indeed, he grew so sick from the severity of the illness that
he could not raise his arm at all or make the sign of the
cross or even bring food to his mouth with his right hand.
Because his health was not restored either by the expensive
aid of physicians or through the merits of the saints of that
land, whom he had devoutly sought out on pilgrimage for about
a year, he went home again at last, not cured or even relieved
at all, and with great devotion there sought his mother church
and nurse, namely, Lincoln.
92   At once he went to the tomb of blessed Hugh which was
his goal and placed on the tomb a wax image of his right arm,

imaginariam brachii dextri similitudinem ceream sinistra sua,
quia dextram ut diximus movere non poterat, super tumbam ap-
posuit. Et sic cum aliquot diebus ibidem victitans circa
tumbam et pernoctans, lacrimosis precibus graciam sacri pontificis pro sanitate recuperanda suppliciter exorasset, paulatim
convalescere cepit, et infra breve temporis spacium plene
sanitatis gaudia recuperavit. Qui statim ad R. decanum et
capitulum accedens, seriatim eis rem gestam totam letabundus
aperuit, faciemque suam, elevata facillime coram ipsis dex-
tera, crucis caractere consignavit. Quo viso et audito,
decanus et capitulum, cum ceteris qui tunc aderant multis,
digna Dei preconia cum graciarum actionibus extulerunt.

III

De Matildide ceca ad tumbam viri *sancti* curata.

93   In provincia de Lindeseia fuit mulier quedam, Matildis
nomine, que cum iter agendo inter villas vicinas ad conpita   150
viarum perveniret, ecce subito irruens venti turbo vehemens
eam obvolvit, et ad terram prostratam visu oculorum ilico
privavit. Quo conperto, quidam forte transiens notus ipsius
eique conpaciens, ipsamque ad manum trahens, secum in hospici-
um duxit. Illa vero, quoniam artificii sui subsidio quo
inopiam suam relevare solebat omnino caruit, solebat enim dum
sana fuerat arte et acu vitam sustentare, palpans ut poterat
et hostiatim irrepens, mendicare conpulsa fuit.
94   Demum autem sano quorundam consilio Lincolniam adiens
sanctique viri ad tumbam accedens, eiusque suffragium devotissime postulans, in atrio ecclesie beate Virginis per annuum
et amplius spacium moram faciens, in cecitate permansit. Ad
tumbam vero precario ducis officio sepius accedens, crebris
et uberrimis eandem lacrimarum fluentis quas eius eduxit tam
devocio quam afflictio, vitam quippe miserrimam tedio ducens,
irrigavit.
95   Accidit autem, anno interdicti primo, quod illa cum aliis
languidis plurimis, vigilia scilicet Pentecostes, ad tumbam
accessit, elemosinario decani, cui nomen Stephanus, ducatum
ei prebente candelamque manui ipsius inponente, quatinus cum
aliis ibidem ea nocte vigilaret graciamque Sancti Spiritus
per merita presulis sancti votis et vocibus invocaret.
96   Videtur his autem et hoc inserendum, qualiter quedam   151
urbis matrone, que illi in atrio ecclesie iacenti elemosi-
narum suarum solacia conferre consueverant, firmiter eidem
asseverabant se per visum vidisse ipsam proculdubio per sancti
Hugonis merita luminis leticiam recepturam. Qua spe mulier

using his left arm since, as I said, he could not move the right. Subsisting there near the tomb for some days and remaining through the night, he implored with tearful prayers the grace of the holy bishop for his recovery. Then little by little he began to improve and soon fully regained the joys of health. He went immediately to R[oger of Rolleston], the dean, and the chapter and happily told them in detail all that had happened. In their presence he easily made the sign of the cross with his right hand. When they saw and heard this, the dean and the chapter, with many others then present, offered worthy praises of God with thanksgiving.

Chapter Three

Of Matilda, a blind woman, cured at the saint's tomb.

93   In the district of Lindsey, there was a woman named Matilda who while on her way among neighboring villages came to a crossroads where a violent whirlwind suddenly burst upon her. It whipped around her and threw her to the ground, instantly causing her to lose the sight of both eyes. An acquaintance who was passing there took pity on her when he discovered this. Taking her by the hand, he led her to a hospice. When she was in good health she had been accustomed to live by her needlework. Since she now entirely lacked the support of the craft by which she had relieved her poverty, she had to beg, feeling her way as she could and creeping from door to door.

94   At last on the good advice of certain persons, she came to Lincoln and went to the saint's tomb, devoutly seeking his intercession. She stayed for more than a year, remaining in her blindness within the precincts of the church of the Blessed Virgin. She often went to the tomb, asking another to lead her, and moistened the tomb with frequent and abundant streams of tears, stirred by her devotion as well as her affliction. In her misery, she led indeed a pitiful life.

95   During the first year of the interdict [1208] she went to the tomb on the vigil of Pentecost with many other sick persons. The almoner of the dean, named Stephen, furnished her guidance.* He put a candle in her hand so that she could keep watch there that night with the others and, by prayers and words, invoke the grace of the Holy Spirit through the merits of the holy bishop.

96   It seems worth mentioning that certain married women of the city who used to comfort her with their alms as she lay in the precincts of the cathedral told her with conviction that

plurimum refecta, et paciencius inediam suam atque miseriam
sustinuit et longe devocius ac confidencius sancti presulis
auxilium imploravit. Noctem autem illam, ut diximus, scilicet
Pentecostes, usque ad diluculum vigiliis et oracionibus duxit
insompnem, et tunc demum fatigata, capite in uno circulari
foramine tumbe marmoree posito, parumper obdormivit. Cui dormienti videbatur quod vir quidam pulcre stature, vultu decor-
us, candidis vestibus decenter indutus, et ornamentis episcopalibus congrue redimitus, de tumba processit et altare proximum, sancti scilicet Iohannis, adiens, missam ibidem celebravit. Qua finita, regrediens ad tumbam, cum corporalibus que
manibus gestabat oculos cece illius ventilabat et ex calice
quoque stillas infundens ait ei, "Surge." Et cum ipsa inpo-
tenciam suam, ut ei videbatur, pretendere vellet, iteravit
ille dicens, "Surge, quia curata es." Ad hanc ergo vocem
expergefacta, mulier surrexit, seque sanam penitus senciens
et visui restitutam, ante tumbam protinus extensis in crucem
brachiis se prostravit, et alta voce Deo sanctoque presuli
Hugoni super sanitate sibi reddita gracias egit. Cuncti vero   152
qui aderant et hec viderant admirantes et congratulantes,
dignas Deo sanctoque suo laudes in hoc facto persolverunt.
97   Huius autem miraculi fama statim civitate repleta, matrone de quibus mencionem antea fecimus, unā cum populi multitudine copiosa, ad contemplandum tante novitatis ostentum accur-
rerunt.

IV

De Iohanne de Plumbard ā gutta festra curato.

98   Vir quidam Iohannes nomine, de villa que dicitur Plumgard,
morbi incomodum qui vulgari vocabulo gutta festra vocatur in
femore multum ingravatus et debilitatus incurrit, adeo quod
nec ad passum unum se movere nec pedibus suis se quoquam
transferre valeret. Qui demum salubri fretus consilio se
Lincolniam ad sanctum Hugonem reda conducta deferri fecit.
Et cum in ecclesia beate Virginis ad tumbam viri sancti per
dies aliquot moram fecisset, cementum quo lapides tumuli
iungebantur, cultello suo abrasum, vulneribus suis que morbus
effecerat et cutem exulceraverat causa recuperande sanitatis
inposuit. Et statim vulnera, sanie defluencia, paulatim
arescere ceperunt, et dolor de die in diem decrescendo preter-
ire, adeo quidem ut infra breve tempus plenam ibidem suscipi-
ens curacionem, qui paulo ante quasi moribundus veiculo ad-
vectus fuerat, iamiam pedes eundo iuxta redam, sanus et   153
hilaris ad propria remearet.

they had seen in a vision that she was sure to receive the
happiness of sight through the merits of Saint Hugh. By this
hope the woman's spirit was renewed and she bore her depriva-
tion and misery more patiently and begged the help of the holy
bishop far more devoutly and confidently. But as I was saying,
on Pentecost she sleeplessly spent the night until dawn in
vigils and prayers. Weary at last, she slept a little, resting her head in one of the circular openings of the marble
tomb. As she slept it seemed to her that a man of beautiful
stature, handsome in face, nobly clothed in white vestments
and fitly decked with a bishop's accoutrements, came in procession from the tomb, went to the adjoining altar of St. John
[the Baptist], and celebrated mass there. That done, he returned to the tomb and, with the corporals he was carrying in
his hands, fanned the blind woman's eyes. He also poured
drops from the chalice on her eyes and said to her, "Arise."
When she wanted to protest that she was powerless, it seemed
to her that he said again, "Arise, for you are cured." Awakened at these words, the woman got up. She felt herself completely well and restored to sight, and she prostrated herself
before the tomb with her arms extended in a cross. Loudly she
thanked God and the holy Bishop Hugh for the recovery of her
health. All those who were present and who had seen these
things, astonished and sharing in her joy, gave fitting
praises for this to God and to his saint.

97   Since the city was filled at once with the report of the
miracle, the matrons I mentioned before, together with a great
multitude of people, ran to observe a marvel of such rarity.

Chapter Four

Of John from Plungar cured of an ulcer.

98   A man named John from the village called Plungar* incurred
the painful disease known as an ulcer. He was so afflicted
and weakened in his leg that he could not move a single step
or go anywhere on his feet. Finally, relying on good counsel,
he rented a wagon and had himself conveyed to Saint Hugh at
Lincoln. After he had stayed for some days at the saint's
tomb in the church of the Blessed Mary, he scraped away with
his knife some of the mortar by which the stones of the tomb
are held together. To get well, he put this on the wounds
caused by the disease, which had ulcerated the skin. Little
by little the wounds that had been running with diseased blood
began to dry up, and the pain, lessening from day to day,
began to pass. Indeed, within a short time he received a

99 Decanus autem Lincolniensis ecclesie Rogerus, tanquam
vir discretus et providus, ne quid dubietatis aut falsitatis
fortefortuitu suboriri posset, super hoc miraculo sicut et
aliis cunctis certificari per omnia volens, quendam vicarium
ecclesie quem idoneum ad hoc elegerat usque ad villam de
Plumgard, propter inquisicionem rei istius diligentissime
faciendam, destinavit. Et ibi, tam ville quam vicinie tocius
testimonio, super rei geste veritate, sicut scripto presenti
declaratur, certificatus fuit.

V

De milite Milone â brachii tumore pariter et dolore
curato.

100 Miles quidam Milo nomine, de familia Ricardi de Sanford,
tercia post minucionem suam die cum domino suo et commilitoni-
bus suis spaciatum equitans, seque cum aliis, calcaribus equis
admissis, militaribus ludis exercens sueque minucionis inmemor existens, finito demum militari preludio domum reversus,
sinistrum quo minutus erat brachium, dicto casu sinistro minus
discrete vexatum, gravi dolore subito correptum sensit et
inflatum. Sed licet anxie nimis morbi puncturas ferens, tota
tamen nocte prima â domino suo familiaque tota incomodum hoc
celavit. In crastino vero, urgente morbi gravamine iam nimio
conpulsus, quod accidit ei domino suo revelavit. Ille vero
cum uxore totaque familia sua valde super hoc anxius existens, 154
quod potuit fecit. Medicorum ei solacium, quamquam sumptuosum
magis et honerosum quam proficuum aut fructuosum, ilico perquisivit. Medici vero, post operas longas et sedulas revera
magis quam utiles, plusque promissionis habentes quam curacio-
nis, de sanitate penitus diffidentes, qui fortunam sequi sol-
ent, militem desperatum reliquerunt, dicentes et conmuniter
asseverantes totum ei mundum ad salutem suffragari non posse.
Audiens autem hec sponsa dicti R. de Sanford, ad militem
visitandum tristis accessit, eique ut votum suum Deo et sancte
Marie Lincolniensi sanctoque Hugoni faceret salubre consilium
dedit. Quo facto, sicut ei fideliter consultum fuerat, militi
sancti Hugonis auxilium devote et obnixe postulanti statim
sanitas est restituta. Cruor namque putridus, cum sanie simul
aspectu horribili, â vulnere brachii quo minutus fuerat undan-
ter erupit et habundanter effluxit. Sicque, sedata grossicie
brachii cum inflacione tota, qui morti paulo ante fuit exposi-
tus, per sancti Hugonis merita plene sanitati est restitutus.
Miles autem, accepti beneficii nec inmemor nec ingratus, cum
intime devocionis affectu versus Lincolniam iter arripiens,

complete cure there, and he who had recently been carried in
a vehicle as if he were dying now returned home healthy and
cheerful, walking beside the wagon.

99   But Roger [of Rolleston], the dean of the church of Lincoln, as a discreet and sensible man, lest any doubt or de-
ception arise, wanted to be entirely sure of this miracle, as
of the others. He sent a vicar of the church, whom he had
chosen as suited for the task, to the village of Plungar to
investigate the matter thoroughly. There he was convinced of
the truth of what happened, just as is told here, by testimony from the village and all the neighborhood.

Chapter Five

Of the knight Milo cured of a tumor and pain in the arm.

100   A knight named Milo belonging to the household of Richard
de Sanford, on the third day after submitting to a blood-
letting, went riding horseback with his lord and his fellow
knights. He exercised himself with the others in military
games and once the horses were spurred on forgot about his
blood-letting. When this military sport was finished and he
returned home, he suddenly felt his left arm where he had been
bled, which was carelessly disturbed by the unlucky game I
mentioned, gripped with great pain and swollen. He could
barely endure the throbbing of the infection, yet the whole
first night he concealed the injury from his lord and all the
household. The next day, driven now by the painful intensity
of his affliction, he revealed to his lord what had happened.
The lord and his wife and all his household were very upset
about this, and doing what he could, the lord immediately
sought the help of physicians for him, though more costly and
burdensome than beneficial or productive. After efforts that
were really longer and more strenuous than useful, more pro-
mising than healing, the physicians, who are accustomed to
follow fortune, lost all hope of his recovery and abandoned
the desperate knight, all of them saying that the whole world
could not avail to make him well. When the wife of Richard
de Sanford heard this, she was saddened and went to visit the
knight, giving him the sound advice to pray to God and Saint
Mary of Lincoln and Saint Hugh. Once he did so, as advised in
good faith, health was immediately restored to the knight,
even as he was devoutly and strenuously begging Saint Hugh's
help. For the putrid flow of blood with corrupted matter,
terrible to look at, burst like waves from the arm wound where
he had been bled. It flowed out in great quantity, and the

ad ecclesiam beate Virginis tumbamque beati presulis gratanter
accessit, statimque formam brachii sui curati de cera expres-
sam et effigiatam super tumbam optulit, et post devotas ora-   155
ciones et largas oblaciones ibidem factas, cum turba stipan-
cium eum et congratulancium, Deumque laudancium, capitulum
intravit. Magistro Philippo subdecano in absencia decani ibidem tunc presidente, cui rem gestam totam sanitatemque plenam
post desperacionem tantam per sancti Hugonis graciam sibi
restitutam in publica audiencia replicavit, multis astantibus
et contestantibus, Deumque et sanctum Hugonem in hoc miraculo,
sicut et in ceteris cunctis, conmuni applausu collaudantibus.

VI

De iuvene paralitico et contracto, ad tumbam
sancti viri curato.

101 Adolescens quidam adeo paralisi percusus erat quod á zona
inferius nec membrum aliquod movere, nec quicquam etiam sen-
tire valeret. Qui et in hac languescens egritudine, per
quatuor annos et dimidium in hospitali Lincolniensi lecto
iacuerat, et per annum postmodum et dimidium in atrio matri-
cis ecclesie se receperat, ante ianuam precentoris habitaculum
habens. Hic autem, exemplo quamplurium denique ductus quos
ad tumbam sancti Hugonis curatos ad propria letos redire vi-
debat, vigilia assumpcionis beate Virginis se in ecclesiam et
usque ad tumbam transferri fecit, et sic nocte eadem tota cum
lacrimis et suspiriis, Deo sancteque matri ipsius, sanctoque
presuli Hugoni, pia fundere precamina non cessavit. Mane vero
facto, cum parumper obdormisset, visum eidem in sompnis fuit
quod clerici duo, stolis albis induti, proximum altare, sci-   156
licet sancti Iohannis Baptiste, tanquam ad missam celebrandam
decenter adornarunt. Quo facto, episcopus quidam mitratus et
episcopalibus conpetenter indutus, vultu pariter et statura
venustus, versus altare per ipsum transiens, dixit ei,
"Surge." Cui ille, "Et quomodo surgam, qui me de loco quo
iaceo movere non possum?" Episcopus autem ad altare accedens, missam ibidem celebravit, eaque conpleta cum ministris
suis per languidum eundem rediens, capudque suum ad ipsum in-
clinans et in vultum eius insufflans, dixit ei, "Surge, tibi
dico, surge," et sic disparuit. Contractus autem ad hanc
vocem evigilans, crura sua et tibias quasi ferro sensit per-
forari. Sed quamvis anxiatus plurimum et vulnerum veluti
recencium dolore gravatus, tanti tamen preceptis viri parere
cupiens, surgere pro posse conatus est. Statimque, cruribus
et tibiis extensis, sese in stacionem erexit, set nutans in

distention of the arm with all the swelling was thus healed,
and he who just before was at the point of death was completely restored to health through the merits of Saint Hugh. But
the knight did not forget or fail to appreciate the benefit
he had received. He traveled to Lincoln with a feeling of
profound devotion. Joyfully, he went to the church of the
Blessed Virgin and the tomb of the blessed bishop and immediately placed on the tomb a wax image of his healed arm. After
saying sincere prayers and giving generous offerings there,
he entered the chapter house with a crowd around him sharing
his joy and praising God. He publicly disclosed to Master
Philip the subdean (then presiding in the absence of the dean)
all that had happened and, after such despair, his restoration
to full health through the favor of Saint Hugh. Many people
stood there as fellow witnesses, and with common applause they
praised God and Saint Hugh for this miracle as for all the
others.

Chapter Six

Of a paralyzed and contracted youth who was cured at
the saint's tomb.

101 A boy was so stricken with paralysis that from the waist
down he could neither move any part of his body nor feel a
thing.* He lay in bed at the hospital of Lincoln suffering
from the illness for four and a half years. For a year and
a half after that he settled in the precincts of the mother
church, having a little dwelling in front of the door of the
precentor. Stirred by the example of so many whom he saw
returning to their homes happy after being cured at the tomb
of Saint Hugh, he had himself carried into the church to the
tomb on the vigil of the Assumption of the Blessed Virgin.
With tears and sighs he spent the whole night in fervent
prayer to God and his holy Mother and to the holy Bishop Hugh.
But when morning came, after he had slept a little, it seemed
to him in his sleep that two clerks wearing white stoles were
properly preparing the adjoining altar, that of St. John the
Baptist, as if for celebrating mass. Then a bishop, mitred
and appropriately clothed in episcopal vestments, handsome in
both face and stature, passed by him on his way to the altar
and said to him, "Rise." He answered, "And how shall I rise,
since I cannot move from where I am lying?" But the bishop
went on to the altar, celebrated mass there, and when it was
done, returned with his ministers past the same sick man.
Bending his head towards him and breathing upon his face, he

primis et titubans, protinus in terram corruit, iterumque per
se surgens, firmius stetit. Sorores autem prescripti hospi-
talis, que in langore suo ei ministraverant simulque in vigiliis et oracionibus tunc presentes extiterant, videntes eum
erectum et pedibus suis ambulantem, gaudio magno gavise sunt,
et muliebriter vociferantes et exultantes, cum universis qui
tunc aderant et hec viderant, mirificum Deum in sanctis suis
et gloriosum in cunctis operibus suis voce conmuniter pre-   157
coniali magnificabant.
102 Precentor autem ecclesie, vir bonus et veneracione dignus,
nomine Gaufredus, cuius ad ianuam diu languens ille iacuerat
de elemosinis eiusdem sustentatus, fama sanitatis illius au-
dita, fide oculata rei certitudinem cum desiderio probans,
Deum omnipotentem letabundis vocibus et votis glorificavit.
103 Publicato vero sic miraculo coram multitudine cleri et
populi in capitulo Lincolniensi, et omnibus Deum in conmune
laudantibus, ecce canonicus quidam de cella de Wirkesope, nomine sancte Margarete Graves, in huius miraculi recitacione
festinus pariter et festivus, ad duplicandam seu pocius multiplicandam sancti sui in terris gloriam, tanquam â Deo missus
advenit. Ait enim et assertive proposuit plurima in ecclesia sua per merita beati Hugonis facta fuisse miracula, quorum unum in publico tale recitavit.
104 In provincia de Len fuit vir quidam multo tempore cor-
porali egritudine lectum tenenset gravi langore laborans.
Accidit autem ut nocte quadam dormienti apparens in visu
sanctus Hugo, sub eadem specie quam vivens habebat, egroto non
incognita, dixit ei, "Vade ad cellam sancte Margarete Graves,   158
et in ecclesia illius desideratam recipies sanitatem." Cui
ille, "Et quomodo," inquit, "illuc irem qui me de loco isto
movere non possum?" Cui sanctus Hugo, "Veniam tibi in auxilium." At ille subiunxit, "Domine, nec prior loci illius nec
conventus, quibus sum prorsus incognitus, etsi illuc etiam
venire possem, verbis meis fidem haberent." Cui iterum sanctus, "Vade secure et nichil hesitans, quoniam et hec intersigna priori loci illius dices, quod cum ultimo tumbam meam
visitavit, eundo ad nundinas sancti Botulfi, devote supplicavit pro quodam negocio, quod et inpetravit." Idemque negocium egro propalavit. Experrectus igitur egrotus et de
visione tali letus effectus, redam ut potuit qua deferretur
perquisivit, eaque inpositus, et per dietas suas usque ad
dictam cellam transvectus, priori, cum quo fandi copiam statim
habuit, causam adventus sui et intersigna que â sancto Hugone
ad ipsum acceperat intimavit. Quibus auditis, quia neminem

101.33-4 *Cf.* Matthew 2:10, "Videntes autem stellam, gavisi
sunt gaudio magno valde." 101.36-7 *Cf.* Psalm 67:36 *and*
Psalm 144:13, 17.

said to him, "Rise, I say to you, rise." And with that he
vanished. But the paralytic woke up at these words and felt
his legs pierced as by a sword. Though in anguish with the
pain, like that of fresh wounds, yet longing to obey such a
great man's commands, he tried with all his might to get up.
After stretching his legs out, he drew himself immediately
into a standing position. He tottered at first and staggered,
then sank forward onto the ground. Getting up again on his
own, he stood more steadily. The sisters of the hospital of
Lincoln who had ministered to him in his sickness were also
there at the time in vigils and prayers. When they saw him
upright and walking on his own feet, they rejoiced with great
joy. Crying out and celebrating as women do, they and everyone there who had seen these things magnified God with praise,
who is wonderful in his saints and glorious in all his works.
102 But as soon as Geoffrey, the precentor of the church--
a good and venerable man at whose door the sick boy had lain
for a long time supported by his alms--heard of the boy's cure,
he eagerly confirmed the fact with his own eyes and glorified
almighty God with joyful words and prayers.
103 When the miracle was thus announced before many of the
clergy and people in the chapter house at Lincoln and all were
praising God together, a canon from a cell of Worksop [Priory]
named Saint Margaret Graves* arrived just as the miracle was
being told. He was as timely as he was devout, having evidently been sent by God to double, or rather multiply, the glory
of his saint on earth. For this canon declared that many
miracles had been done in his church through the merits of
blessed Hugh, one of which he recounted publicly as follows:
104 In the district of Lynn, a man was confined to his bed
for a long time, sick in body and very debilitated. One night
Saint Hugh appeared to the man in a vision as he slept, looking
just as he had while alive, for he was not unknown to the sick
man. He said to him, "Go to the cell of Saint Margaret Graves,
and in its church you will receive the health you desire."
The sick man answered him: "And how," he said, "shall I go
there, since I cannot move from this place?" Saint Hugh said
to him, "I shall come help you." But the sick man added,
"Lord, neither the prior of that place nor the community, to
whom I am quite unknown, would have faith in my words, even if
I were able to go there." The saint said to him again, "Go in
confidence, without hesitation. For you shall report these
secret signs to the prior of the place: that when he last
visited my tomb, on his way to the weekly markets of St. Botolph
[at Boston], he prayed for a certain business transaction,
which he obtained." And the saint told the sick man what the
transaction was. Then the sick man woke up, happy after such
a vision. He sought out any wagon he could get to carry him.

preter se solum huius secreti conscium habuerat, prior ipsum
in ecclesia sua gaudenter admisit. Qui et eadem nocte, divine
pietatis gracia, perque viri sancti merita, promisse sanitatis
gaudia recuperavit.
105 Prior autem loci illius et conventus, tam super visione   159
tali quam etiam miraculo tanto non mediocriter exhilarati,
dictum canonicum suum hec referente, et una cum visione miraculum hoc recitantem, Lincolniam destinarunt. Quod etiam quasi pro miraculo quodam reputari potuit, quod in ipsa quoque
tam solempni prioris miraculi recitacione, divina bonitate ad
multiplicandam sancti viri gloriam id totum ordinante, de
remotis finibus ex insperato novi miraculi cum visione laudabili fidelis et fide dignus recitator advenit.
106 Intererant autem horum recitacionibus miraculorum in
capitulo Lincolniensi, persone eiusdem ecclesie tres, Gaufredus
precentor, Reimundus archidiaconus Leicestrie, Willelmus archidiaconus de Westredinge, et canonici ac clerici ecclesie plurimi, necnon et laici multi, Deum publice laudantes, et vocibus
ac votis in huiuscemodi preconia Deique magnalia prorumpentes,
"'Mirabilis Deus in sanctis suis,' et magnus in omnibus operibus suis." Item, "'Magnus Dominus et laudabilis nimis, et
magnitudinis eius non est finis,' quique de fine in finem
attingens fortiter, et disponens omnia suaviter, vivit et
vincit, regnat et imperat, in secula seculorum. Amen."

                              Explicit.

106.7 Psalm 67:36 (Vulgate). 106.7-8 *Cf.* Psalm 144:13, 17,
which verses read, "sanctus in omnibus operibus suis."
106.8-9 Psalm 144:3. 106.9-10 *Cf.* Wisdom 8:1, "Attingit ergo
a fine usque ad finem fortiter, et disponit omnia suaviter."

He was put in it and was carried to the cell for his meetings
there. He revealed to the prior, to whom he had a great many
things to say at once, the reason he had come and the secret
signs he had received for him from Saint Hugh. After the
prior had heard these signs, since he was aware of no one but
himself who knew the secret, he gladly admitted the man into
his church. That same night, through God's compassion and the
merits of the saint, the man regained the joys of health he
had been promised.

105 Both the prior of that place and the community felt more
than ordinary joy in such a vision and so great a miracle.
They sent the canon I mentioned to Lincoln, who reported it,
narrating both the miracle and the vision. In this formal
report of the prior's miracle, it could also be judged a miracle, ordained by God's goodness to increase the saint's glory,
that there arrived unexpectedly from far away a true and reliable witness of a new miracle and a wonderful vision.

106 At the public recounting of these miracles in the chapter
house at Lincoln, three officials of the church were present,
Geoffrey the precentor, Reimund the archdeacon of Leicester,*
William the archdeacon of the West Riding [of Lincolnshire,
i.e., Stow], and many canons and clerks of the church and many
laymen as well. They publicly praised God and broke into
words and prayers of tribute, magnifying God with praises such
as these: "Wonderful is God in his saints, and great in all
his works." And: "Great is the Lord and greatly to be praised,
and there is no end to his greatness. Reaching strongly from
end to end and ordering all things sweetly, he lives and
conquers, reigns and rules for ever and ever. Amen."

The End

APPENDIX

The Rebuilding of Lincoln Cathedral,
from *The Metrical Life of St. Hugh*

Soon after the canonization of St. Hugh in 1220, a metrical life of him was written by an author having access to Adam
of Eynsham's *Magna Vita*, the lives by Gerald of Wales, and the
papal commissioners' report, as well as other sources that
would include the author's acquaintance with the cathedral as
the building then stood (the main or western transepts were
finished, with their rose windows, and the chapter house was
under construction). The *Metrical Life* was edited by James F.
Dimock and printed at Lincoln in 1860 by W. and B. Brooke.
The author is identified as the prolific European poet, Henry
of Avranches, in J.C. Russell and J.P. Hieronimus, *The Shorter
Latin Poems of Henry of Avranches Relating to England* (Cambridge, Mass.: The Mediaeval Academy of America, 1935), pp. 5,
8, 79-80. On the evidence for this attribution, David Townsend
has given me the following note:

  The metrical Life of Hugh is probably by Henry of Avranches.
  I would go so far as to say that the burden of proof lies
  upon someone who contests the attribution. As is frequently
  the case with the book by Russell and Hieronimus, a valid
  conclusion is presented without a clear or ample presentation
  of the evidence. The poem is anonymous in both MSS. The
  only external evidence is a reference to a "Vita S. Hugonis
  Lincol. Ep. versifice sec. Mag. H. de Hariench." in the
  fourteenth-century *Matricularium* of the library of Peter-
  borough Abbey published by M.R. James. James suggests that
  "Hariench" is a corruption of "Avranches," which seems entirely likely. Parallels with Henry's Life of Francis support
  the identification of the life edited by Dimock with Henry's
  poem on Hugh. In the Hugh there is a discursus, for example,
  into the technicalities of contemporary medicine which recalls
  several passages in the Life of Francis, not so much by specific style or vocabulary as by the simple presence of such

disquisitions in a saint's life. But what I consider most
persuasive of the affinities of the two lives is the striking similarity of two long passages, one in each poem, describing a ship struggling in a storm. If the two lives have
drawn from a common source, I am not aware of it. The
passages are Hugh, 618-653, and Francis, VIII.25-39.

For the most part, the *Metrical Life* versifies what we
know from Adam and Gerald. The following incidents versified
in the *Metrical Life* are evidently derived from Gerald's *Vita
Sancti Hugonis*, since they match Gerald's narrative in details
and sequence and are not in the *Magna Vita* (except the passage
on the swan which Adam quotes from Gerald):

ML 604-610: Hugh's pet hedge sparrow at Witham (*VSH* 12).
ML 734-822: Hugh's perseverance in administering confirmations
until nightfall (*VSH* 15); his confirmation of a testy old
man (*VSH* 16); his refusal to change a boy's name through a
second confirmation (*VSH* 17); his conceding an ox to the
widow of a feudal tenant (*VSH* 18); a similar concession to
a knight's son (*VSH* 19).
ML 974-1005: his concern for burying the dead, as once during
Lent when he buried two bodies late in the day at Lincoln
(*VSH* 22); his burial of four bodies on his way to the king's
court at Le Mans (*VSH* 23); his punishing his almoner for not
reporting a body in need of burial (*VSH* 24); his rebuking
Hugh of Coventry for hurrying through mass (*VSH* 25).
ML 1055-1061: his response to William de Montibus regarding
the leper (*VSH* 46).
ML 1106-1135: his swan at Stow (*VSH* 50-1).
ML 1191-1205: the healing of the knight of Lindsey (*VSH* 68).

Some information and insights are found only in the
Metrical Life. For example, the *Metrical Life* gives the names
of St. Hugh's parents as William and Anna, and describes the
mother, Anna, as being kinder than a lamb and devoted to the
care of the sick and the poor (lines 44-6, 52-4):

> Cujus et insignem vitam duxere parentes,
> Willelmus flos militiae, vir nobilis, Anna
> Matronale decus, omnique benignior agna. . . .
> Anna lavare pedes ipsis assueta leprosis,
> Spes miseris, oculus caecis, solamen egenis,
> Ut caput in membris Christum veneratur in illis.

(The parents who formed his remarkable life were William,
the flower of knighthood, a noble man, and Anna, the glory of
mothers, kinder than any lamb. . . . Anna used to wash the

feet of the very lepers--a hope for the unfortunate, an eye
for the blind, a relief for the needy--that she might honor
Christ, the head, in these members.)

A particularly interesting and original passage in the
Metrical Life is the account of the rebuilding of Lincoln
Cathedral begun by St. Hugh in 1192 (lines 833-965). A year
before Hugh became bishop an earthquake destroyed much of the
cathedral. Hugh undertook to rebuild the cathedral, beginning
with the east end and working towards the still standing west
end of the cathedral. His architect is traditionally identified as an Anglo-Norman named Geoffrey de Noiers, though John
Harvey argues that the man responsible for the design of the
rebuilt cathedral was probably St. Hugh's master mason named
Richard; see *English Mediaeval Architects: A biographical
dictionary down to 1550* (London: Batsford, 1954), 195, 225.
At Witham, Hugh had built using stone vaulting, as may be seen
in the surviving lay brothers' church, which now serves as the
parish church of Witham (Thurston 102-4). How much of the
cathedral was rebuilt by the time of Hugh's death we do not
know. In his last illness, in London, Hugh ordered Geoffrey
de Noiers to prepare the altar of St. John the Baptist for
dedication by the bishop of Rochester at the general council
of bishops and magnates scheduled to be held in Lincoln that
November (*MV* 2:189). The chapel of St. John the Baptist may
have been located behind the high altar, a place of honor
reflecting the devotion of Hugh and the Carthusians to the
saint. Hugh gave instructions to his chaplain that he was to
be buried in front of the altar of St. John the Baptist, to
the side and near the wall so as not to take up too much of
the pavement or obstruct those passing by (*MV* 2:191-92). When
the cathedral was later extended to provide a larger shrine
for St. Hugh, with a square east end filled with glass, the
apse he had had built was torn down; but its outline is known
and is marked today on the floor of the cathedral. Hugh's
east end was an apse with ambulatory and side chapels, the
two sides converging to an apex at a polygonal chapel behind
the high altar. This design, like other features of Hugh's
cathedral such as the lavish use of Purbeck marble pillars,
resembles Canterbury Cathedral as rebuilt after 1174. Thurston argues that it was regarding the apex chapel that St. Hugh
gave his deathbed instructions to his architect and chaplain:

> A misunderstanding has long prevailed as to the position of
> this chapel of St. John the Baptist, in which St. Hugh's
> remains were interred. There can, I think, be no room for
> doubt that in St. Hugh's new cathedral the chapel of St. John
> the Baptist was the chapel in the apse, directly behind the

high altar, and consequently in the position usually occupied
in other churches by the Lady chapel. As the Cathedral itself
was dedicated to our Lady, it was not likely that a second
chapel should be consecrated to her in such an important
position, and the site was thus left free for St. Hugh's
special patron, St. John the Baptist. St. Hugh's extreme
anxiety that the chapel should be finished in time for the
great assembly at Lincoln becomes much more intelligible
when we recognize that it meant equivalently the completion
of the east end of the church. (Thurston 527, n. 2)

Thurston has a further note on this subject, explaining the
specification in the *Magna Vita* (2:232) that Hugh was buried
on the north side of the building (*a boreali ipsius edis re-
gione*) as meaning that his tomb was placed against the north
wall of the chapel of St. John the Baptist (Thurston 555-57).

Although St. Hugh's apse has been replaced by the Angel
Choir, much remains that can be identified as work associated
with St. Hugh and his architect. Gerald of Wales names the
wonderful stone roofing (*miro lapideo tabulatu*) in his title
to chapter five of part one of his *Vita Sancti Hugonis*, and
in that chapter, he mentions the little columns of white stone
and black marble, *sicut nunc cerni potest* ("as can now be
seen"). Gerald was writing after Hugh's death when the rebuilding was still going on, but he credits the beauty of the
new cathedral to Hugh as the one who authorized and inspired
it. And his earlier testimony in chapter 26 of the *Life of
St. Remigius* indicates that there was already much to see
before Hugh died (*Op.* 7:40-41). Various features of the work
attributed to St. Hugh and his masons are described and ana-
lyzed in Paul Frankl, *Gothic Architecture* (Baltimore: Penguin
Books, 1962), 73-75; and Nikolaus Pevsner and John Harris,
Lincolnshire, The Buildings of England Series (Harmondsworth:
Penguin Books, 1964), 31-32, 85-105. Pevsner estimates that
Geoffrey de Noiers was at work on the cathedral from 1192 to
about 1210-15 (Pevsner, 32), approximately the period when
Gerald witnessed the rebuilding and described it in the *Vita
Sancti Hugonis*. In "St. Hugh's work" the Early English style
of Gothic architecture appears, with the pointed arches and
stiff-leaf capitals characteristic of that new style. St.
Hugh and his masons were innovative, and their innovations
show an imaginative concern for effect. After acknowledging
that Remigius had built the original cathedral well, in the
[Romanesque] style of his age, Gerald describes the new
[Gothic] style in which Hugh built as in "conformity with the
more delicate craftsmanship of modern invention, far more
subtly and ingeniously finished" (*VSH* 20). With all the
changes time has brought to the building, Lincoln Cathedral

yet preserves that moment when Gothic was new.

As one looks up into the choir vault or along the decorative double arcading of the aisles or at the little columns
that shimmer around their pillars, a modern visitor recognizes
that he is being transported by an artist of *trompe-l'oeil*.
Pevsner quotes with amused approval Frankl's word "crazy" for
the choir vault, and he provides these other apt terms for
distinctive elements in "St. Hugh's work": "unexpected"
(pp. 32, 87); "syncopated" (pp. 32, 88, 94); "transparency . . .
letting you see one thing behind the other" (p. 94). In St.
Hugh's work, things are often unexpected in the historical
sense of being new, perhaps invented at Lincoln Cathedral.
The tierceron or third rib in the choir vault may be a Lincoln
invention (Frankl, 74). Certainly the way it is used in that
vault is boldly experimental. The decorative enrichments of
St. Hugh's work are also arresting in that they add not weight
but lightness, not massive grandeur but intriguing mystery,
by perspectives that partly reveal and partly conceal. For
example, the double arcading presents two rows of arcade-
pillars, with the pillars of one row at the apex of the arches
of the other. An illusion of depth between the two rows is
created to suggest that there is a passageway between them.
It is like the illusion of depth in a confined space achieved
by a baroque architect such as Borromini. But Lincoln Cathedral
is not (and was not in 1220) a confined space. Rather, the
great spaces of the cathedral are made intimate and dramatic
by St. Hugh's work. Beneath the north rose window is a row
of seven arched openings with a sequence of five lancet windows beyond them, and the whole composition is framed by a
vault that closes in at the top. One must move closer to see
it all, wondering if the shielding vault was a miscalculation.
Moving forward and gazing intently upward turn out to be what
must have been intended and reason enough for the partial con-
cealment.

The architectural effect of transparency, drawing your
eye to see something yet farther off, finds a rationale in the
allegorical commentary set forth in the *Metrical Life*. The
building, says the poet, springs toward heaven. He perceives
the "crazy" vault of St. Hugh's choir as a ceiling that opens
up through flight. Speaking of the roof (*tectum*), he writes:

> Nam quasi pennatis avibus testudo locuta,
> Latas expandens alas, similisque volanti,
> Nubes offendit, solidis innisa columnis. (lines 863-65)

(For like winged birds, the vault I spoke of, resting on
firm columns, spreads wide wings and as if in flight soars to
the clouds.)

My illustration of the design and visual effect of the choir
vault, which follows my translation below, shows how the lines
of the vault may suggest wings moving in flight.

Here is the Latin text of the description of the cathedral
in the *Metrical Life*, from Dimock's edition of 1860, and my
translation. In the opening lines is an allusion to the fact
that on one Good Friday, Hugh of Avalon helped the builders by
carrying mortar and stones in a hod. A cripple was permitted
to carry the same hod later and thereby recovered the power
to walk. This is one of Hugh's miracles reported by the papal
commissioners (Farmer 94, 97-98).

Quomodo aedificavit ecclesiam Lincolniensem.

Pontificis vero pontem facit ad Paradisum
Provida religio, provisio religiosa;
Aedificare Sion in simplicitate laborans,   835
Non in sanguinibus. Et mirâ construit arte
Ecclesiae cathedralis opus: quod in aedificando
Non solum concedit opes, operamque suorum,
Sed proprii sudoris opem; lapidesque frequenter
Excisos fert in calatho, calcemque tenacem.   840
Debilitas claudi, baculis suffulta duobus,
Illius officium calathi sortitur, inesse
Omen ei credens; successivêque duorum
Indignatur opem baculorum. Rectificatque
Curvum, quae rectos solet incurvare diaeta.   845
O gregis egregius, non mercenarius immo
Pastor! Ut ecclesiae perhibet structura novella.
Mater nempe Sion dejecta jacebat et arcta,
Errans, ignara, languens, anus, acris, egena,
Vilis, turpis: Hugo dejectam sublevat, arctam   850
Ampliat, errantem regit, ignaram docet, aegram
Sanat, anum renovat, acrem dulcorat, egenam
Fecundat, vilem decorat, turpemque decorat.
Funditus obruitur moles vetus, et nova surgit;
Surgentisque status formam crucis exprimit aptam.   855
Tres integrales partes labor arduus unit:
Nam fundamenti moles solidissima surgit
A centro, paries supportat in aera tectum:
Sic fundamentum terrae sepelitur in alvo,
Sed paries tectumque patent, ausuque superbo   860
Evolat ad nubes paries, ad sidera tectum.
Materiae pretio studium bene competit artis.
Nam quasi pennatis avibus testudo locuta,
Latas expandens alas, similisque volanti,

Nubes offendit, solidis innisa columnis.   865
Viscosusque liquor lapides conglutinat albos,
Quos manus artificis omnes excidit ad unguem.
Et paries ex congerie constructus eorum,
Hoc quasi dedignans, mentitur continuare
Contiguas partes; non esse videtur ab arte,   870
Quin a naturâ; non res unita, sed una.
Altera fulcit opus lapidum pretiosa nigrorum
Materies, non sic uno contenta colore,
Non tot laxa poris, sed crebro sidere fulgens,
Et rigido compacta situ; nulloque domari   875
Dignatur ferro, nisi quando domatur ab arte;
Quando superficies nimiis laxatur arenae
Pulsibus, et solidum forti penetratur aceto.
Inspectus lapis iste potest suspendere mentes,
Ambiguas utrum jaspis marmorve sit; at si   880
Jaspis, hebes jaspis; si marmor, nobile marmor.
Inde columnellae, quae sic cinxere columnas,
Ut videantur ibi quamdam celebrare choream.
Exterior facies, nascente politior ungue,
Clara repercussis opponit visibus astra: 885
Nam tot ibi pinxit varias fortuna figuras,
Ut si picturam similem simulare laboret
Ars conata diu, naturam vix imitetur.
Sic junctura decens serie disponit honestâ
Mille columnellas ibi: quae rigidae, pretiosae,   890
Fulgentes, opus ecclesiae totale rigore
Perpetuant, pretio ditant, fulgore serenant.
Ipsarum siquidem status est procerus et altus,
Cultus sincerus et splendidus, ordo venustus
Et geometricus, decor aptus et utilis, usus   895
Gratus et eximius, rigor inconsumptus et acer.

De fenestris vitreis

Splendida praetendit oculis aenigmata duplex
Pompa fenestrarum; cives inscripta supernae
Urbis, et arma quibus Stygium domuere tyrannum.
Majoresque duae, tamquam duo lumina; quorum   900
Orbiculare jubar, fines aquilonis et austri
Respiciens, geminâ premit omnes luce fenestras.
Illae conferri possunt vulgaribus astris;
Haec duo sunt, unum quasi sol, aliud quasi luna.
Sic caput ecclesiae duo candelabra serenant,   905
Vivis et variis imitata coloribus irim;
Non imitata quidem, sed praecellentia; nam sol,
Quando repercutitur in nubibus, efficit irim;
Illa duo sine sole micant, sine nube coruscant.

De allegoriâ singulorum

Haec, descripta quasi pueriliter, allegoriae 910
Pondus habent. Foris apparet quasi testa, sed intus
Consistit nucleus; foris est quasi cera, sed intus
Est favus; et lucet jucundior ignis in umbrâ.
Nam fundamentum, paries, tectum, lapis albus
Excisus, marmor planum, spectabile, nigrum, 915
Ordo fenestrarum duplex, geminaeque fenestrae,
Quae quasi despiciunt fines aquilonis et austri,
In se magna quidem sunt, sed majora figurant.

De partibus ecclesiae integrae

Est fundamentum corpus, paries homo, tectum
Spiritus; ecclesiae triplex divisio. Corpus 920
Terram sortitur, homo nubes, spiritus astra.

De albis lapidibus

Albus et excisus castos lapis et sapientes
Exprimit: albedo pudor est, excisio dogma.

De marmoribus

Marmoris effigie, planâ, splendente, nigellâ,
Sponsa figuratur, simplex, morosa, laborans. 925
Rectē nimirum designat simplicitatem
Planities, splendor mores, nigredo laborem.

De vitreis fenestris

Illustrans mundum divino lumine, cleri
Est praeclara cohors, claris expressa fenestris.
Ordo subalternus utrobique potestque notari; 930
Ordine canonicus exstante, vicarius imo.
Et quia, canonico tractante negotia mundi,
Jugis et assiduus divina vicarius implet,
Summa fenestrarum series nitet inclita florum
Involucro, mundi varium signante decorem; 935
Inferior perhibet sanctorum nomina patrum.

De duabus orbicularibus fenestris

Praebentes geminae jubar orbiculare fenestrae,
Ecclesiae duo sunt oculi: rectēque videtur
Major in his esse praesul, minor esse decanus.
Est aquilo zabulus, est Sanctus Spiritus auster; 940

Quos oculi duo respiciunt. Nam respicit austrum
Praesul, ut invitet; aquilonem vero decanus,
Ut vitet: videt hic ut salvetur, videt ille
Ne pereat. Frons ecclesiae candelabra coeli,
Et tenebras Lethes, oculis circumspicit istis.   945

Consummatio totius allegoriae

Sic insensibiles lapides mysteria claudunt
Vivorum lapidum, manualis spiritualem
Fabrica designat fabricam; duplexque refulget
Ecclesiae facies, duplici decorata paratu.

De crucifixo, et tabulâ aureâ in introitu chori

Introitumque chori majestas aurea pingit: 950
Et propriè propriâ crucifixus imagine Christus
Exprimitur, vitaeque suae progressus ad unguem
Insinuatur ibi. Nec solum crux vel imago,
Immo columnarum sex, lignorumque duorum
Ampla superficies, obrizo fulgurat auro.   955

De capitulo

Astant ecclesiae capitolia, qualia nunquam
Romanus possedit apex; spectabile quorum
Vix opus inciperet nummosa pecunia Croesi.
Scilicet introitus ipsorum sunt quasi quadra
Porticus; interius spatium patet orbiculare,   960
Materiâ tentans templum Salomonis et arte.
Si quorum vero perfectio restat, Hugonis
Perficietur opus primi sub Hugone secundo.
Sic igitur tanto Lincolnia patre superbit,
Qui tot eam titulis ex omni parte beavit.   965

Note: Dimock's text is based on the two extant manuscripts
of the *Metrical Life*, British Museum MS Bib. Reg. 13.A.iv,
folios 9-22, and Bodleian MS Laud 515, folios 116-139. The
British Museum manuscript he dates about 1220-1230; the Bodleian, later but before 1250. The British Museum manuscript
he judges more correct, though the Bodleian has several passages which Dimock incorporates in brackets in his edition.
These bracketed additions include all the headings and these
lines from the section I translate: 859-861; 931-965. The
latter passage occurs at a point where the British Museum
manuscript is missing two folios (Dimock, *ML*, xix-xxiii).

Translation

How he built the church of Lincoln

Farsighted religion and religious foresight construct the
bishop's bridge to Paradise. He labors to build Zion in innocence, not by deeds of blood, and with marvelous art he raises
the edifice of the cathedral church. In building it, he not
only spends wealth and the toil of his people, but the abundance of his own sweat. Often he carries the hewn stones and
mortar in a hod. A disabled cripple supported on two crutches
gets to use the bishop's hod. The cripple believes there is
good luck in it for him and afterward scorns to use the two
crutches. Day-labor that usually bends the straight of limb
straightens up the stooped man.

O distinguished pastor of the flock, by no means a mer-
cenary, as the rebuilding of the church shows! Zion the Mother
[i.e., the Mother Church of Lincoln] lay downcast and confined,
erring, unenlightened, frail, a bitter old woman, needy, poor,
and ugly. Hugh raises her up who is downcast, frees the confined, corrects the erring, teaches the unenlightened, heals
the sick, renews and sweetens the embittered old woman, en-
riches the needy, adorns the poor, beautifies the ugly one. The
old foundation is completely destroyed, and a new one rises.
The rising structure exhibits the appropriate form of the cross.
Hard work joins three integral parts. For the solid mass of
the foundation rises from the center [i.e., the earth]; the
wall supports the roof in the air. So the foundation is buried
in the belly of the earth, but the wall and the roof are vis-
ible, and with bold pride the wall flies up to the clouds, the
roof to the stars. The investment of art matches the cost of
the material. For like winged birds, the vault I spoke of,
resting on firm columns, spreads wide wings and as if in flight
soars to the clouds. Mortar glues together the white stones,
all of which the hand of the artisan cuts precisely. And the
wall constructed by laying them upon one another as if mocking
that makes the contiguous parts seem to join. It seems to be
not by art, but by nature, not a thing joined, but a single
thing. A second precious material of black stones supports
the structure. It is thus not limited to one color, nor is
it weakened by so many apertures, but shines with innumerable
stars and is held solidly in place. And the material will not
be mastered by iron till subdued by art, as the surface is
smoothed by many applications of sand and the solid stone is
penetrated by strong vinegar. On inspection, the stone raises
doubts whether it be jasper or marble. If jasper, it is a dull

jasper, but if marble, a noble marble. Of this stone are made
the little columns that so encircle the piers that they seem
to be dancing in a ring there. The outer surface, carefully
polished, rivals bright stars in its shimmerings. For chance
has drawn so many different designs there that if art should
try long and hard to produce a like image, it could hardly
equal nature. So a fine conjunction arranges a thousand little
columns there in worthy sequence. Firm, rich, shining, they
extend the structure of the church with utter steadiness, en-
rich it with value, brighten it with splendor. If their appearance is noble and lofty, their craftsmanship is genuine and
fine, the pattern graceful and geometrical, the beauty decor-
ous and useful, the use pleasing and excellent, the firmness
sure and dazzling.

The glass windows

A brilliant double array of windows shows mysteries to
the eyes. The figures depicted are citizens of the heavenly
city and the arms by which to subdue the Stygian tyrant. [In
lines 6-9 of this poem, the poet has named the arms by which
virtue withstands vices: the shield of justice, the spur of
the cross, the greave of the law, the lance of hope, the hel-
met of faith, the sword of religion.] There are two greater
windows, like two lamps. Their circular radiance facing north
and south imparts a twin light to all the windows. They can
be likened to familiar stars: one of the two resembles the sun,
the other the moon. Thus two lamps brighten the head of the
church that have imitated the rainbow in living and varied
colors--not imitated indeed, but excelled. For when the sun
is reflected in clouds, it makes the rainbow. These two shine
without the sun, are iridescent without a cloud.

The allegorical significance of each part

These things, described as a child might describe them,
carry a weight of allegory. Outside one sees as it were a
shell, but inside is the nucleus. The outside is like wax,
but within is the honey, and fire flashes more brightly in
the darkness. For the foundation, the wall, the roof, the
white cut-stone, the smooth marble, beautiful and black, and
the double series of windows, and the twin windows that face
north and south are certainly great in themselves, but they
symbolize greater things.

The parts of the whole church

The foundation is the body, the wall is man, the roof is
the spirit--a threefold division of the church. The body wins
the earth, man wins the clouds, the spirit wins the stars.

The white stones

The white cut-stone stands for chaste and wise men. The
whiteness is modesty, the cutting is instruction.

The marble stones

By the appearance of the marble--smooth, lustrous, dark--
the bride is symbolized, simple, meticulous, industrious. The
even surface well represents simplicity; the lustre, virtue;
the darkness, industry.

The glass windows

Illuminating the world by divine light is the bright
company of the clergy, represented by the clear windows. A
subordinate rank can be seen on each side. The series that
stands above corresponds to the canons; the lower series, to
the vicars. And since the faithful and devoted vicars carry
out the worship of God while the canons attend to worldly
business, the bright upper row of windows shines with a
covering of flowers, symbolizing the varied beauty of the
world; the lower group displays the names of the holy fathers.

The two circular windows

The twin windows that impart a circular radiance are the
two eyes of the church. Rightly, the greater of these is seen
to be the Bishop, the lesser, the Dean. The devil is the
north, the Holy Spirit is the south; the two eyes look in
those directions. The Bishop looks to the south, to attract
it. But the Dean looks to the north, to avoid it. The former sees in order to be saved, the latter sees in order not to
be lost. With these eyes, the face of the church carefully
considers the lamps of heaven and the shades of hell.

A summing up of the whole allegory

Thus do unfeeling stones enclose the mysteries of living stones, a building made by hands represents a spiritual building, and the double form of the church blazes forth embellished with twofold art.

The crucifix and the gold painting at the entrance to the choir

Golden majesty adorns the entrance to the choir, and fittingly the crucified Christ is shown by a faithful likeness and the course of his life is skillfully represented there. And not only the cross or the figure, but the large surface, with six columns and two wooden panels, shines with pure gold.

The chapter house

Next to the church stands the chapter house, such [a Capitol] as the Roman crown never possessed. The great wealth of a Croesus could hardly undertake its beautiful construction. Its entrance resembles a square gallery. Inside, a circular space spreads out, competing in material and art with the temple of Solomon. If its completion should be achieved, the work of Hugh the First will be finished under Hugh the Second. Thus Lincoln takes pride in so great a father who has blessed her in every way with so many glories.

Western towers of Lincoln Cathedral, showing earlier Romanesque round arches and later Gothic pointed arches. Atop the pinnacle to the left is a restored statue traditionally said to be of St. Hugh. The Romanesque work, of course, preceded St. Hugh's rebuilding of the cathedral, while the Gothic extension of the towers is work in the Perpendicular style raised in the early fifteenth century.

LINCOLN CATHEDRAL

Illustrations relating to St. Hugh and the work he inspired.

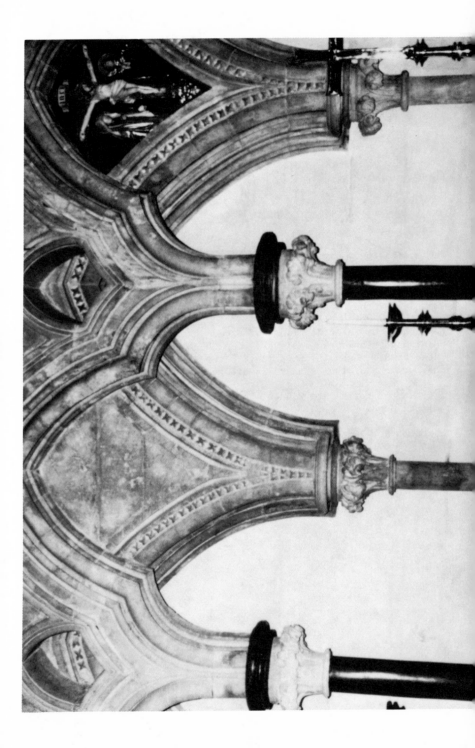

The North Rose Window

Opposite page: A drawing of the panel in the North Rose Window showing archbishops and kings carrying the body of St. Hugh, with God's hand in blessing above and a priest kneeling below the bier. This is a reproduction of figure *d* of plate LXVII in N.H.J. Westlake, *A History of Design in Painted Glass*, vol. 1 (London, 1881), 115. The painting has lost detail since the time of this drawing, but still surviving are the principal outlines and colors (white, yellow, red, a blue background, and the bier in green). Jean Lafond dates the medallion as early thirteenth-century work. It was not originally in the North Rose Window. Lafond notes a tradition associating this glass with a chantry in a chapel adjoining the nave that had an altar dedicated to St. Hugh and had been founded by Bishop Hugh of Wells (who died in 1235). The St. Hugh medallion is located in the lower left quadrant of the bottom circle of the four large circles of the North Rose. The window is shown on pages 102-103. The medallion is described and catalogued (no. 47) in Jean Lafond, "The Stained Glass Decoration of Lincoln Cathedral in the Thirteenth Century," *The Archaeological Journal* 103 (1946): 137-38. It is also listed (no. C1) in N.J. Morgan, *The Medieval Painted Glass of Lincoln Cathedral*, Corpus Vitrearum Medii Aevi, occasional paper no. 3 (London: The British Academy, 1983), 16.

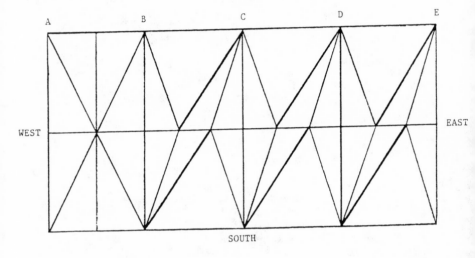

The Vault of St. Hugh's Choir

The figure above is a schematic representation of the ribs of
the vault of St. Hugh's Choir, shown as in an architectural
plan, that is, as if looking directly down from above on each
part of the plan. The tiercerons or third ribs are shown in
darker lines. The westernmost vault, rebuilt after the collapse
of the central tower in 1237, is in a balanced and centered
pattern, contrasting with the syncopated lines of the other
vaults. In a letter to me, P.R. Hill, Clerk of the Works at
Lincoln Cathedral, describes the tiercerons thus: "The double
ribs which are, in effect, a diagonal rib divided longitudinally
and pulled apart, run in plan from south west to north east."
This may be seen in the drawing above.

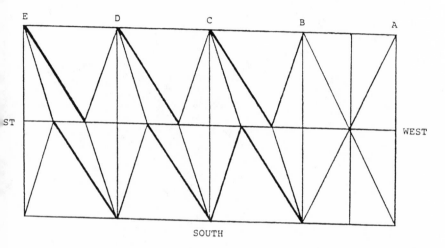

NORTH

E   D   C   B   A

ST   WEST

SOUTH

An observer standing on the floor of the cathedral and looking
up at the vault sees the roof differently from what appears in
an architectural projection. First, the vault lines are reversed,
as in a mirror image. This is illustrated in the drawing above.
Second, only a crossing rib directly overhead appears straight
to an observer below, while the other ribs are seen as curving
arches. Third, the spaces of roof defined by the ribs assume
a different outline as one changes position on the floor of the
cathedral. To illustrate these effects, the photographs and
drawings on pages 106-107 show from two perspectives the section
of roof between the ribs I have labelled C and D that run
from north to south, perpendicular to the central rib. The
photograph on page 106 is a view taken from just east of rib D.
The alternating narrow and wide spaces and the reversed curves
of the ribs impart a sense of movement to the roof, fitting the
description in the *Metrical Life* that likens the vault to birds
spreading wide wings in flight. Historians have called it a
daring experiment, influential but never exactly repeated
elsewhere, and critics have objected that it is disorienting
and lopsided. Yet this unique if "crazy" vault seemed wonderful
to Gerald of Wales. It is certainly consistent with those other
features of St. Hugh's work that produce effects of depth,
opening-up, and variation. Where so much is ordered and
symmetrical, syncopation gives stone the surge of life.

THE CHOIR VAULT AS SEEN FROM UNDER RIB D

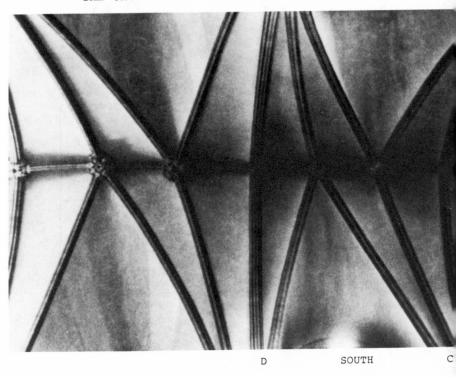

D   SOUTH   C

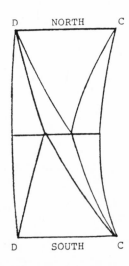

EAST

THE CHOIR VAULT AS SEEN FROM UNDER RIB C

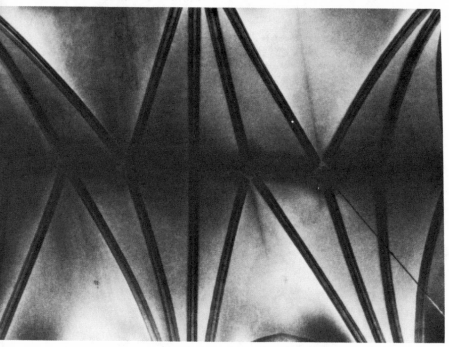

D   SOUTH   C

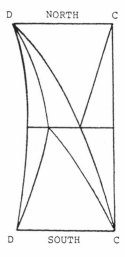

WEST

Medieval catalogue of books from the Great Bible at Lincoln. Reproduced courtesy of the Lincoln Cathedral Library. Photograph by George Tokarski.

These notes are numbered by the paragraph and line numbers of the translation. An asterisk in the translation indicates that a note is provided here.

2.10. Cf. C.R. Cheney, *From Becket to Langton: English Church Government 1170-1213* (Manchester, 1956), p. 87: "I translate *sacerdotium* and *regnum* as ecclesiastical and royal government, for this seems to be the usual meaning of the terms when they appear conjoined."

5.1. Gerald's heroic phrase for St. Hugh, "virorum vir perpaucorum," is echoed in other of his works. In *Gemma Ecclesiastica*, he uses the phrase "viri virorum perpaucorum" to characterize good bishops (*Op.* 2: 362). Hagen translates it "the very, very few real men" (*Jewel* 276). The source of the phrase is not known, though in the *Gemma*, Gerald cites it as "illud comicum," perhaps meaning Terence as the author; see Hagen's note 32 on the passage (*Jewel* 340-41). In *Speculum Duorum,* Gerald speaks of Roger of Rolleston, Dean of Lincoln, as "vir revera virilis animi, virque virorum perpaucorum," which Brian Dawson translates, "a truly noble man, a man as few men are" (*SD* 10-11).

5.2. Hugh was born at his father's castle of Avalon, located in a mountain valley along the River Isère, northeast of Grenoble. Adam of Eynsham quotes a reference to Hugh as "Hugh of Avalon" (*MV* 1: 47-48) and quotes Hugh's allusion to his brother William as owning the castle of Avalon (*MV* 1: 131). The French biography translated and expanded by Thurston begins with a description of the scene, its background being the Alps: "Near the borders of Dauphiné and Savoy, the lovely and fertile valley of Graisivaudan opens out and then narrows again, enclosing the townships of Pontcharra and Saint-Maximin" (Thurston 1). Thurston comments: "The Castle of Avalon is situated upon territory now belonging to the commune of Saint-Maximin" (Thurston 2, n. 1). The diocese of Grenoble is in the north of the region that in the ninth century became the kingdom of

Provence, its boundaries being the Rhone, the Alps, and the
Mediterranean. In the tenth century the German emperor Otto
the Great joined Provence with the kingdom of Trans-Jurane
Burgundy to its north and made of these a united kingdom of
Burgundy which became a protectorate of the empire. In the
eleventh century its northern portion, the duchy of Burgundy,
was allied with the Capetian monarchy of France, though the
emperors contested control. Gerald's words that Hugh's origins were on "the distant borders of imperial Burgundy" are
quoted in the canonization report of the papal commissioners
(Farmer 95). Adam of Eynsham records that Hugh was in his
sixtieth year when he died in 1200 (*MV* 2: 208), so that the
year of his birth would have been 1140.

5.13. According to Adam, Hugh was eight, not ten, when he
and his father, after his mother's death, went to live with the
Augustinian canons at the church of Villarbenoît near Avalon
(*MV* 1: 5-7). There were two older brothers, William and Peter,
who inherited the father's estates (*MV* 2: 171).

5.19. In the patristic tradition of allegorical interpretation, Gerald refers to the sensuality the father mastered
as his "Dalila" [Delilah].

6.9. Adam of Eynsham says that boys were sent to Villarbenoît to be instructed in secular as well as religious authors
(*secularibus simul et ecclesiasticis litteris imbuendi*); but
among his first lessons, the senior canon who was his teacher
especially encouraged Hugh to study the scriptures and to love
spiritual doctrine (*MV* 1: 7).

7.7. According to Adam, Hugh was nineteen when he was
ordained a deacon by the bishop of Grenoble; as deacon, he
preached effective sermons and publicly rebuked sinners
(*MV* 1: 16). Consequently, his former teacher, now his prior,
put him in charge of the cell or dependent religious house of
St. Maxime's. An older canon, a priest, was his companion
there. Deacon Hugh was now administering a small parish, giving religious instruction to the people and managing the modest
material resources of the church--vineyards and sheep that he
entrusted to the care of reliable laymen (*MV* 1: 18-19).

8.7. As "Dalila" was synonymous with "sensuality," so
"Mars" could stand for fighting; thus Gerald achieves the
punning *arte magis quam Marte*. Thurston expresses the sense
of this paragraph thus: "that St. Hugh was troubled at the
freedom with which women were permitted to come and go in such
outlying chaplaincies, where the Canons lived like the ordinary

secular clergy, and that he resolved, according to the asceti-
cal ideas of the early centuries, to seek safety in flight"
(Thurston 42).

9.9. Thurston's biography provides details on the Carthusian cell. It is not a mere chamber, but a small two-
storied, five-roomed house with its own garden and passageway:
"An old tradition still points out the cell which St. Hugh
inhabited during his sojourn at the Grande Chartreuse. It is
at the end of the Gothic cloister, and is surmounted by the
letter F. . . . With the exception that stone walls have replaced the wooden ones of the twelfth century, the cell presents much the same appearance now as it would have done in
the time of St. Hugh. Passing through the door which opens on
the cloister, we find ourselves in a short covered passage
used to pace up and down in wet weather. This communicates
with the solitary's little garden, and further on with his
wood-shed, and the room which serves him for carpentry or other
manual work. At the end of the passage, a staircase takes us
to the upper floor, and here we enter first a room used as a
kitchen in the time of the Saint, and then the cell proper,
in which he lived and prayed. On one side of it, in a sort of
oratory, stand a stall and a *prie-dieu*, on the other is a bed
which shuts up like a cupboard, containing only a straw
paillasse and woollen coverings. A small table, fitting into
the recess of the window, served for his solitary meals, and
a crucifix and a few holy pictures are the sole ornaments of
the humble dwelling. Adjoining is a little work-room, a few
wooden shelves holding the books which were required by the
monk for his studies" (Thurston 46-47). The medieval Carthusian
labored at the copying of manuscripts in his cell. Thurston
translates the list of tools and supplies provided for this
purpose: Dom Guigo enjoins that each monk should be provided
with "a desk, pens, chalk, two pumice stones, two horns, a
scalpel, two knives, or razors, for shaving smooth the parch-
ment, a bodkin, an awl, lead, a rule and ruler to rule with,
tablets, and ink" (Thurston 52, n. 1). Thurston also mentions
a weekly walk outdoors: "Once also in the week, the merciful
Rule prescribes for the health of mind and body that he shall
take his *spatiamentum*, or walk abroad, which is made a matter
of obligation, and lasts between two and three hours" (Thurston
47). A plank bench between two fir trees was pointed out as
the place where Hugh (who was short and stout) stopped to rest
on a return visit to the Grande Chartreuse and where he had
rested in earlier years when he accompanied St. Peter of Tarentaise, a retired Cistercian abbot, on their mountain walks
together (*MV* 1: 39-40).

11.6. According to the article on St. Hugh in David Hugh
Farmer, *The Oxford Dictionary of Saints* (Oxford: Clarendon
Press, 1978), Hugh joined the Carthusians about 1165 and went
to Witham about 1179-80 (cf. *MV* xxiv-xxv). In about 1175 he
was appointed procurator at the Grande Chartreuse, a position
that placed him in charge of the lay brothers and made him
responsible for receiving and welcoming guests to the monastery
(Thurston 70). The distinction with which he fulfilled this
office brought him to the attention of Henry II, who had under-
taken to found a Carthusian monastery in England as part of his
public reparation for the murder of Becket (*MV* xxiv). The first
two priors sent to the chosen site of Witham in Somersetshire
had failed to establish a viable community. Hugh was recommended as one who could succeed (*MV* 1: 46-49). Hugh accepted the
task with the reluctant consent of the community at the Grande
Chartreuse and at the urging of the bishop of Grenoble, whose
judgment the prior had sought (*MV* 1: 54-59). Hugh succeeded
in launching the Witham Charterhouse by selfless energy and
tact, winning the friendship of the local folk by seeing that
they were generously compensated for lands and buildings bought
from them, and patiently persuading Henry II to fulfill his
pledge of financial support (*MV* 1: 60-68). W.L. Warren concludes his *Henry II* (Berkeley, 1973) with the story of how
Hugh's calm faith in the king won Henry to be true to his
pledge. Hugh's spirituality attracted able and learned men
to join the community at Witham and gained him renown throughout Britain (*MV* 1:77).

11.9. Eilert Ekwall's *The Concise Oxford Dictionary of
English Place-Names*, 4th edition (Oxford, 1960), derives the
name of Witham in Somersetshire neither from "white" nor "wit,"
but from a personal name: "Witta's Hām," that is, Witta's home
or settlement. Although Gerald's etymological conjectures were
therefore incorrect, his spellings, "Witham" or "Wittham," with
a single or double *t*, are attested in the period: *Witham* in
1160 and *Wuttheham* in 1212. The modern name of the river that
flows through Lincoln is also Witham, but was differently
spelled in the Middle Ages. Ekwall cites *Widme*, *Withma*, from
the Danelaw Charters of about 1150 and *Widhem* from the Close
Rolls, 1243. He derives the name from a Romano-British name,
Widumanios, the first part probably being the same as the
Welsh word, *gwydd*, meaning "forest," the second part perhaps
related to the Latin verb, *manare*, "to flow." Thus the name
of the river is ancient, antedating Saxon and Danish settlement. So also is the name of Lincoln itself, which is a com-
pound of British *Lindon* (corresponding to the Welsh *llyn*,
"lake") and the Latin *colonia*, "settlement" (for veterans).
The lake at Lincoln is a widening of the River Witham now known
as Brayford Pool.

12.19. In his note to line 605 of the *Metrical Life of
St. Hugh*, Dimock observes that *Burneta*, the name which Gerald
here gives to this pet bird, is the clear reading of both manuscripts, but asks whether *berneca*, "Bernicle goose," may have
been intended, and he cites Du Cange, under *Bernaca*. In the
glossary to his later Rolls Series edition of the *Vita Sancti
Hugonis*, Dimock gives for *Burneta*, "a bird," adding, "I am
unable to identify it." Thurston follows Dimock's earlier
suggestion that Gerald meant a "bernacle-goose" (Thurston 143).
But in R.E. Latham, *Revised Medieval Latin Word-List from
British and Irish Sources* (London: The British Academy, 1965),
burneta is identified conjecturally as "(?) hedge-sparrow."
The name would presumably be derived from the bird's brown
plumage; another attested twelfth-century meaning of *burneta*
given by Latham is "burnet, brown cloth." The modern name of
the plant burnet is derived from the Middle English word meaning "dark brown," from the Old French *burnete*. In Fascicule I:
A-B of Latham's *Dictionary of Medieval Latin from British Sources* (London: The British Academy, 1975), under *brunettus*, 3,
the conjectural identification of "hedge-sparrow" for *burneta*
is repeated, with three citations: the present passage from
Gerald's *Vita Sancti Hugonis*, the versification of that in the
Metrical Life, and a quotation from the *Fabulae* of Odo of
Cheriton (who died in 1247): "cucula quandoque ponit ovum in
nido burnete," that is, "the hen cuckoo sometimes puts its egg
in the nest of the *burneta*." The hedge sparrow is the most
familiar of the various small birds whose nests are thus in-
vaded by cuckoos. Lear's Fool alludes to the phenomenon:
"For you know, nuncle, 'The hedge-sparrow fed the cuckoo so
long/ That it had it head bit off by it young'" (*King Lear*
1.4.234-36). The hedge sparrow is an accentor, not related to
the house sparrow or tree sparrow. It is also called dunnock,
its Latin name being *Prunella modularis*. It builds its nest
in a bush or hedge. Its plumage is striated brown above and
slate-gray beneath. See S. Vere Benson, *The Observer's Book
of Birds* (London: Frederick Warne, 1977), p. 182. The *Metrical
Life* retells Hugh's friendship with this bird to illustrate
Hugh's gentleness, in contrast to the severity of the Carthusian
rule:

  Ordo quidem gravis est; Hugo tam mitis, ut ipsae
  Attestantur aves: sicut Burneta probavit,
  Quae cellam celebrando diu, mansueta, manuque
  Sueta Prioris ali, fidente domestica rostro
  Dulces carpebat micas, gelidumque papaver;
  Et solo deerat ponendi tempore nidi;
  Solaque discedens, multis comitata redibat. (lines 604-610)

(The Order indeed is stern, Hugh just as gentle, and to this
even the birds testify. The *Burneta* which long frequented his
cell demonstrated that. Tamed and accustomed to being fed
from the Prior's hand, it would take tasty crumbs and cold
grain with its confident beak. And it would be absent only
during the time of nest-building; departing alone, it would
return with a throng.)

13.8. Hugh's election was canonical only because he in-
sisted on that. His appointment came through the favor of
Henry II, who had him elected at a royal council held at the
Abbey of Eynsham. But bishops were to be freely chosen by
clerics in the chapter house of their own church, not at an
assembly supervised by a secular ruler. Hugh therefore re-
jected this election at Eynsham. Pleased by his respect for
their authority, the canons of Lincoln overcame all their
initial misgivings about this foreign monk and again unanimous-
ly elected him their bishop. He would still not accept the
post without the approval of the Prior of the Grande Chartreuse, who was Hugh's religious superior as General of the
Carthusian Order. This approval was obtained upon sending
emissaries there (*MV* 1: 92-99; Thurston 128-33). Subsequently
Hugh did not allow his critics to forget that he had not sought
to be bishop of Lincoln. He sometimes gained leverage in
political and financial crises by offering to resign his see
and return to the cloister (*MV* 2: 35-37; 2: 99). From an evident longing for the peace of the cloister, he made that request in the last year of his life, while revisiting the Grande
Chartreuse, but Innocent III denied him his wish (*MV* xx; 2:
149-50).

14.8. Gerald's conception of the duties of a bishop is
developed in *Speculum Duorum*, in Letter 6 to Bishop Geoffrey
of St. David's, which affirms that a bishop should be a prudent
administrator and a temperate pastor, not harsh or arrogant.
The penultimate chapter of *Gemma Ecclesiastica*, chapter 38 of
part two, argues that bishops must be eminent in virtue and
specifically that they should not prefer worldly goods and the
favor of a temporal ruler to the service of God. The sacraments and ceremonies for which a bishop is specially responsible
include, besides confirmation and the dedication of churches,
the ordination of priests; the consecration of a bishop
(effected in company with other bishops); the blessing of the
holy oil or chrism used in confirmation, baptism, and the
anointing of the sick; and supervising in accord with the
norms of canon law all the liturgical observances and sacra-
mental ministries within his diocese (see relevant articles
in the *New Catholic Encyclopedia*). Hugh was also often called

upon to act as a judge delegate of the pope, mediating eccle-siastical disputes outside his diocese (*MV* xxx-xxxii). Within his diocese, the bishop of Lincoln presided over what Dorothy Owen calls "an elaborate administrative machine," with wide-ranging responsibilities: "The centre and fount of authority was the bishop, who was at once pastor, judge, and disciplin-arian of his entire flock. He moved perpetually through his diocese, from one to another of his estates, or to London to his residence in the Old Temple" (*Church and Society in Medi-eval Lincolnshire* [Lincoln: History of Lincolnshire Committee, 1971; rpt. 1981], p. 20).

16.4. The *Magna Vita* draws attention to Hugh's not con-firming from on horseback by citing the case of another reck-less bishop who did (*MV* 1: 128).

16.19. As Thurston points out, correcting Dimock's mis-judgment that Hugh's slapping the old man was rude (*Metrical Life*, p. xi), the slap is part of the rite of confirmation: "Mr. Dimock is evidently unaware that the *alapa* or buffet forms part of the ordinary rite of Confirmation, and is in-tended to be symbolical of the endurance which is to be ex-pected of a soldier of Christ" (Thurston xx). But the vigor of Hugh's slap seems understood by Gerald to be special.

17.6. The chrismatory is the vessel containing chrism or holy oil used in the rite of confirmation.

17.13. Gerald elsewhere alludes to "God's grace" as the meaning of the name John: in *De Principis Instructione*, he comments on King John, "Would that John's life agreed with his name" (*Op.* 8: 310).

19.3. The "relief" (*relevatio*) was the payment by the heir upon the death of the holder of a tenement, paid to the feudal lord who owned the property. 100 shillings on the knight's fee--a fief assessed as owing one knight's service--had come to be the agreed payment by this time. For an account of relief and heriot, see F. Pollock and F. W. Maitland, *The History of English Law before the time of Edward I*, vol. 1 (Cambridge, 1898), pp. 312-14.

20.4. The meaning "roofing" for the word *tabulatus* in the title to this chapter (*miro lapideo tabulatu*) is given in J.F. Niermeyer, *Mediae Latinitatis Lexicon Minus* (Leiden: E.J. Brill, 1976). For further discussion of Hugh's rebuild-ing of Lincoln Cathedral, see my appendix on the *Metrical Life*. In a letter of March 1880, John Ruskin faults James Anthony

Froude for paying scant attention to the cathedral in his
essay on St. Hugh (*Fraser's Magazine*, n.s. 1 [Feb. 1870],
220-36). Ruskin says that Froude "has no knowledge of art,
nor care for it; and therefore, in his life of Hugo of Lincoln,
passes over the Bishop's designing, and partly building, its
cathedral, with a word, as if he had been no more than a wood-
man building a hut" (*Works*, vol. 29, p. 389). In a letter of
January 1883, Ruskin writes: "I have always held (and am prepared against all comers to maintain my holding) that the
Cathedral of Lincoln is out and out the most precious piece of
architecture in the British islands, and--roughly--worthy any
two other cathedrals we have got" (*Works*, vol. 37, p. 433).

22.3. On fulfilling the "natural hours" (*reales horas*),
Dimock has an entry in his glossary (*Op.* 7: 255), quoting from
the Prologue to Book 5 of a thirteenth-century commentary on
the liturgy, the *Rationale Divinorum Officiorum* by Durandus,
that is, William Duranti the Elder. This is my translation of
the passage from Durandus; it is an explanation of the "natural
day" (*dies naturalis*): "The natural day has seven different
periods. The first is infancy, which is represented by matins
and lauds. The second is childhood, represented by prime.
The third is adolescence, represented by terce. The fourth
is youth, represented by sext. The fifth is maturity, represented by nones. The sixth is old age, represented by vespers.
The seventh is decrepitude or the end of our life, which is
signified by compline." Dimock adds, "'*Reales horas explere*'
is to realize and fulfill the duties appertaining to these
several natural hours." The liturgical hours were a framework
for Hugh's day, as for all the life of the cathedral. The
names of the hours were conventionally used in the Middle Ages
to designate the times of day, following the ancient Roman
division of the twelve hours of daylight:

Prime: Sunrise
Terce: The third hour or midmorning
Sext: The sixth hour or midday
Nones: The ninth hour or midafternoon
Vespers: Sunset

Matins and lauds are the night office, for which the medieval
clergy rose at midnight or later, but before the ordinary day
began. Often, as mentioned in *VSH* 82, a cleric would go back
to bed after matins, to rise again at daybreak. Compline was
chanted just before retiring to bed. From the *Black Book of
Lincoln*, we learn specific features of the liturgy of Lincoln
Cathedral. Henry Bradshaw notes these observances: "The
curfew, still rung, and twice mentioned in our '*Consuetudinar-
ium*' [in the *Black Book*], carries us back still further, to
the time of Remigius himself. The sailors pulling the bells

on Christmas morning, and making a point of coming five and
twenty miles inland for the occasion, the watchman playing the
flute to tell the hours of the night in the still Cathedral,
the Canon's men bringing drink to the ringers at night, are
details not forgotten" (*BBL* 73). Among the specifications for
the ringing of the bells and the lighting of candles is this
(in my translation of the Latin of the *Black Book*): "At the
first bells for matins, all the doors of the church are opened
and candles are then lit in the choir and in the nave of the
church, so that those who enter the church and choir may see
where they are going" (*BBL* 384). Adam of Eynsham tells us that
St. Hugh loved an abundance of lights and ordered that his
church be well lit (*MV* 2: 220). A feast-day procession had
these features: "There will be three clerics carrying three
crosses and wearing silken copes, while a lesser cleric precedes them carrying and sprinkling holy water. In the second
rank will be two wax-bearers wearing albs and carrying lighted
candles in candle-holders. Third, two thurifers [incense-
bearers] with thuribles [incense-boats] in their hands, wearing albs and tunics. Fourth, three poor clerks carrying
relics, wearing surplices. Fifth, the second subdeacon carrying at his breast the Gospel book with a silver or gold image
of the Crucified [Lord] and Mary and John. Sixth, the second
deacon carrying at his breast a silver or gold cross. Seventh,
the presiding [priest] with two ministers wearing silken copes"
(*BBL* 375). There is provision for a candle-lit scrutiny of
the church at night, lest anyone evil be lurking in its corners.
And then:

> Hoc facto quiescere qui volunt possunt excepto illo qui vo-
> catur vigil quia ille astrictus est vigilare per totam noc-
> tem quia racione huius officii vocatur vigil. (*BBL* 386.)

(After that, those who wish can sleep, except the one called
the watchman, for he is obliged to keep watch all night long,
since by reason of that office is he called the watchman.)

26.2. Henry II died on July 6, 1189, at Chinon and was
buried at the nearby convent of Fontevrault. His surviving
sons, Richard and John, were at that time both in league with
his enemy, King Philip II of France. Gerald of Wales was
attending the court then and gives an account of Henry's death
in *De Principis Instructione*. It is likely that Gerald is
writing from personal recollection of Hugh's observance of the
major feast-days that spring and summer.

31.6. The Old Temple was acquired as the London residence
of the bishops of Lincoln by Bishop Robert de Chesney (1148-
1166). The site was in the parish of St. Andrew, Holborn, and
included a chapel and a garden (*Op.* 7: 35). See *The Book of*

John de Schalby, trans. J.H. Srawley (Lincoln Minster Pamphlets, no. 2, rpt. 1966), pp. 7; 25, n. 11.

31.14. At his coronation feast on September 3, 1189, Richard I excluded women and Jews from the banquet. It was an act that had consequences the king deplored. The Jews of England were under the king's protection, and on this occasion some of their leaders sought to enter the palace to present gifts to him. But the crowd at the gates attacked them, apparently thinking the king would sanction that. A riot ensued, with killing, burning, and looting which lasted through the night and afflicted both Christians and Jews. Richard was enraged that the peace had been broken on his coronation and that the Jews whom he protected and whose financial assistance he needed had been plundered. It was on September 5 that he received the homage of the bishops mentioned by Gerald. See John T. Appleby, *England Without Richard: 1189-1199* (Ithaca: Cornell Univ. Press, 1965), pp. 10-13.

33.6. Hugh's opposition to the Angevin kings was not simply a defense of religion. It was often occasioned by differences of judgment on issues of state, such as Hugh's challenge to the privileges of foresters (*MV* 1: 114), his liberal extension of the right of sanctuary (*MV* 2: 126-29), his support for Geoffrey Plantagenet against William Longchamp, and his resistance to being taxed to support troops for overseas warfare (cf. *MV* xlii-xlvii). Yet defense of the liberty of the church was a consistent element in his stance in these controversies.

34.10. In December of 1197, Hubert Walter, Archbishop of Canterbury and chief justiciar, summoned a meeting at Oxford of all tenants-in-chief of the realm of England. He asked them to supply 300 knights (or funds to support 300 knights) to serve King Richard for a year in his war with Philip Augustus in Normandy. St. Hugh argued that the church of Lincoln was not obliged to supply troops for overseas warfare. Other prelates also appear to have regarded the demand as an unfair infringement, but only one other bishop, Herbert of Salisbury, joined Hugh in open resistance. Salisbury was compelled to make an expensive settlement with the king. Hugh employed the vigor and charm of his own personality to achieve the reconciliation described in this chapter. See Appleby, *England Without Richard*, pp. 202-209.

37.9. The manuscript reads "absque mare." Dimock asks what this means and suggests "without any heavy sea" (*Op.* 7: 104, n. 1). But the repetition of *mare* after *mare Gallicum*

may be a scribal error rather than an obscure pun. Accordingly, I have emended *mare* to *mora* ("delay"). Yet Gerald's fondness for puns and the correctness of this scribe's work argue
in favor of the riddling reading, "mare Gallicum absque mare
transfretavit."

37.14. King Richard's fortress of Château Gaillard ("High-
spirited Castle") was built in 1196 on the banks of the Seine
midway between Paris and Rouen. Richard boasted that even if
it were made of butter (it was not; it was a formidable, three-
moated rampart), he would defend it against King Philip (*De
Principis Instructione, Op.* 8: 290). His brother John lost
the castle--and Normandy--to Philip Augustus in 1204.

40.7. In the later Middle Ages, the kiss of peace was
replaced by an embrace given among the clergy and the circu-
lation of an object such as a crucifix or pax-board, to be
kissed by others at the mass. But what Gerald describes
appears to have been the primitive ceremony: the priest celebrating the mass kisses the Host--the Body of Christ--and then
kisses the other ministers, who in turn extend the kiss to
members of the congregation. See the article "Kiss, Liturgical" in the *New Catholic Encyclopedia.*

40.11. The excesses of which Hugh accused King Richard on
this occasion included his infidelities to his wife Berengaria
and his practice of selling offices, including bishoprics
(*MV* 2: 104, n. 4); their conference occurred on Aug. 28, 1198.

46.10. The incident of St. Martin's healing a leper by
kissing him is in chapter 18 of the *Life of St. Martin* by
Sulpicius Severus (Migne's *Patrologia Latina* 20: col. 170);
see the translation of this work by Bernard M. Peebles (New
York: Fathers of the Church, 1949), p. 127. Benedicta Ward
cites this saying of St. Hugh's as illustrating the shift of
interest in the twelfth century from physical miracles that
would identify a man of God with some earlier saint to the
ethical miracles of that man's "present virtues"; see *Miracles
and the Medieval Mind* (Philadelphia, 1982), p. 175.

49.7. The second bishop of Lincoln, Robert Bloet, gave
King Henry I a sable mantle worth 100 pounds and bound his
successors to make similar gifts (*Op.* 7: 33). King Richard's
government now claimed that Hugh should pay this amount for
each year of his episcopate, as well as for that of his pre-
decessor, Walter of Coutances. Hugh offered to withdraw to
Witham for a period and use the revenues from the bishopric
to pay the great sum. But the clergy of his diocese contributed

funds from their own revenues rather than lose Hugh's presence
in office. Hugh settled the tax forever by one payment of
3000 marks, the settlement being confirmed by a royal charter
dated at Le Mans, June 23, 1194 (*MV* 2: 34-37; *Op.* 7: 108, n. 1).

50.24. Gerald uses the word *olor* for Hugh's swan and
cygnus for the other swans it overpowers. From Gerald's description, Hugh's swan may be identified as a whooper swan, a
wild swan whose bill is yellow and black, without a knob, and
which holds its neck in an erect line. The other swans would
be mute swans, which are domesticated birds having a deep
orange bill with a black knob at the base of the bill and
which hold the neck in an S-curve. The mute swan has a barking
note, while the whooper makes clear trumpeting notes. See
S. Vere Benson, *The Observer's Book of Birds* (London: Frederick
Warne, 1977), pp. 46-47.

51.7. Dimock draws attention to the fact that the reading
attactus ("touch") appears here and in the transcript of Gerald's account of the swan included in the *Magna Vita*, whereas
the account in the *Vita Sancti Remigii* reads *attractus*. Dimock judges *attactus* "probably the true reading" (*Op.* 7: 74, n. 3).
Both the *Vita Sancti Hugonis* and the *Magna Vita* appear then to
be following a more correct text, possibly the first edition
of the *Vita Sancti Remigii*, of which Gerald had donated a copy
to the Lincoln cathedral library.

51.25. This bracketed passage from the account of the swan
in the *Vita Sancti Remigii* is also found in the *Magna Vita*.
Why is it omitted from the *Vita Sancti Hugonis*? Is the omission
only a scribal oversight? Dimock speculates (*Op.* 7: 75, n. 1)
that Gerald added the passage to the *Vita Sancti Remigii* when
preparing the second edition of that work (the Corpus Christi
College manuscript 425 is the only extant copy of the *Vita
Sancti Remigii*, as of the *Vita Sancti Hugonis*). But there is
evidence that both the *Vita Sancti Hugonis* and the *Magna Vita*
are based on a more correct text than that found in the extant
Vita Sancti Remigii, perhaps the now lost first edition of the
Vita Sancti Remigii (see my note above on line 7 of paragraph
51 of *VSH*). The bracketed passage might have been an insert
in the first edition that a scribe could overlook in copying.

52.12. For a recent discussion of the swan as an emblem--
a tradition amply and variously attested in antiquity--see
Frederick M. Ahl, "Amber, Avallon, and Apollo's Singing Swan,"
American Journal of Philology, 103 (Winter 1982), 373-411.
Gerald's allusion to the swan as a sign follows the well-
established patristic tradition of reading creation as a

system of signs revealing spiritual truths. One may note three wonders in Gerald's account: the saint's extraordinary kindness, which attracts animals to him; the corresponding prodigy of the bird's friendship for Hugh; and the bird itself interpreted as a sign of God's favor for the bishop. In his title, Gerald refers to the swan's behaving *miro modo, vel etiam miraculoso*, "in a remarkable, even miraculous way," implying a distinction between an event that provokes wonder and one that is in a narrower sense miraculous, that is, produced by God's intervention in the normal course of nature. For a comment on Gerald's attitude towards miracles, prodigies, and signs, which merged a newer, more scientific interest with a basic traditionalism, see Benedicta Ward, *Miracles and the Medieval Mind*, pp. 7-8. St. Hugh himself embraced the Augustinian view of creation as the first of miracles (*MV* 1: 90-91; cf. Ward, pp. 3-4).

54.3. Hugh's mortal illness in London followed a long trip he had made on the continent. King John had invited him to be present on May 22, 1200, near Les Andelys, at the signing of a peace treaty between England and France (Thurston 456). France was then under an interdict provoked by King Philip's effort to repudiate his wife; he was eventually reconciled with the queen and the interdict lifted, but his son Louis, who was married at the time of Hugh's visit, had to go to Normandy for the ceremony, outside the interdicted territory. Louis' wife was Blanche of Castile, whom Hugh met on this occasion; their son would become the warrior saint, King Louis IX. After his participation in these political events, Hugh visited La Grande Chartreuse and his birthplace at Avalon, as well as several shrines in France, including Cluny, Cîteaux, and Clairvaux. He was already fatigued and ill when he arrived at Wissant to embark on his return crossing to England in September (*MV* 2: 149-81).

54.13. Adam of Eynsham reports that Hugh did take some meat during his last illness, in obedience to the Archbishop of Canterbury (*MV* 2: 195-96).

55.3. The feast of St. Edmund, the ninth-century king of East Anglia who was martyred by the Danes, is on November 20.

56.5. Hugh died after sunset on November 16, 1200. Consistent with the liturgical practice of beginning the next day's office at vespers, the date November 17, the day of his deposition or preparation for burial, was designated as his feast day in the bull of canonization. He was sixty, not fifty, when he died (*MV* 2: 208).

58.6. The body was disemboweled on Friday, November 17, and the long funeral journey from London to Lincoln began on November 18. It included overnight stays at the following places (the manors belonged to the bishop of Lincoln):
Saturday, November 18, at Hertford.
Sunday, November 19, at Biggleswade Manor.
Monday, November 20, at Buckden Manor.
Tuesday, November 21, at Stamford.
Wednesday, November 22, at Ancaster (20 miles from Lincoln). The body was finally carried in procession up the central street of Lincoln and into the cathedral on Thursday, November 23. Hugh was buried in his tomb in the cathedral on Friday, November 24. The royal council had convened on November 22. On that day William the Lion, King of Scotland, took an oath of fealty to King John. In April of the previous year, John had been proclaimed king by English barons doing fealty to him in obedience to the deathbed command of Richard. St. Hugh had officiated at Richard's funeral at Fontevrault and later counseled John there and also attended his coronation at Westminster in May 1199. In November 1200, John was therefore in the second year of his reign. The Council of Lincoln which by chance coincided with the funeral of St. Hugh was an occasion of dignity and peace for the new king. Among those attending the council were Gruffydd ap Rhys, Prince of South Wales, whom Hubert Walter had helped to win recognition as successor to the Lord Rhys (who had died in April 1197). William the Lion had been king of Scotland since 1165 and so belonged to an earlier generation. John had refused him the earldom of Northumberland, which William had long and vainly sought from the Angevin kings. William knew and venerated St. Thomas Becket and had met St. Hugh upon the accession of Richard I (*MV* 2: 219-32; Thurston 332; 525; 540-53).

59.4. Anselm was the archbishop of Ragusa in Dalmatia. Forced into exile, he was given refuge in England. In 1203, King John granted him the bishopric of Carlisle. Other sources name him Bernard. See Dimock's comment, *Op.* 7: 114, n. 4.

60.9. Adam of Eynsham tells of the throngs that pressed forward to touch the bier and help carry it to the cathedral. They were not deterred by the condition of the rain-soaked road or the deep mire in which they sank to their ankles and even knees. He reports that William of Scotland wept at one side and did not actually carry the bier, but that King John and the archbishops did, from about a mile outside the city and up the steep hill to the minster. There they permitted the crowd of ordinary layfolk to finish carrying the body into the church (*MV* 2: 225-29).

62.6. Adam counts fourteen, not twelve, bishops present. Gerald's less accurate count yields the significant number of 12 + 1, the number of the Apostles and Christ.

70.4. Hugh's successor, William of Blois, was not elected bishop until the summer of 1203. In his dream, the dean of Marnam is advised to mould a wax image of his afflicted head. As soon as he wakes up and proceeds to make the image, he begins to recover health. Benedicta Ward suggests that the wax figures of cured limbs that were offered at shrines were tokens of devotion that could later be used for candles (*Miracles and the Medieval Mind*, p. 94). She also notes that shrine offerings modelled in the shape of human limbs have a long history dating from pre-Christian times to the present, and she cites the wax figures discovered in 1943 in a bishop's tomb at Exeter Cathedral (p. 261, n. 90). The dean's making a wax figure as an offering would therefore be an act of generosity as well as faith, while placing such an image at the tomb was yet another mode of physical contact with the shrine. Other instances of this use of wax figures are recounted by Gerald in the *Vita Sancti Hugonis* (see paragraphs 92 and 100).

73.3. The devout observance of Sunday would begin with Saturday vespers. The French abbot, Eustace of St. Germer de Flay, preached throughout England in 1200 and again in 1201, recruiting for the Fourth Crusade and denouncing profanation of the sabbath. C.R. Cheney notes in *From Becket to Langton* (Manchester Univ. Press, 1956), p. 170, that in response to Eustace's sermons some nineteen Sunday markets were moved to week-days and that miraculous retribution fell upon many of those who broke the sabbath. The papal commissioners' report gives the name of this woman from Keal as Alicia (Farmer 102).

77.42. The letter about this cure from the chapter of Beverley to the dean and chapter of Lincoln is extant, being included in the dossier on the canonization of St. Hugh (Farmer 110-11). This letter gives the woman's name as Matilda and notes that she returned to Beverley cured of dropsy a year after leaving Beverley.

78.2. The papal commissioners' report names this boy Symon and notes that after his cure he was recognized by his speech rather than by his face (Farmer 99-100)--his appearance evidently being so changed after the albumen-like substance had flowed from his eyes.

83.2. The papal commissioners' report gives this boy's age as about twelve and names Conan the priest as another witness

in the case. Farmer identifies Conan as sacristan at the
cathedral from sometime before 1214 until before 1221 (Farmer
106, n. q). The boy was a frequent guest in the household of
Adam son of Reginald. Though he was often hit to force him to
speak, not a word could be wrung from him before his cure at
the saint's tomb (Farmer 103).

84.3. The papal commissioners' report notes that only
Philip the Deacon was present at this second cure of a dumb
boy (Farmer 103). This conflicts with Gerald's account of
crowds thronging around the tomb and pressing upon the boy
till he wakes up and speaks. The point may be that Philip the
Deacon was the sole witness of the boy's first words, but that
news of his being able to speak was quickly spread abroad.

88.11. Hugh of Wells, "Hugh the Second," was bishop of
Lincoln from 1209 to 1235.

90.8. Following the death of Hubert Walter in 1205, two
candidates were put forward to succeed him as archbishop of
Canterbury. One was favored by bishops loyal to King John,
the other was elected by the monks of Canterbury, who enjoyed
by papal privilege the right to choose the primate of England.
The dispute was brought to Rome where Innocent III voided both
elections and recommended the election of Stephen Langton, a
biblical scholar whom the pope had met in Paris. Langton was
elected by representatives of the monks and consecrated by the
pope in June 1207. But King John refused to accept this election and challenged the right of appeals to Rome. In response
Innocent III put England under an interdict in March 1208.
This meant that the administering of the sacraments was suspended in England, except for persons at the point of death or
in other extraordinary circumstances. Shrines such as St. Hugh's
tomb became the only places where the people could have open
access to religious ministry. Gerald often notes how the dean
and chapter extend a welcome to the pilgrims, some of whom were
tended and supported by the canons or local citizens. This
heightens the interest of those dreams Gerald tells in this
part of the *Vita Sancti Hugonis* in which the bishop is seen
celebrating mass and caring for the sick at the tomb. Citing
Gerald's account of St. Hugh's miracles during the interdict,
C.R. Cheney discusses the impact of the interdict on religious
life in England in "King John and the papal interdict,"
Bulletin of the John Rylands Library, 31 (1948), 295-317.

91.2. Dimock draws attention to the significance of the
primo added to this passage in the margin (*Op.* 7: 137, n. 3).
King John first led an army into Poitou in the summer of 1206,

a year and a half before the interdict. It was "about a year"
after being injured during this campaign, in the seige of
Montauban on the far southeastern border of Angevin territory,
that John Burdet returned to his home in Lindsey (the northern
portion of Lincolnshire, bounded by the North Sea and the
rivers Humber, Trent, and Witham). King John's second expedition
into Poitou was in February 1214, an event we may judge con-
temporaneous with the completion of this part of the *Vita
Sancti Hugonis*, since it entailed distinguishing the earlier
expedition as "the first."

95.4. Of Stephen, the almoner of Dean Roger of Rolleston,
Dr. Major has given me this information derived from the archives of the Dean and Chapter of Lincoln (A/1/8 no. 773):
"He had a wife Amabel and a son Roger and had land in Eastgate
and Northgate at the northeastern end of Minster Yard. He
sold the land to Geoffrey of Wicham, also called Geoffrey de
Magdalena, and it was later used to endow Geoffrey's chantry.
It was for a time held by Nicholas Grecus, one of Grosseteste's
clerks and later a canon."

98.1. The name of the village appears as "Plumgard" in
this and the following paragraph of the Latin text, as well
as in the table of contents. Dimock therefore regards the
spelling "Plumbard" in the title of the chapter as a scribal
error and identifies the village as the modern Plungar in
Leicestershire (*Op.* 7: 141, n. 1).

101.3. The papal commissioners' report gives this paralytic's name as John and notes that a priest of Wigford also
named John testified that he had known him to be paralyzed
for three years before the cure and that immediately after the
cure the priest went to the tomb and saw the once paralyzed
youth standing on his own beside an altar (Farmer 103).

103.4. Only one dependency, Felley, is listed for Worksop
Priory in David Knowles and R. Neville Hadcock, *Medieval Religious Houses: England and Wales* (London: Longmans, 1971),
pp. 157, 180. Both Worksop and Felley are located in Notting-
hamshire, west of Lincolnshire. According to Knowles and
Hadcock, Worksop was designed for eighteen Augustinian canons
and their prior; Felley was for five or six religious.

106.3. Reimund the archdeacon of Leicester was a kinsman
of St. Hugh, who made him a canon of Lincoln. He studied
theology in Paris and entertained Hugh there in his hospice in
1200, when Hugh visited the Grande Chartreuse and various
shrines in France. Adam of Eynsham reports that he too was a

guest of Reimund's in Paris for nearly three months during the
interdict (*MV* 2: 154-56). Dimock notes that Reimund's name
occurs as archdeacon of Leicester as late as 1222 (*Op*. 7: 147,
n. 1). Reimund went to Paris during the interdict, Adam reports, rather than stay in England and come to dishonorable
terms with King John as most of the English prelates had done.
At what time during the interdict did he return to Lincoln,
then, if Gerald is correct in saying that Reimund witnessed
this report in the chapter house there? Stephen Langton, whose
election in Rome as archbishop of Canterbury had led to the
dispute between King John and Innocent III which resulted in
the interdict, returned to England in July 1213. Perhaps
Archdeacon Reimund returned to Lincoln then too, while the
interdict--which was not finally lifted until July 1214--was
still in force, but after some reconciliation had been achieved
between Langton and John. In that case, we might date this
last event of Gerald's *Vita Sancti Hugonis* as having occurred
during the second half of the year 1213.

INDEX

This is an index to the text and translation, appendix, and notes to the text. Unless the Latin text is cited, the page references are to the facing English translation. Notes are cited by the number of the page where the topic is treated and the number of the note (i.e., paragraph and line numbers of the annotated passage). The following topics are also treated in the Introduction to this edition, in the sections indicated:

Gerald of Wales: his years at Lincoln and his acquaintance with St. Hugh, in "Life of the Author"

St. Hugh of Avalon: his life from other sources, principally the *Magna Vita Sancti Hugonis* by Adam of Eynsham, in "Artistic Achievement"

Carthusians: Gerald's esteem for Carthusian customs, in "Life of the Author"

Jews: Hugh's suppression of an anti-Semitic cult and the attendance of Jews at his funeral, in the summary of Hugh's life and work in "Artistic Achievement"

Miracles at the tomb of St. Hugh: Gerald's miracle-accounts and their relationship to the report of the papal commissioners, in "Sources and Influences"

Vita Sancti Hugonis: the extant manuscript, dedicated to Stephen Langton, in "Editorial Policy for this Text and Translation"; the scope and style of the work, in "Artistic Achievement"; its place in the tradition of lives of the saints, in "Sources and Influences"

Vita Sancti Remigii: Gerald's history of the Church of Lincoln and his estimate of Hugh's career in that context, in "Artistic Achievement"